HOW TO GET BETTER VALUE HEALTHCARE

We need to learn from the military. This is from the Intelligence Corp!

Muir Gray

With Gwyn Bevan, Chantelle Rizan, Walter Ricciardi
Caroline Clarke, Rachel Stancliffe, Anant Jani
& Alison Tonge

HOW TO GET BETTER VALUE HEALTHCARE

ISBN 978-1-904202-19-6

First edition 2007
Second edition 2011
Third Edition 2017
www.OffoxPress.com

Printed in the United Kingdom

A catalogue version of the book can be found at the British Library

Interior layout by The Book Refinery Ltd
www.TheBookRefinery.com

Cover designed by Muir Gray

CONTENTS

PREFACE

The arrival of Dave Sackett as the Founder Director at the Centre for Evidence-Based Medicine in 1994 had a revolutionary effect, creating a new paradigm that had a few strong critics as well as many supporters. One of the principles that helped establish the paradigm of evidence-based decision making was Dave's emphasis on the need to focus not just on evidence but also on the value individuals placed on outcomes, both good and bad, that might result from interventions. Evidence-based medicine applied to individuals evolved into evidence-based healthcare focused on commissioning in the NHS in England. This was based in part on the explicit allocation of finite financial resources, while the term value-based healthcare (VBHC) was perhaps first used in 2001 in describing how in 'the era of value-based healthcare... the situation that is set to become the prevailing system of resource allocation in which those who pay for healthcare will require that interventions are provided only when their outcomes give greater benefits than any of the alternative uses of equivalent resources'.[1] The NHS in England explicitly adopted the concept of value in 2004 and published the first Annual Population Value Review in 2006, publicising the scale of variation in the allocation of resources to different segments of the population defined by need, for example people with cancer or people with mental health problems.

The best definition of value is that provided by the European Union Expert Panel on Effective Ways of Investing in Health in 2019,[2] which concluded that there are four perspectives on value, not counting the perspective of industry:

- Personal value: appropriate care to achieve a patient's personal goals
- Technical value: achievement of best possible outcomes with available resources [for all the people in need in a population]
- Allocative value: equitable resource distribution across all patient groups
- Social value: contribution of healthcare to social participation and connectedness

Useful though this list may be its brevity needs amplifying, particularly with respect to technical value. As the text makes clear this aspect of value is in fact broader than at first reading, on which it sounds like a synonym for efficiency, but in Europe – committed to universal healthcare – it is necessary to emphasise that the appraisal needs to focus on all people with a need, such as hip pain, and not just those people who have had a hip replacement. The reason for this is to be sensitive to the possibility of inequity, namely the underuse of services by people from the most deprived sub-groups of the population.

We are very encouraged to see the moves taking place worldwide on value-based healthcare, all of which fully support the continuation of efforts to improve quality and safety for patients who reach health services, but which also emphasise the need for healthcare policymakers, payers and providers to focus on value not only for individuals but also for populations. In England the white paper titled *Innovation and integration: working together to improve health and social care for all,*[3] which led to the Health and Care Act of 2022, emphasised the need to focus not only on patients but also to 'improve outcomes for the population as a whole' and 'improve outcomes and value for citizens'. There is one country that is not involved – the United States of America. They use the term value often but with a meaning closer to efficiency, and assessment of their 'value-based payment' policy suggests that it has made inequity worse, in that value-based payment models implemented over the past decade have often been regressive, moving dollars away from patients, providers and communities with fewer resources and towards those with more.[4]

We are a team of people from different backgrounds and with different perspectives but we are all committed to the promotion and development of value-based healthcare and have produced the fourth edition of this book with excitement, because it does seem that the paradigm is shifting towards value-based healthcare, in line with the mission of the Oxford Value and Stewardship Programme (OVSP).

The OVSP strategy for achieving better value is described in four linked books on value: this book, and three other linked books on population healthcare, systems and culture. These are supported by online learning resources at www.ovsp.net. Our strategy is to:

- Base health services on populations, remembering the key role of personal value as well, rather than on hospitals and health centres, important as they are
- Deliver better value through systems and networks, for example a system for people with atrial fibrillation, not through primary, secondary and tertiary care, important as they are
- Create a culture of stewardship to ensure the survival of universal healthcare

This is the era of value-based healthcare, for both populations and individuals, enabled by digital development but requiring real leadership to create the new culture.

Muir Gray

Oxford, 2023

Note: I would like to acknowledge how much I learned from the late Major Shaun Brogan, MA, MC, including the importance of the Tactical Aide Memoire, which was the inspiration for the section devoted to checklists.

References

1. Gray JAM. *Evidence-based Healthcare: How to Make Health Policy and Management Decisions.* 2nd Edition. 2001. Churchill Livingstone.

2. European Commission. Defining Value in Population-Based Healthcare. Published 19 July 2019. Available at: https://ec.europa.eu/health/sites/default/files/expert_panel/docs/2019_defining-value-vbhc_factsheet_en.pdf

3. UK Department of Health & Social Care. Policy paper: *Integration and innovation: working together to improve health and social care for all.* Updated 11 February 2021. Available at: www.gov.uk/government/publications/working-together-to-improve-health-and-social-care-for-all/integration-and-innovation-working-together-to-improve-health-and-social-care-for-all-html-version

4. Gondi S, Maddox KJ, Wadhera RK. '"REACHing" for equity—moving from regressive toward progressive value-based payment'. *New England Journal of Medicine.* 2022; 387(2): 97–99. doi: 10.1056/NEJMp2204749

PART 1

EVOLUTION OF THE VALUE PARADIGM AND BEYOND

1

THE NEED FOR VALUE-BASED HEALTHCARE

This chapter will:

- Describe the challenges to sustaining universal healthcare in the next decade
- Analyse the reasons need and demand are increasing faster than resources
- Give an account of the evolution of the paradigms of healthcare
- Define what is meant by the value-based healthcare paradigm
- Look ahead to zero carbon healthcare.

By the end of the chapter you will have an understanding of:

- How to engage professionals and the public in debating and defining the social trends that will influence how care is managed and delivered
- The concept of paradigm shift and the need for a revolution
- How the paradigm now focuses on increasing value for both populations and individuals.

The turmoil we see in healthcare across the world post-COVID 19 was decades in the making - the pandemic just brutally exposed the weaknesses that were already there. Anyone taking a critical look at healthcare systems will have noticed them but it was much easier, much more convenient and much less painful to simply continue with business as usual…

What we have ended up with in many cases are healthcare services that are failing their patients and healthcare professionals – as evidenced by the massive waiting lists and huge increase in unmet need as well as a demoralized and exhausted workforce. And all of this in societies where a large proportion of disease burden (around 70% in the West) is linked to completely preventable non-communicable diseases.

The COVID-19 pandemic increased the need and demand for healthcare, but it had been steadily – some say relentlessly – increasing in the years before the pandemic and will continue to do so in the decades to come. The steepness of the gradient and its size can, however, be influenced, and we should not conclude that we just need to continue pouring money into healthcare systems. Indeed, one of the many lessons of the pandemic is that money is not the most important resource. Services that had for years been desperate for more money suddenly had governments providing huge amounts of extra cash only to meet other, more difficult constraints, such as a lack of oxygen or personal protective equipment, or – even more importantly – human resources.

Here is what the challenge looks like:

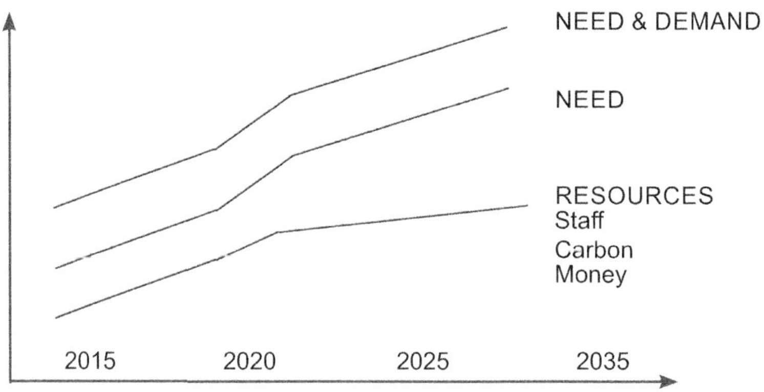

Figure 1.1: Forecasted challenges for healthcare systems

How value-based healthcare can mitigate the drivers of need and demand

Increasing need and demand should not be accepted as inevitable, because steps can be taken to influence both, which occur as a result of four main factors:

- Population ageing
- New diseases and epidemics
- New technology
- The relentless increase in the volume and intensity of clinical practice.

The contribution of these four drivers to increased need and demand for healthcare was covered in some detail in our previous book, *How to Design and Deliver Population Healthcare*,[5] so we will concentrate here on how value-based healthcare can mitigate these factors.

Mitigating the impact of population ageing

The impact of population ageing should not be overemphasised, and in many countries it is not the main driver of increased healthcare demand compared with new health problems, new technology and the relentless increase in the volume and intensity of clinical practice.

Nevertheless, at one time older people were often denied treatment solely on account of their chronological age. The sterling work done by the speciality of geriatric medicine has reversed this ageist prejudice and older people are now rarely denied diagnostic or treatment technology. However, the other lesson that geriatric medicine has tried to teach – namely that the ageing process decreases resilience, and combined with the fact that multimorbidity becomes more common the longer we live, this means that clinical care is much more complex – has been less readily absorbed. Furthermore, as a UK Department of Health report on polypharmacy titled *Good For You, Good For Us, Good For Everybody*[6] pointed out, 'clinical trials typically involve people between the ages of 18 and 64, which means that the effects of the medicine on older patients is less well understood' and 'some classes of medicines, such as those to reduce blood pressure, can increase the risk of falls amongst the frail and elderly, often leading to broken bones. This will often mean a long hospital stay and extended recovery, and may result in the patient experiencing ongoing pain, and a loss of mobility, confidence and independence. …around 6.5% of hospital admissions are caused by adverse effects of medicines. This rises to up to 20% in the over 65 age group and two thirds of medicines-related hospital admissions are considered preventable.'

Currently 30% of people over the age of 80 are receiving eight or more repeat prescriptions, compared with 10% of people aged 50–60.[7] However, it is not only drugs that need to have their value as well as their cost-effectiveness considered: similar considerations apply to laboratory tests, imaging and hospital admission; the latter is now recognised as causing deconditioning and loss of ability so quickly that even an admission deemed essential for an acute problem can lead to loss of function such that an older person is unable to be discharged back home.[8]

Value-based healthcare for older people would see a switch of resources from 'pointless' drug prescribing, estimated in the 'Good For You' report as costing about £1 billion a year, to promoting and enabling physical, cognitive and emotional activity.

Mitigating the impact of new diseases and epidemics

Let us hope that the COVID-19 pandemic was atypical and that most new conditions will either be those created by new definitions of disease, for example a lower level of blood pressure for defining 'high blood pressure', or by the development of new drugs for previously untreatable diseases, remembering that one definition of a health need is a condition for which there is an effective intervention. Due to advances in genetic science we are seeing the development of new drugs for rare conditions that were previously untreatable, and one feature of these treatments is the high cost of prescribing these drugs for people, often children, with rare disease conditions. The total cost for the population may not be great, because the condition is rare, but the cost per case is high because the developer's costs are often similar when developing a drug for a rare disease to what they would be if that drug was for a common condition, and the price per patient, determined in part by the need to recover development costs, needs to be higher when there are fewer patients.

What is called value-based pricing may help, because when a drug is given in the first year of life its benefits need to be assessed taking into account its effects over the next 70 or 80 years. However, it is probable that there would still be a higher cost per patient. Again, the cost may seem high considered in isolation, but value-based healthcare offers another solution. The rare disease and its treatment costs should be considered not in isolation but in the context of the total spend for people with that type of disease. One of the key principles of value-based healthcare is that budgets need to be organised not just by the level of care – primary and secondary, or health centre and hospital to put it another way – but by the segments of the population defined by need, for example people with cardiovascular disease, which is about £100 million per million population in many countries. This is a method called service line accounting or programme budgeting, which we will consider in more detail later. If, therefore, a new treatment for a previously untreatable genetic disorder causing heart disease was invented, costing £10,000 for each child, and there were 100 such children, then the source of that money would be within that programme budget. The question addressed by clinicians, with patient representatives involved, would be 'Can we identify £1 million's worth of expenditure that is of lower value, or, to put it another way, is being wasted?', where one of the four definitions of waste, which we will discuss in Chapter 2, is the use of resources that would give more value if used for another group of people in need.

Mitigating the impact of new technology

The excitement generated by innovation should not divert attention from the need to deliver low-cost, high-value interventions, such as smoking cessation, particularly because the people who are not receiving such interventions are often those with the greatest need due to deprivation. Inequity also needs innovation, and often the innovation lies in the ways in which services are organised rather than in new technology.

The development of programme budgeting as part of the development of value-based healthcare also offers the opportunity to engage clinicians and patient representatives in ensuring that only interventions of high value are introduced. Take, for example, the management of glaucoma. There was concern about the late diagnosis of glaucoma and the National Screening Committee in the UK was asked to review the evidence on the effectiveness of screening. They came to the conclusion that there was no evidence to support the development of a national screening programme.[9] However, several years later a low-cost means of measuring intra-ocular pressure was developed and introduced by every optometrist, resulting in a large increase in referrals to hospital ophthalmology services, which in turn had a huge impact on resources for the treatment of cataracts and macular degeneration. If the cost and benefit of the equipment and these referrals of people with minor degrees of raised intra-ocular pressure had been considered in the context of a population-based budget for eye and vision problems, then a decision would have been made not to invest in this new equipment.

Thus value-based healthcare changes the discussion and decisions about new drugs and equipment.

Mitigating the relentless increase in the volume and intensity of clinical practice

The programme budgets that will help to mitigate the effect of new technology and new conditions on the need and demand for healthcare will make a contribution to reducing the 'relentless increase in volume and intensity', but of much greater importance than the development of population-based systems with a budget will be a change in culture.

Value-based healthcare has a number of distinguishing features. It is focused on populations rather than hospitals and health centres, it has systems running from self-care to tertiary care and it has a distinctive culture – the culture of stewardship, which we will discuss in more depth in Chapter 6, but which is best captured in a quote from the Academy of Medical Royal Colleges report on promoting value and protecting resources:[10]

> *Reducing waste in today's climate of constrained resource is really about creating the health care system that we want to have. It is not just about cutting corners or reducing spending. As responsible stewards, doctors can provide a more effective use of constrained economic and environmental resources... A cultural shift is required which calls upon doctors and other clinicians to ask, not if a treatment or procedure is possible, but whether it provides real value to the patient and genuinely improves the quality of their life or their prospects for recovery.*

The adoption of the principles and methods of value-based healthcare is essential both to preserve the principles of universal healthcare and to mitigate all four of the drivers of increased need and demand.

The need for a new paradigm shift

The Second Healthcare Revolution of the past 50 years involved not only the development of new technology, with COVID-19 vaccines being a startling example of this, but also advances in the leadership and management of healthcare, for example the introduction of evidence-based decision-making and the explicit and public recording of variations in quality and safety.

There have been other fantastic achievements, both technologically and in the management of services, but more of the same is not enough – a new paradigm is needed, or to put it another way, a third, Value-Based Healthcare Revolution. That paradigm shifts are revolutions is epitomised in the title of the book that brought the concept of paradigm shifts into both scientific and public debate, Thomas Kuhn's *The Structure of Scientific Revolutions*. Here is his definition:

> *Aristotle's* Physica, *Ptolemy's* Almagest, *Newton's* Principia *and* Opticks, *Franklin's* Electricity, *Lavoisier's* Chemistry, *and Lyell's Geology – these and many other works served for a time implicitly to define the legitimate problems and methods of a research field for succeeding generations of practitioners. They were able to do so because they shared two essential characteristics. Their achievement was sufficiently unprecedented to modes of scientific activity. Simultaneously, it was sufficiently open-ended to leave all sorts of problems for the redefined group of practitioners to resolve.*[11]

A simpler definition is given by General Sir Rupert Smith in his widely respected book about shifting paradigms in warfare, titled *The Utility of Force: The Art of War in the Modern World*:

> *Universally recognized scientific achievements that for a time provide model problems and solutions to a community of practitioners.*[12]

The paradigm shift described by Smith is a shift from relying on increasing force and more sophisticated technology to a paradigm in which the focus is on understanding, communicating with, and seeking to win over not necessarily the guerrilla forces but the communities that sustain them. There are interesting parallels for the health service in the modern world, in which a third revolution is taking place thanks to citizens having unparalleled access to knowledge, both accurate and inaccurate, through the internet. A paradigm shift entails:

- A new way of thinking, with…
- A new language, which…
- Creates a new culture, which…
- Creates a new social reality, the result of the revolution

The dominant paradigm of the past 50 years has been to have big bureaucracies, both public and private, develop technology and services, with clinicians being trained to make evidence-based decisions and then deliver high-quality care safely. This paradigm has to change, but first let us reflect on the current paradigms.

The rise of the bureaucratic paradigm

In 1948, with the start of the National Health Service (NHS), a new paradigm was introduced in the United Kingdom, namely that the provision of healthcare was to be free for everybody at the point of access. Similar paradigm shifts had taken place in other countries. In fact, universal healthcare coverage and access (with co-payments in some countries), funded by taxation or insurance, is the dominant paradigm in all developed countries with the exception of the USA.

In the fledgling NHS, reliance was placed on a bureaucracy with a long chain of command to deliver healthcare, with the Secretary of State ultimately responsible for, to use one famous example, the cleanliness of the floor of a hospital ward. Then in 1990 in England a new paradigm was introduced – 'the internal market'. The National Health Service and Community Care Act 1990[13] posited that an internal market and and not tiers of bureaucracy was the best way to manage the health service, and this introduced purchasers, later rebranded as 'commissioners', and providers. The 2021 White Paper, *Innovation and integration: working together to improve health and social care for all,*[14] introduced a new managerial paradigm – the integrated system, mentioned 251 times. This paradigm is based on the widely accepted principle that for complex challenges like meeting the health needs of a population from a finite budget, neither a bureaucracy nor the market is the appropriate solution. The principle is based on the work of Oliver Williamson and Elinor Ostrom – winner of the 2011 Nobel Prize for Economic Science[15] – which showed that what is needed is for people who are responsible for finite resources to develop a system for protecting those resources 'collaboratively'. The term collaboratively is mentioned 55 times in the White Paper.

The rise of the clinical paradigm of effectiveness and quality

While these shifting paradigms in funding and management were taking place another set of paradigms was evolving to change the way decisions were made about the provision of treatment and care to individual patients and populations – a significant paradigm shift in clinical practice. From 1948 onwards it was assumed that the medical profession collectively and individually knew what was best. This changed in 1971 when Archie Cochrane published *Effectiveness and Efficiency.*[16] This publication led to the development of the 'effectiveness' paradigm, summarised as a slogan carried by Cochrane at a protest rally: 'All effective treatments should be free.' In time the effectiveness paradigm evolved into the 'evidence-based' paradigm. Then, it was superseded by 'cost-effectiveness' paradigms as concern about the costs of healthcare began to escalate, and over the past two decades the dominant clinical paradigm has focused on the quality and safety of healthcare, and, more recently, on efficiency – for good reason.

This focus on quality, safety and efficiency has been essential but is not sufficient; new concerns emerged, based principally on the work of Jack Wennberg and colleagues at the Dartmouth Institute, New Hampshire, on unwarranted variation.[17]

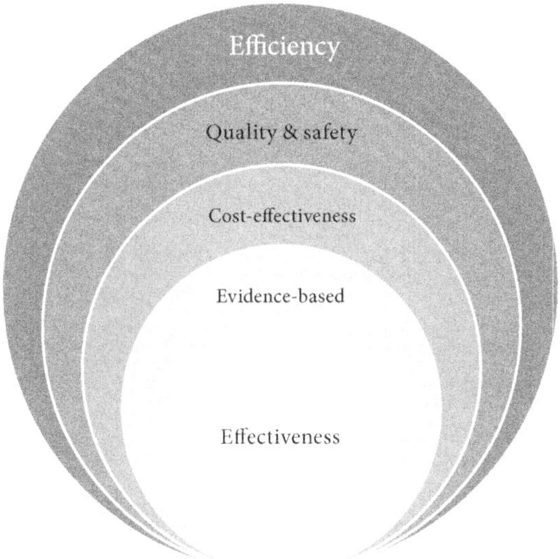

Figure 1.2: Previous paradigm shifts in clinical practice

Explosions in the 20th century bureaucratic and clinical paradigms: unwarranted variation, overuse and underuse

What Wennberg and his team demonstrated was that at the end of these decades of progress three huge problems could be seen in every country, no matter how their healthcare was organised or financed.

The first of these problems is huge and unwarranted variation in access, quality, cost and outcome. Unwarranted variation is defined by Wennberg, creator of the brilliant *Dartmouth Atlas of Healthcare*, as variation that cannot be explained by discrepancy in need or patient preference.[18] Analysis of the unwarranted variation published in the NHS Atlases,[19] and atlases in many other countries inspired by Wennberg, reveals the other two problems:

- Overuse, leading to:
  - waste, that is anything that does not add value to the outcome for patients or uses resources that could give greater value if used for another group of patients
  - patient harm, even when the quality of care is high

- Underuse, leading to:
  - failure to prevent the diseases that healthcare can prevent, such as stroke and vascular dementia in atrial fibrillation
  - inequity, namely lower rates of intervention in the most deprived groups of the population, which also often have higher levels of need.

These problems cannot be solved by the current paradigm and the set of activities that have dominated the thinking of leadership and management for the past decade, namely:

1. Preventing disease, disability, dementia and frailty to reduce need. (Although controlling epidemics of the 21st century, caused by disruption in the social environment, will be much more difficult than controlling epidemics of the 19th century, achieved by modifying the physical environment.)
2. Improving outcome by providing only interventions with evidence of cost-effectiveness
3. Improving outcomes by increasing the quality and safety of processes
4. Increasing productivity by reducing cost.

These are all necessary but not sufficient, and a new paradigm is needed to tackle the challenges of unwarranted variation, overuse and underuse: value-based healthcare within a culture of stewardship – defined with respect to our natural environment by Peter Block as being 'to hold something in trust for another'.[20]

The value-based healthcare paradigm

For the next decade, perhaps for the rest of the 21st century, the dominant healthcare paradigm will be focused on value (Figure 1.3). The new paradigm of value-based healthcare will encompass and adopt the previous paradigms and at the same time challenge the assumptions not only that increased investment in healthcare is always better, but also that increased investment in quality and safety always increases value.

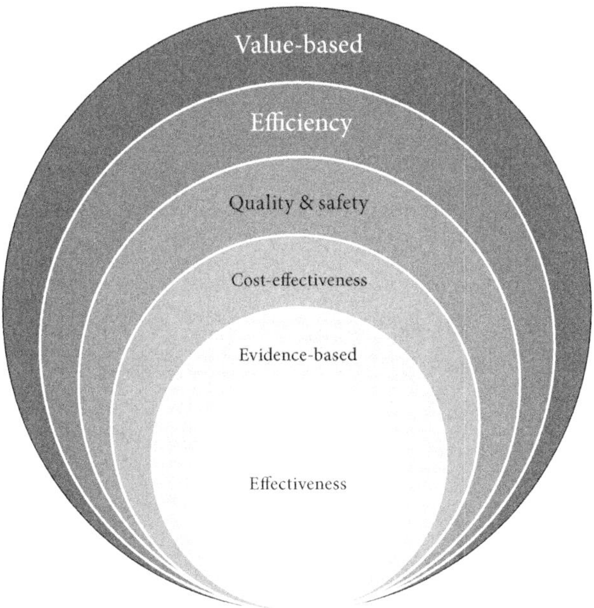

Figure 1.3: The newest paradigm shift

The European Union Expert Panel on Effective Ways of Investing in Health (EXPH) definition of value emphasises four different dimensions:[21]

- **Personal value:** appropriate care to achieve a patient's personal goals
- **Technical value:** achievement of the best possible outcomes with available resources
- **Allocative value:** equitable resource distribution across all patient groups
- **Social value:** contribution of healthcare to social participation and connectedness.

The meanings of these terms and other related terms, notably stewardship, will be clarified in the next chapter, but before going into more depth it is appropriate to summarise how this paradigm has evolved around the world.

How the revolution is spreading

The emergence of a new paradigm does not make the preceding paradigms redundant; Newtonian physics survived the work of Einstein, for example. Similarly in healthcare the development of evidence-based decision-making did not invalidate the paradigm in which it was recognised that the effectiveness of a procedure or intervention had to be proved by a randomised controlled trial, as described by Cochrane in *Effectiveness and Efficiency*.[16]

England

In England, evidence-based healthcare was launched at the same time as evidence-based medicine, and as long ago as 2001 the term value-based healthcare was used for the first time in a book on evidence-based healthcare,[22] describing how in 'the era of value-based healthcare. . . the situation that is set to become the prevailing system of resource allocation is that in which those who pay for healthcare will require that interventions are provided only when their outcomes give greater benefits than any of the alternative uses of equivalent resources'. The NHS in England explicitly adopted the concept of value in 2006, when it released the first Annual Population Value Review, publicising the scale of variation in expenditure and activity. By this time, however, the quality improvement paradigm was in full flow, with every health service focused on the need to improve quality, including safety, and reduce cost. Important though this was and is, it is also essential to bear in mind Peter Drucker's cautionary principle that: 'There is nothing so useless as doing efficiently that which should not be done at all.'[23]

The 'Choosing Wisely' campaign[24] in the USA (see below) stimulated the Academy of Medical Royal Colleges in the United Kingdom to take up the challenge, producing in 2014 a major report called *Protecting Resources, Promoting Value*,[10] subtitled: 'A doctor's guide to cutting waste in healthcare.' This radical report describes the new paradigm clearly:

> *. . .avoiding waste and promoting value are about the quality of care provided to patients – which is a doctor's central concern. One doctors' waste is another patient's delay. Potentially, it could be that other patient's lack of treatment. There is a clinical cost to wasted resources and also, as the report shows, a cost to the environment.*
>
> *This process creates a higher value health care system where resources: cash, carbon and staff time, are released from some parts of the system to develop new services or support struggling services. Reducing waste in today's climate of constrained resource is really about creating the health care system that we want to have. It is not just about cutting corners or reducing spending. As responsible stewards, doctors can provide a more*

effective use of constrained economic and environmental resources.

A cultural shift is required which calls upon doctors and other clinicians to ask, not if a treatment or procedure is possible, but whether it provides real value to the patient and genuinely improves the quality of their life or their prospects for recovery. . . Doctors should embrace the values of resource stewardship in their clinical practice.

In England in 2021 the principles of value-based healthcare were expressed through the White Paper *Integration and Innovation*,[14] which set out the Triple Aim that the NHS needs to have as its focus:

- to support better health and well-being for everyone
- better quality of health services for all, and
- sustainable use of NHS resources.

So, as well as the continuing commitment to universal healthcare it is emphasised that resources need to be used sustainably – which implies both consideration of their environmental impact and the need for a culture of stewardship to protect the principle and the practice of universal healthcare for future generations.

The principal means of delivery described in the White Paper is the system, and the four 'purposes' of these systems clearly position value and equity as part of the new paradigm:

- Improving population health and healthcare
- Tackling unequal outcomes and access
- Enhancing productivity and value for money
- Helping the NHS to support broader social and economic development.

The United States

The 'Choosing Wisely Campaign'[24] in the United States challenged physicians to identify activities of low value and to stop or at least reduce them. The scope for doing this had been highlighted since 1999 by Jack Wennberg's team at Dartmouth College, who introduced the concept of unwarranted variation. The term value was also used in the United States from 2008, when a widely quoted report from Harvard Business School defined value in the following way: 'the patient health outcomes relative to the total cost (inputs) of attaining those outcomes'.[25] This actually would be considered a definition of efficiency in countries committed to universal healthcare, which have to consider value from a population perspective, and therefore also take into account allocative and social value as well as technical value.

Europe

The EXPH was commissioned to define value and make recommendations for action. Their definition of value-based healthcare is that it is a '**comprehensive concept** built on the four value pillars – personal, technical, allocative and social'.[21] (Figure 1.4)

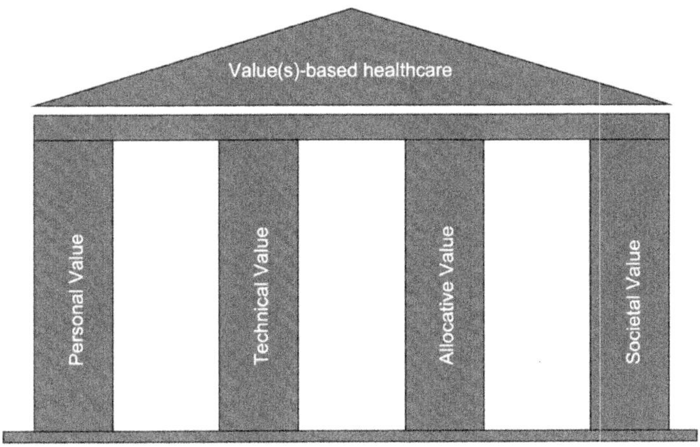

Figure 1.4: The four value pillars

The EXPH report, published in June 2019, made clear the need for a 'reallocation of resources – the freeing of resources and accordingly the reinvestment – from low to high value care – as the utmost necessity for sustainable and resilient European healthcare systems.' The report emphasised that the meaning of the term value as used in the United States was not appropriate for countries committed to universal healthcare in the following way: 'Currently, "value" in the context of healthcare is often discussed as "health outcomes relative to monetized inputs", aiming at increasing cost-effectiveness. This interpretation is perceived by the EXPH as too narrow and the notion of "values-based healthcare" seems more suitable in conveying the guiding principles underlying solidarity-based healthcare systems.'

The EXPH emphasis of the importance of a value-based healthcare approach to securing the future of universal healthcare epitomises the principle of solidarity on which the European Union (EU) is based.

Globally

The Group of Twenty (G20) organised a 'side event' at their Riyadh meeting in November 2020, entitled, 'Accelerating Transformation Towards Sustainable Health System through Value-Based Healthcare'. Their report of this meeting stated: 'We acknowledge the success of the G20 side event. . . We support the establishment of a Global Innovation Hub for Improving Value in Health (the Hub), with a five-year mandate. We recognize the importance of accelerating learning and the adoption, measurement and evaluation of different approaches to improve value in countries at all stages of development.'[26]

New programmes are opening in many countries. In Saudi Arabia the Council of Ministers has set up a Centre for Improving Value in Health and is also supporting the G20 Global Innovation Hub for Improving Value in Health. In Latin America a new academy – the

Academia VBHC – has been launched in Sao Paulo. In China the new School of Population Medicine in Beijing is leading work on value-based healthcare. In Europe the European Academy for Healthcare Leaders has been launched in Rome, a Network for Value Improvement has been launched in Spain, NOVA University in Portugal launched a Value CoLab and NHS Wales has appointed a National Clinical Director of Value-Based Healthcare.

Carbon neutrality paradigm

Even as value-based healthcare, with a culture of stewardship, is being adopted, another, closely related shift is gathering momentum: the Net Zero Carbon paradigm shift, aimed at maximising value within the context of finite natural resources. Climate change is the greatest threat to public health of the 21st century.[27] Human health and planetary health are intricately linked, and even the provision of healthcare itself has a major carbon footprint, with the healthcare sector being responsible for 4.4% of global greenhouse gases.[28]

The Academy of Medical Royal Colleges 2014 report on protecting resources[10] highlights the importance of 'the carbon cost of wasted resources', and in its summary describes the relationship between savings in financial resources and carbon reduction:

> *The NHS remains the largest single contributor of greenhouse gases in the public sector. Most of these emissions come not from heating or lighting clinics or hospitals, but directly from clinical practice. Reducing waste in the clinical domain has a triple imperative:*
>
> - *it improves value,*
> - *lowers costs, and*
> - *reduces CO2 emissions.*

> *A good example of this is a project that provided specialist geriatric services within nursing and residential homes, which led to a reduction in unplanned admissions. This initiative improved care and saved the Trust £65,000 and 23 tonnes of carbon in one year.*

They also made one of their top recommendations that: 'All those working in health should take steps to increase their understanding of the carbon costs of healthcare activities.'

As a growing number of healthcare professionals seek to improve the sustainability of health and healthcare systems globally, the Net Zero Carbon paradigm shift is gathering momentum in health services, as we will describe in the final chapter. The UK has been paving the way, with the creation of Oxford-based charity the Centre for Sustainable Healthcare,[29] in 2008, and the launch of the Greener NHS programme in 2020.[30]

The next chapter describes the meanings of the key terms in the new paradigm.

Questions for reflection when teaching or engaged in professional and organisational development

If using these in network building or teaching, give one of the questions to the group and ask them to work in pairs to reflect on the question for 3 minutes. Try to get people who do not know one another to work together. When taking feedback, let each pair make only one point. In the interests of equity, if you start with the pair on the left-hand side of the room for the first question, start with the pair on the right-hand side of the room for the second question.

- What three steps would you take to reduce the demand for healthcare?
- How could the internet be used to help health services cope with the challenges they face?
- What technological innovations could reduce the cost of healthcare?
- What technological innovations could reduce the need for healthcare?
- What technological innovations could reduce the demand for healthcare?

References

5. Gray JAM. *How to Design and Deliver Population Healthcare*. 2022. Offox Press.

6. UK Department of Health & Social Care. *Good for you, good for us, good for everybody: A plan to reduce overprescribing to make patient care better and safer, support the NHS, and reduce carbon emissions*. Published 22 September 2021. Available at: https://assets.publishing.service.gov.uk/government/uploads/system/uploads/attachment_data/file/1019475/good-for-you-good-for-us-good-for-everybody.pdf

7. NHS England. Blog: Time to move: Get up, get dressed, keep moving (Amit Arora). Published 24 January 2017. Available at: www.england.nhs.uk/blog/amit-arora

8. Arora A. 'Time to move again: from deconditioning to reconditioning'. *Age and Ageing*. 2022; 51(2): afab227.

9. UK National Screening Committee. Adult screening programme: glaucoma. Available at: https://view-health-screening-recommendations.service.gov.uk/glaucoma (accessed September 2022)

10. Academy of Medical Royal Colleges. *Protecting Resources, Promoting Value: a Doctor's Guide to Cutting Waste in Clinical Care*. Published November 2014. Available at: www.aomrc.org.uk/wp-content/uploads/2016/05/Protecting_Resources_Promoting_Value_1114.pdf

11. Kuhn TS. *The Structure of Scientific Revolutions*. 2nd Edition. 1970. The University of Chicago Press, p. 10.

12. Smith R. *The Utility of Force: The Art of War in the Modern World*. 2012. The Penguin Group, p. 3.

13. The National Archives. *National Health Service and Community Care Act 1990*. Available at: www.legislation.gov.uk/ukpga/1990/19/contents (accessed September 2022)

14. UK Department of Health & Social Care. Policy paper: *Integration and innovation: working together to improve health and social care for all*. Updated 11 February 2021. Available at: www.gov.uk/government/publications/working-together-to-improve-health-and-social-care-for-all/integration-and-innovation-working-together-to-improve-health-and-social-care-for-all-html-version

15. Earl PE, Potts J. 'A Nobel Prize for Governance and Institutions: Oliver Williamson and Elinor Ostrom'. *Review of Political Economy*. 2011; 23(1): 1–24. doi: 0.1080/09538259.2011.526291

16. Cochrane AL. *Effectiveness and Efficiency: Random Reflections on Health Services*. 1972. Nuffield Provincial Hospitals Trust.

17. Dartmouth Medical School, Center for the Evaluative Clinical Services. *The Dartmouth Atlas of Health Care*. 1996. American Hospital Association.

18. Wennberg JE. *Tracking Medicine: A Researcher's Quest to Understand Health Care*. 2010. Oxford University Press.

19. NHS England. Atlases. Available at: www.england.nhs.uk/rightcare/products/atlas (accessed June 2022)

20. Block P. *Stewardship: Choosing Service Over Self-Interest.* 1993. Berrett-Koehler Publishers.

21. European Union. *Defining Value in "Value-Based Healthcare".* Published November 2019. Available at: https://health.ec.europa.eu/system/files/2019-11/024_defining-value-vbhc_en_0.pdf

22. Gray JAM. *Evidence-based Healthcare: How to Make Health Policy and Management Decisions.* 2nd Edition. 2001. Churchill Livingstone.

23. Drucker P. *The Practice of Management.* 1955. Heinemann.

24. ABIM Foundation. Choosing Wisely. Available at: www.choosingwisely.org (accessed September 2022)

25. Porter ME. *What is Value in Health Care?* Harvard Business School. Institute for Strategy and Competitiveness White Paper. 2008. Adapted in New England Journal of Medicine, 2010; 363(26): 2477–2481. doi: 10.1056/NEJMp1011024

26. G20 Research Group. *G20 Health Ministers' Declaration.* Published 19 November 2020. Available at: www.g20.utoronto.ca/2020/2020-g20-health-1119.html

27. Costello A, Abbas M, Allen A, et al. Managing the health effects of climate change: Lancet and University College London Institute for Global Health Commission. *The Lancet.* 2009; 373(9676): 1693–1733. doi: 10.1016/S0140-6736(09)60935-1

28. Health Care Without Harm/Arup. *Health Care's Climate Footprint.* Published September 2019. Available at: https://noharm-global.org/sites/default/files/documents-files/5961/HealthCaresClimateFootprint_092319.pdf

29. The Centre for Sustainable Healthcare. Available at: https://sustainablehealthcare.org.uk (accessed June 2022)

30. NHS. Delivering a net zero NHS. Available at: www.england.nhs.uk/greenernhs/a-net-zero-nhs (accessed September 2022)

2

THE MEANINGS OF VALUE

This chapter will:

- Clarify the different meanings of the terms value and waste
- Show how the meanings of these terms can be explained in both words and numbers
- Introduce the concept of social value
- Describe what is meant by stewardship.

By the end of this chapter you will have developed an understanding of:

- The difference between the moral meaning of the term value and its economic meaning
- The relationship between value and efficiency
- How to define the meaning of the term value from the perspectives of clinicians, patients, and those who invest in healthcare or manage it
- The perspective of industry on value
- How to help a management or clinical team reach agreement on the way in which they use the term value.

Words are weapons in a cultural revolution. Words change not only dialogue but also how people think, feel, make decisions and act, the culture of organisations and the social reality in which people live. Just as 'liberté, égalité, fraternité' was a powerful three-word slogan associated with the French Revolution, the paradigm shift to value-based healthcare is associated with two words – value and stewardship.

Value is a complex concept. As is the case with many words, 'value' has more than one meaning:

- When used in the plural, as in 'the values of our service', it can be a statement of principles. For example, 'respect for the autonomy of the individual patient is one of our core values'.
- When used in the singular, it has an economic meaning relating outcomes achieved to the resources invested.

The multiple meanings of 'value' illustrate Wittgenstein's principle that many arguments result from a failure of the parties concerned to realise that they have failed to agree on the meaning of the terms they are using.[31] For example, two people can debate whether a hospital service is offering good value, but one may be talking about efficiency and the other productivity.

Dictionary definitions of value

There are two types of dictionary. The first, such as Dr Johnson's original dictionary, gives only the lexicographer's definition of a word. The second, such as the *Shorter Oxford English Dictionary*, gives the lexicographer's definition in conjunction with examples of the word in use. This type of dictionary of course requires considerable resources to compile.

In the *Shorter Oxford English Dictionary*, there is a clear distinction between two different meanings of the word 'value', both of which are in common use in the healthcare sector:[32] the moral meaning and the economic meaning.

The moral meaning of 'value'

According to the *Shorter Oxford English Dictionary*, based on a definition from late Middle English, the moral meaning of value is: '. . .the status of a thing or the estimate in which it is held according to its real or supposed worth, usefulness, or importance.'

Examples of statements in which health services would use the term value in its moral sense are:

- 'this hospital values patient choice'
- 'at this primary care practice we value openness and honesty.'

The economic meaning of 'value'

The economic meaning of value has four variants in the *Shorter Oxford English Dictionary*, one of which is: '. . .that amount of some commodity, medium of exchange, etc. which is considered to be an equivalent for something else.' An example of the economic meaning of the term value in use in 1806 given is: 'We could hardly be said to have value for our money.'

In the specialised *Healthcare Economics Dictionary*,[33] published by Anthony Culyer in 2005, the lexicographer defines value by saying that: 'In economics, value is usually taken as a maximum amount that an individual or group is willing to pay for a particular good or service rather than go without it.' He also defines 'marginal value' as: '. . .the value of marginal benefit: the maximum an individual is willing to pay for an increment of benefit'.

The four healthcare perspectives on value

Although the term value has the same general meaning for the main actors involved in the provision of health services – payers for healthcare, patients, clinicians and managers, and for the industries that produce drugs, equipment and information technology (IT) –

there are four aspects of value pertinent to a health service in the useful taxonomy developed by the European Commission's EXPH,[34] which are reproduced below, this time ordered from the population to the individual; there is, of course, no correct ordering because the four are inter-related:

- **Allocative value**: equitable resource distribution across all populations and within each population across all patient groups
- **Social value**: the contribution of healthcare to social participation and connectedness
- **Technical value**: achievement of the best possible outcomes with available resources
- **Personal value**: appropriate care to achieve a patient's personal goals (Figure 2.1).

In countries in which universal healthcare is funded from insurance funds rather than direct investment of government finance, the situation is less clear-cut but the same principles apply.

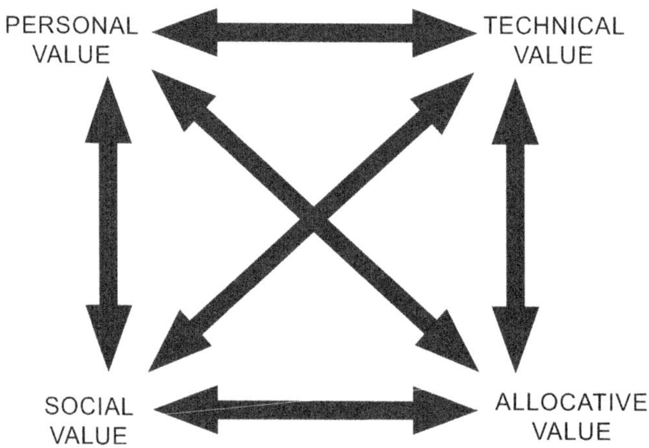

Figure 2.1: The four types of value in healthcare

Before discussing each of these four types of value in more depth, let us reflect on the term 'waste' – previously thought of as any resource that was not essential to complete a task and which could therefore be thrown away. The Academy of Royal Colleges report[35] reminds us that 'One doctor's waste is another patient's delay. Potentially, it could be that other patient's lack of treatment. There is a clinical cost to wasted resources.' Thus another definition of waste is that it is the use of resources that would deliver more value if used for other interventions or another group of patients, and waste is now an accepted term with this broader meaning, which will be discussed in more detail later.

Allocative value

There are different levels of allocation that can be seen in every health service that has to cover the whole population from a finite budget, depending on the structure. From the perspective of payers for healthcare, whose responsibility it is to allocate resources among different segments of the population, value is at its maximum when it is not possible to increase the benefit or decrease the harm by re-allocating a single pound, euro or dollar from one group of patients to another. Some economists refer to this as 'the point of indifference', a term developed by Vilfredo Pareto:[36]

> *When the consumption and production markets are in equilibrium, and when consumers' rates of indifference are equal to the economy's ability to transform one good into the others, we are in a position called Pareto optimality, named after economist Vilfredo Pareto. In an economy that is in a Pareto-optimal state, it is impossible to make someone better off (that is, increase that person's welfare) without making someone else worse off. Under such a situation, the economy has reached a state of allocative efficiency, although. . . this rests on a number of assumptions.*

In public services we do not aim to measure value solely in monetary units. Individual patients place a value on certain aspects of their health that cannot be captured in financial terms, and populations also have perceptions about value not governed by financial considerations, a concept referred to as 'public' or social value.

Social value (and the need for stewardship of health services)

Mark Moore's seminal book on public value, *Creating Public Value: Strategic Management in Government*, describes how public services can create 'public value'.[37]

Moore's definition of public value is synonymous with social value:

> *. . .things produced by public organizations are (more or less imperfect) reflections of the desires that citizens express through the institutions of representative government. It follows that managers of public sector enterprises can create value (in the sense of satisfying the desires of citizens and clients) through two different activities directed at two different markets. The most obvious way is to deploy the money and authority entrusted to them to produce things of value to particular clients and beneficiaries. Public managers can also create value by establishing and operating an institution that meets citizens' (and their representatives') desires for properly ordered and productive public institutions.*

Moore and co-author John Benington subsequently elaborated on the concept of public value as having two different dimensions: 'Public value can be thought of in two main ways: first, what the public values; second, what adds value to the public sphere? These two aspects are often in tension and sometimes in conflict with each other, but it is necessary to link both dimensions if the theory is to be robust.'[38]

The UK's population places a high value on the NHS. Moreover, the importance of public value was recognised by the passing of the Social Value Act 2012,[39] which aimed to ensure that local authorities take social value into account by, for example, helping local entrepreneurs develop job creation schemes to employ local people to deliver services.

The radical NHS white paper on integration and innovation,[40] which demolished the reliance on 'the market' introduced to the NHS in England in 1990 by Margeret Thatcher and Kenneth Clarke, was very clear. It set out the 'triple aim' for the NHS, namely:

- to support better health and well-being for everyone
- better quality of health services for all
- sustainable use of NHS resources.

The term 'sustainable' is a broad term that includes the need to take the environmental impact of the NHS into consideration given finite natural resources. We are reminded, however, that the very survival of the NHS, its 'sustainability', depends on the way in which those resources are used. The white paper also emphasised the need for the NHS to increase social value, defining one of the four purposes of the integrated systems that are proposed as the key organisational form – rather than relying on bureaucracies and 'the market' – as being to help 'the NHS to support broader social and economic development'. This is a clear call for organisations like hospitals to focus on social as well as technical value, and Nigel Crisp's provocative book *Health is Made at Home, Hospitals are for Repairs* challenges hospitals to think more broadly.[41] Many hospitals are becoming what are termed 'anchor hospitals', committed to just this principle, although technical value remains of vital importance.

One of the key contributors to social value in healthcare is the voluntary sector, whose principal resource is the work of volunteers, who usually live in the population served by a hospital, and whose work not only improves the health of that population but also makes a major contribution to the sustainability of the health service – often without any investment from that health service.

The need to think of sustainability in an environmental sense is of great and growing importance. The concept and language of stewardship re-entered common use in relation to the future of the planet, initially with regard to biodiversity (a more visible issue than climate change in the early days), as highlighted in Rachel Carson's book *Silent Spring*, published in 1962.[42] Many individuals, including healthcare professionals, are conscious of planetary stewardship and take action to mitigate their environmental impact in their personal lives, yet this strategy must also be applied to clinical practice and health service management. The healthcare sector is not exempt from wider issues of sustainability. A growing number of health service organisations have a target and plan for meeting net zero carbon. Within sustainability strategies it has also been important to recognise that the activities that contribute most to the carbon footprint of health services are not heating, lighting and waste, but the use of medical equipment, pharmaceuticals, staff commuting and patient travel to and from appointments.

Some clinicians may be unmoved to optimise resource use by appeals to increase financial efficiency or to 'make savings' and reduce costs in a way that will release money for reallocation. However, many may become strongly motivated when an appeal is made to reduce carbon, and maximising resource use in this way will almost always reduce financial cost. The Centre for Sustainable Healthcare in Oxford is committed to this aspect of sustainability and is working with clinicians on a wide range of clinical technologies and services to make them more sustainable.

Technical value

The meaning of value to a health service manager is similar to that for a payer, because managers are responsible for groups of patients, not individuals. Managers want healthcare to be:

- Effective and safe for individuals. Not only because this is obviously desirable, but also because the downsides of failure are errors that are troublingly common, have serious iatrogenic consequences for patients, and waste resources to remedy and deal with complaints, investigations and lawsuits that are time-consuming and bad for morale.
- Productive, and of high quality.

The manager of a healthcare facility such as a hospital is rarely told how much to invest for each patient group by the payer. They may be told to invest in a service where there are obvious deficiencies, usually manifest by long waiting times. A manager has to allocate resources into three main types of spend:

- direct clinical care
- clinical support services, such as biochemistry or imaging
- management.

A health service management team also has to decide which services should get more money and, in times of retrenchment, which should get less. A health service manager values most highly their ability to deliver care of a standard that will maximise the possibility of benefit and minimise the possibility of harm while satisfying the payer's requirements and continuously improving the service.

People who work in healthcare are sometimes classified as being either 'clinicians' or 'managers'. This is a false distinction because all clinicians manage resources. Busy clinicians place a high value on the opportunity to use their scarcest resource, their time, to a). see those patients most likely to benefit from their skill, and b). provide the 'best care' quickly and easily as needed by each individual patient. Most clinicians now accept that the definition of 'best care' is relative and means the best that can be provided by the service in which they are working. This type of care provision may be different from the care that would be possible for individual patients if cost were not a consideration. The clinician working in a service where resources were limitless might try treatments that could give hope to, and which might work for, one in a million patients. When payers have to derive maximum value for the entire population for which they are responsible, however, treatments with this level of benefit – the offer of hope combined with a one in a million chance of success – are of too low a value to be acceptable, and would not be included in the range of treatment options available to the clinician working in the service. Not all clinicians find this tension easy to bear, but the phenomenon of unwarranted variation is forcing clinicians to face up to the fact that they are making value decisions unconsciously.

There are often several reasons to explain why a particular intervention is used either much more or much less in one population than another, such as:

- Supply-sensitive care: a service in which the patterns of use are not related to any underlying medical evidence but to the availability of the services. For instance, if there are more surgeons in one population than another, it is highly likely that there will be more operations in the population that has a greater number of surgeons. It is important to remember also that supply rarely takes into account the challenges faced by people in the most deprived sub-groups of society – not just the challenge, for example, of literacy, but practical problems such as the difficulty people may have in reaching a service and the fact that they may lose pay by attending a clinic.

- Preference-sensitive care: in medicine there are many scenarios in which more than one option for action exists; both patients and physicians have preferences for certain interventions or types of care, and physician preference is often shared by a group of physicians working in the same population. Physician preference influences what is offered to patients, how it is offered and what is done. In 2013 two major papers on variation in surgery and how to reduce it were published in *The Lancet*.[43,44] The bottom line, dramatically presented in large type on the cover, reads: 'A patient's odds of undergoing surgery often depend more on where he/she lives rather than on clinical circumstances.' The implications of this are of great importance to both individuals and populations. For instance, for the treatment of prostate cancer, surgeons recommend surgery more often than do radiotherapists, who recommend radiotherapy more frequently than surgeons. Clinicians who have spent years developing a sophisticated skill set believe their particular skill to be of high value, and this belief influences not only the way clinicians interact with individual patients but also the way they use resources.

The work of Jack Wennberg and his collaborators[45] in documenting the scale and pervasiveness of variations in rates of treatment over small areas may be seen as a driver of the development of evidence-based medicine (EBM), along with an increasing recognition of the importance of engaging clinicians in drawing up practice guidelines. This developed over the past 40 years, when there were, in most countries, annual real increases in the financial resources available for health services. This has now largely come to an end. The new era of financial constraint entails the need to develop a new culture of 'stewardship', alongside continued progress in EBM.

In recent years, 'stewardship' as a term has experienced a resurgence in use, particularly by the environmental movement, which emphasises that as human beings we do not own the planet but hold it in trust for the next generation. The same can be said of health services. Clinicians need to accept that as well as having the responsibility for bidding for more resources for their speciality or department, they are also the stewards of resources already allocated to them. The importance of the work of Wennberg has been to shift the focus from measuring the outcomes of patients treated by an institution and relating outcomes to costs, which is a measure of efficiency, to instead emphasising the importance of using the population in need – rather than the patients treated – as the denominator. It is now accepted that there is a need to distinguish three terms: productivity, efficiency and value:

- The **productivity** of a health service relates inputs to outputs, e.g. the number of cases per bed or the number of operations per surgeon.
- The **efficiency** of a health service relates outcomes to inputs, e.g. the number of people cured per number of operations conducted.

Anthony Culyer defined 'productivity' as 'the output of goods and services produced by one or more factors of production'.[3] 'Factors of production' here means inputs. Hence, if a hospital were to increase the number of cases treated, which would tend to mean a fall in costs per case (as many costs do not increase *pro rata* with increases in activity), then the hospital would be more productive. The American literature on value usually relates to outcomes for the patients treated,[46] and this focus on value has been very helpful. However, the concept of value in a society in which the needs of the whole population have to be met from a finite budget is broader, because payers have to be on the alert for both overuse and underuse, as well as efficiency. So efficiency is broader than productivity, and utilisation value is broader than efficiency and includes equity. In future payers will not only expect the provider to use the resources to achieve the best outcomes for people who happen to reach a service but also to make the best use of resources for all people with a particular need, and remain aware of the possibility that there may be underuse of a service by people in the most deprived sub-groups of the population.

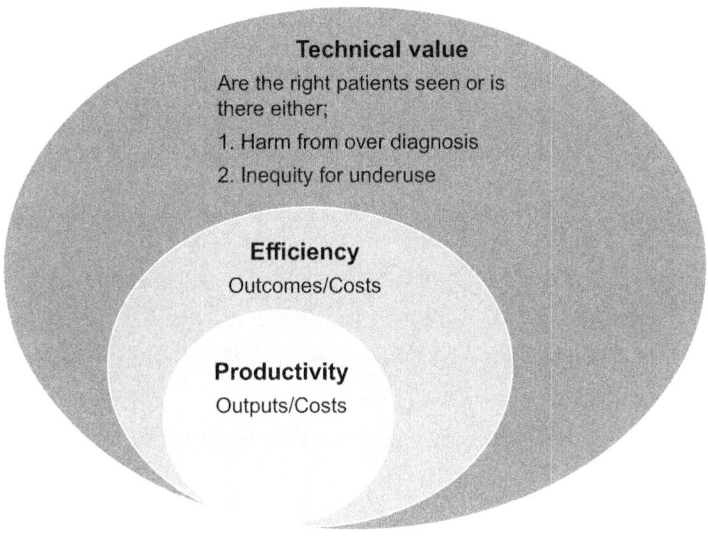

Figure 2.2: Productivity and efficiency in relation to technical value

The 2021 NHS White Paper was very clear. It defined one of the four 'purposes' of the integrated systems it proposed as the organisational form to ensure sustainability of the NHS as being to enhance 'productivity and value for money'.

It is also important to distinguish efficiency from cost-effectiveness. The latter is a feature of an intervention such as a new drug, but productivity, efficiency and value relate to the performance of a service serving a defined population. In times of growth the innovations that are developed from biomedical research can improve value provided they are proven to be effective and cost-effective (as in the recommendations of the National Institute of Health and Care Excellence, or NICE, for England and Wales), and NHS commissioners decide whether these are affordable given their costs and the availability of growth money.

In an era of austerity, however, innovation cannot be funded from growth money, and so decision-makers can either decide that they cannot afford to implement changes that would improve value from biomedical research or find ways to finance them from efficiency savings. Unfortunately the nature of the problem is not widely understood: too many involved in making policy decisions believe that interventions that are cost-effective are cost-saving, and hence affordable. Hence, the first requirement of enabling a health service to avoid ossification from failure to innovate in austerity is basic understanding of the key economic concept of opportunity costs and distinctions between cost-effectiveness, cost-saving and affordability. This has been clearly described by Chris Whitty, the Chief Medical Officer of England, in an article on providing evidence for policy-makers, including those who pay for and manage healthcare. Here is a key section:

> *The first is the relatively limited range of things policy-makers can do. They can exhort; in some cases they can legislate; most commonly they deploy resources but this means moving resources from one priority to another rather than creating new resource. The second follows from the fact that their main lever is moving constrained resources around and choosing between different ratios of financial allocation; they tend to think like economists or be advised by them, and economics is the training for many policy-makers, whether civil servants or politicians. This does not mean good economic analysis is essential to influence policy (although it certainly helps), but good policy-makers will always be asking the question 'what is the opportunity cost of this new*

> *initiative?' Policy-makers also therefore can be more numerate than scientists often give them credit for, and have access to well trained statisticians.*[47]

Policy-makers can also take action to ensure that discussion about the relative value of different interventions is not only prompted by the need to fund an innovation but is part of a continuous cycle of value improvement. It is important to remember that we are where we are not only as a result of formal decisions about the allocation of resources – part of a logical process designed to increase allocative and technical value – but also as a result of decades of drift, with those clinicians who were better organised increasing activity and using more resources that were funded by the payers as a result of bills sent in by the organisations employing them - with both clinicians and payers, and governmental bodies and insurance companies, unaware of the fact that increasing expenditure is not necessarily reflected in a parallel increase in value. This was first described by Avedis Donabedian in his classic diagram from 1980, which we will discuss in more detail in the next chapter.[48]

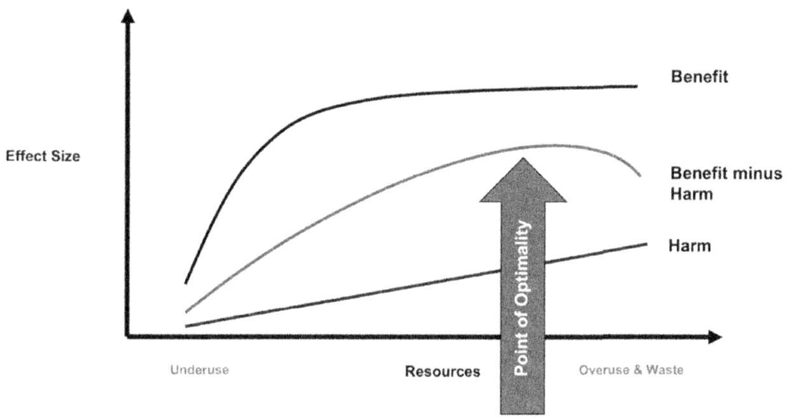

Figure 2.3: Donabedian's depiction of the relationship between investment benefit, harm and value

Increasing expenditure, as distinct from an explicit decision to invest more resources in an intervention, also has implications for personal value.

Personal value

The need to focus on the value of the individual patient is increasingly receiving attention. Maureen Bisognano, the charismatic Director of the Institute of Healthcare Improvement, advocates that we move from 'what's the matter? medicine' to 'what matters to you? medicine'.[49] The vignette in Box 2.1 illustrates the transformational shift necessary.

Box 2.1: 'What matters to you? medicine': A patient with mitral valve disease

Mrs X is 86 years old and has mitral valve disease. She receives care from a compassionate and high-quality cardiology and cardiac surgery team who have advised her that a mitral valve operation (open-heart surgery) is the only treatment that will effectively deal with the mitral valve narrowing that has been diagnosed – an example of 'what's the matter? medicine'.

When Mrs X was asked what her problem was, however, she expressed concern that she felt tired after two hours of gardening. The key issue in 'what matters to you? medicine' is not whether Mrs X has mitral valve disease, but whether cardiac surgery will significantly reduce the level of tiredness she feels after two hours' gardening, taking into account not only the quality of the intervention, known to be high for this particular service, but also the implications of a considerable period of time in hospital and intensive care for a person 86 years of age.

Professor Al Mulley of Dartmouth University and his colleagues coined the term 'the silent misdiagnosis'[50] to describe the common situation in which clinicians have accurately diagnosed a disease but failed to identify the patient's preferences. They argue that not only do decisions need to be based on the best current evidence but also that decision-making needs to be sensitive to the preferences of individual patients. When seeking to explain the causes of unwarranted variation, Wennberg highlighted that patients' preferences were often either not elicited or, if they were, their preferences would be ignored.

> *...elective, or 'preference-sensitive' care, interventions for which there is more than one option and where the outcomes will differ according to the option used because patients delegate decision making to doctors, physician opinion, rather than patient preference, often determines which treatment patients receive. I argue that this can result in a serious but commonly overlooked medical error: operating on the wrong patients – on those who, were they fully informed, would not have wanted the operation they received.*[45]

From the perspective of the patient, the value of the care received is measured not only by the outcome of the care but also by the way it is delivered. The value that patients are prepared to place on the care received will be influenced not only by the outcome but also by what has been termed the burden of treatment, and this requires services to measure outcomes from the perspective of patients as well as clinicians.

When considering costs, economists recognise the importance of capturing costs to patients as well as to providers of care. This has been recognised in the concept of the burden of treatment. Even patients who are appreciative often complain about the number of clinic visits they and their carers have had to make and the demands on their time.

> *Treatment burden includes the work of developing an understanding of treatments, interacting with others to organize care, attending appointments, taking medications,*

enacting lifestyle measures, and appraising treatments. Factors that patients reported as increasing treatment burden included:

a. too many medications and appointments,
b. barriers to accessing services,
c. fragmented and poorly organized care,
d. lack of continuity, and
e. inadequate communication between health professionals.[51]

Again we see how different perspectives on value are interrelated. As more interventions are carried out in a population people who are less severely affected are treated. They will get a smaller benefit than those who are severely affected but run the same risk of side effects of the same magnitude. This is recognised by clinicians who classify interventions as being necessary, appropriate, inappropriate or even futile, and the Donabedian diagram can be adapted to reflect this.

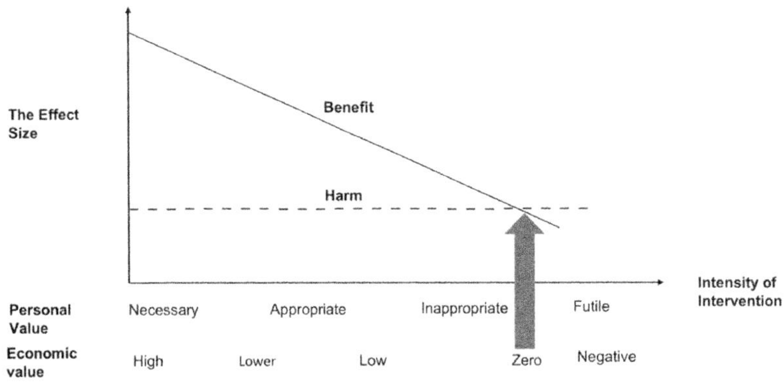

Figure 2.4: Healthcare value from a population perspective

This will be discussed in more detail in Question 7, namely: 'Are we sure that every individual patient is getting the right intervention in the way that is right for them?' In addition to these four health service perspectives on value, however, it is also essential to consider the perspective of industries that have contributed so much to the Second Healthcare Revolution.

The perspective of industry on value

Health services stimulate and support the pharmaceutical, medical equipment, diagnostic and IT industries. Frequently, the developers of products or services are disappointed by the lack of enthusiasm generated by their latest creation. The reason for this lack of enthusiasm is not simply the added cost incurred by any new technology, at least in the short term, but a failure to appreciate the different meanings given to the term 'value'. The situation is further complicated by the fact that many health services are financially hard-pressed and unable to create a fund (an 'invest-to-save' fund) that would allow investment in the short term to increase value in the long term.

For the past two decades, industry has recognised the need to present health service payers and providers with evidence of effectiveness and cost-effectiveness associated with new products or services, and in England and Wales NICE has played a very important part in this revolution (it also has an influence globally as one of the leading healthcare technology assessment agencies). In some cases this has led to differences of opinion between industry and those who pay for healthcare regarding the strength of evidence used by industry. For instance, the pharmaceutical industry has been criticised for generating evidence by comparing a new drug with a placebo rather than with the best existing treatment. Nevertheless, there has been a perception within industry that if they can demonstrate effectiveness and cost-effectiveness funds should flow.

In a period of financial constraint, when health service funds are not increasing – and may even be decreasing – the payer's interest is in how much **value** is added to a service for a particular group of patients, not just whether a treatment is effective. Effectiveness and cost-effectiveness will be taken for granted by health services but they need to see, or be convinced, that value will be increased.[52]

Some principles have been discussed with industry as examples of new types of skills that people need to acquire, not only in the established industry but when working in a start-up business, taking an idea or innovation on the long journey from bench to bedside. Listed below are five skills that people need, in addition to being able to demonstrate effectiveness and cost-effectiveness:

- Being able to explain how a particular drug or technology increases value for individual patients
- The ability to show how a drug or technology increases value for the population served
- Knowing how to describe the system that can be created using a drug or technology as the catalyst for change
- Being able to demonstrate that a technology is of higher value than some other intervention for the same condition, and how it could be funded by reducing investment in that alternative intervention
- How to demonstrate that a drug or technology is of higher value than interventions for other conditions covered by the same programme budget, and how it could be funded by switching resources from those interventions.

The introduction of value-based pricing in the NHS in England was challenging for the pharmaceutical industry,[53] but it is very important to understand that generalisations about 'big pharma' or even 'the pharma industry' have to be made or interpreted with caution because there are two different types of industry, with different perspectives on value. One type consists of the companies that invest to create new drugs, which need to recover the cost of research and development (R&D) before the patent expires, allowing the other type of company to produce generic versions at lower cost. The latter type of company is primarily interested in volume of sales and in producing generic drugs at relatively low cost. The former type of company, the big companies with well-known names, are obviously also interested in keeping costs down, but when they produce a new treatment that is more cost-effective than an existing treatment, as approved by NICE, they know that the NHS will need to find the money to pay for this new and better treatment and understand that one source of this money is the money being spent on drugs of little or no value. The potential for achieving this was excellently described in a powerful report prepared by the Chief Pharmaceutical Officer of the Department of Health and Social Care (DHSC), Keith Ridge, titled *Good for you, Good for us, Good for Everybody, and sub-titled: A plan to reduce overprescribing to make patient care better and safer, support the NHS, and reduce carbon emissions.*[54] The key points of this report on value are that:

- Our best estimate is that at least 10% of the current volume of medicines may be over-prescribed (though this will be less than 10% by value)
- As well as the direct negative effects for individual patients, over-prescribing is also a waste in that the NHS is buying medicines and giving them to people who don't want or need them

The term 'value' features very prominently in the DHSC work on medicines, for example in their Medicines Value Programme, which is based on the evidence that:

- 5–10% of all hospital admissions are medicines-related

- Two-thirds of medicines-related hospital admissions are preventable
- The overall NHS drugs bill is £16.8 billion a year.

Those companies that make the new cost-effective drugs know that one source of funding for these drugs needs to come in part from reducing the over-prescribing of generic drugs of low, zero or even negative value, and they are therefore fully committed to value-based healthcare.

Numerical definitions of value

While all these verbal definitions of value are open to different interpretations, an alternative approach is to use numbers.

The Vienna School of Philosophy flourished in the 1920s and 1930s and became very influential in Britain, where it gave rise to what is known as 'logical positivism'. Their leading light in Britain was A. J. Ayer, whose book *Language, Truth and Logic*,[55] published in 1936, had considerable impact. The logical positivists took an approach to the definition of the meaning of a term that did not rely on words alone. Ayer proposed that:

> *Instead of trying to understand the meaning of a proposition by analysing the meaning of the individual words that compose it, another approach should be taken. The criterion which we use to test the genuineness of apparent statements of facts is the criterion of verifiability. We say that a sentence is factually significant to any given person if, and only if, he knows how to verify the proposition which it purports to express – that is, if he knows what observations will lead him, under certain conditions, to accept the proposition as being true, or reject it as being false. And with regard to questions, the procedure is the same. We enquire in every case what observations will lead*

> *us to answer the question one way or the other, and, if none can be discovered, we must conclude that the sentence under consideration does not, as far as we are concerned, express a genuine question, however strongly its grammatical appearance may suggest that it does.*

In 1978, Rachel Rosser and Paul Kind published a seminal paper entitled 'A Scale of Valuations of States of Illness: is There a Social Consensus?',[56] which led to the development of a measure known as the quality-adjusted life year (QALY). The QALY is a measure of health-related quality of life, encompassing both quantity and quality. A year of perfect health was deemed to be worth 1 and death was usually given 0 – although society agrees that there are some situations that could be regarded as worse than death and which need negative numbers. Although there has been much debate about the use of the QALY, it is a measure that can be used to assess the value of a particular intervention.

In 1996, in *The Global Burden of Disease*, the World Health Organization included quality-adjusted measures of disability (disability-adjusted life years, DALYs), as well as mortality, in a ground-breaking review of healthcare priority setting edited by Christopher Murray and Alan Lopez.[57] This major work changed the way in which diseases were ranked within the assessment of a country's burden of disease (BoD), and in particular it increased the level of significance of mental health problems to the BoD.

Reaching agreement on meanings of value...

As there are multiple meanings and definitions of the word 'value', it is essential to reach agreement on how the term will be used before starting a discussion. In any meeting at which value is to be discussed, either implicitly or explicitly, a consensus must be achieved on a single meaning that will be used, if only for the duration of that particular meeting. Some things that may help:

- Prepare copies of the definition you want to use, or display it on a PowerPoint slide
- If you have sufficient time, you can allow the group to come to the conclusion that there are two different types of meaning for the term 'value': the moral meaning and the economic. However, in most meetings there is usually not time to explore this and the group should be told to focus on the economic meaning.
- Ask people to work in pairs and give them no more than two minutes to agree on words that come to mind when they think of the value derived from resources invested in health services; remind them that value is different from quality.
- Take feedback, with each pair putting forward one word; record the words on a flipchart. The aim, if possible, is to develop a meaning close to the definition in the *Shorter Oxford English Dictionary*. After the group has finished brainstorming, it can be fruitful to reveal a selection of definitions, including that in the *Shorter Oxford English Dictionary*; it may also be helpful to present the Donabedian optimality curve and to emphasise the distinction between allocative and technical efficiency.

...and of stewardship

It is also important to reach agreement on the meaning of stewardship, which is a longstanding concept found in the Bible – the good steward leaves the land in better condition than he found it, even though he does not own it. The concept became broader with its adoption by environmental activists such as David Holmgren: 'The stewardship concept demands that we constantly ask the question: Will the resource be in better shape after my stewardship?'[58]

There is also a need to discuss the consequences of poor stewardship, first articulated by botanist William Forster Lloyd in Buckinghamshire in 1833, who wrote:

> *If a shepherd put more than his allotted number of sheep on the common, overgrazing could result. For each additional animal, a shepherd could receive additional benefits, but the whole group shared damage to the commons. If all shepherds made this individually rational economic decision, the common could be depleted or even destroyed, to the detriment of all.*[59]

This was called the 'Tragedy of the Commons' by Garrett Hardin in an article in *Science* in 1968,[60] which was given great credit by Elinor Ostrom who won the Nobel Prize for Economics in 2008 for her work on stewardship.[61] She concluded that 'If those using the resources are allowed to manage those common pooled resources themselves, then sustainability is possible. They become stewards.'

The term stewardship was adopted by people in healthcare initially to describe the growth of antibiotic resistance, which illustrates the tragedy of the commons perfectly. It is now entering the broader debate, for example through the Academy of Medical Royal Colleges Report that we cited in Chapter 1, with a key quote being that 'Doctors should embrace the values of resource stewardship in their clinical practice.'[35]

Perhaps the best way to gain an understanding of the meaning of stewardship is to debate these issues with a group and ask for examples of good stewardship and examples of the tragedy of the commons.

Clarifying the meanings of value and stewardship will be helpful, but it does not solve all the problems involved in increasing value. We also need to focus on the decisions that have to be made in healthcare – and many of them, not just clinical decisions, are hellish. These are the subject of the next chapter.

Questions for reflection when teaching or developing networks

If using these in network building or teaching, give one of the questions to the group and ask them to work in pairs to reflect on the question for 3 minutes. Try to get people who do not know one another to work together. When taking feedback, let each pair make only one point. In the interests of equity, if you start with the pair on the left-hand side of the room for the first question, start with the pair on the right hand side of the room for the second question.

- Is it possible for those who pay for, and those who manage, healthcare to reach agreement on the meaning of value?
- Is it possible for a clinician to be more concerned about the consequences of their decisions regarding an individual patient for the whole population without their behaving unethically towards that patient?
- If you were the chief executive of a large pharmaceutical company, how would you assess the value of a new drug?
- Can you identify a service that has passed the point of optimality, or will do so if growth is not slowed or stopped?
- How well are we dealing with the challenge of prioritisation of our allocation of resources?
- Are we seeking to identify waste and switch resources to higher-value interventions?

- Are we identifying inequity? Are we collecting the data that would allow us to do so?
- How would you explain 'more is not necessarily better inhealth services' if you were given two minutes on local radio?

References

31. Kenny A. *The Wittgenstein Reader.* 1994. Blackwell.

32. *Shorter Oxford English Dictionary.* 6th Edition. 2007. Oxford University Press.

33. Culyer AJ. *Healthcare Economics Dictionary.* 2005. Edward Elgar.

34. European Commission. *Defining Value in "Value-Based Healthcare".* Published November 2019. Available at: https://ec.europa.eu/health/sites/default/files/expert_panel/docs/2019_defining-value-vbhc_factsheet_en.pdf

35. Academy of Medical Royal Colleges. *Protecting Resources, Promoting Value: a Doctor's Guide to Cutting Waste in Clinical Care.* Published November 2014. Available at: www.aomrc.org.uk/wp-content/uploads/2016/05/Protecting_Resources_Promoting_Value_1114.pdf

36. Rice TH. *The Economics of Health Reconsidered.* 1998. Health Administration Press.

37. Moore MH. *Creating Public Value: Strategic Management in Government.* 1995. Harvard University Press.

38. Benington J, Moore MH. *Public Value Theory & Practice.* 2011. Macmillan Education UK.

39. The National Archives. *Public Services (Social Value) Act 2012.* Available at: www.legislation.gov.uk/ukpga/2012/3/enacted (accessed June 2022).

40. UK Department of Health and Social Care. Policy paper: *Integration and innovation: working together to improve health and social care for all.* 11 February 2021. Available at: www.gov.uk/government/publications/working-together-to-improve-health-and-social-care-for-all/integration-and-innovation-working-together-to-improve-health-and-social-care-for-all-html-version

41. Crisp N. *Health is Made at Home, Hospitals are for Repairs.* 2020. SALUS Global Knowledge Exchange.

42. Carson R. *Silent Spring.* 1962. Houghton Mifflin.

43. Birkmeyer JD, Reames BN, McCulloch P, et al. 'Understanding of regional variation in the use of surgery'. *The Lancet.* 2013; 383(9898): 1121–1129.

44. McCulloch P, Nagendran M, Campbell WB, *et al.* 'Strategies to reduce variation in the use of surgery'. *The Lancet.* 2013; 382(9898): 1130–1139.

45. Wennberg J. *Tracking Medicine: A Researcher's Quest to Understand Health Care.* 2010. Oxford University Press.

46. Porter ME. *What is Value in Health Care?* Harvard Business School. Institute for Strategy and Competitiveness White Paper. 2008. Adapted in *New England Journal of Medicine*, 2010; 363(26): 2477–2481.

47. Whitty CJM. 'What makes an academic paper useful for health policy?' *BMC Medicine*. 2015; 13: 301.

48. Donabedian A. *An Introduction to Quality Assurance in Healthcare*. 2002. Oxford University Press.

49. Bisognano M. *Why "What Matters to You?" Matters Around the World. Institute for Healthcare Improvement*. 24 February 2017. Available at: www.ihi.org/communities/blogs/why-what-matters-to-you-matters-around-the-world

50. Mulley A, Trimble C, Elwyn G. 'Stop the silent misdiagnosis: patients' preferences matter.' *British Medical Journal*. 2012; 345: e6572.

51. Gallacher K, May CR, Montori VM, Mair FS. 'Understanding patients' experiences of treatment burden in chronic heart failure using normalization process theory'. *Annals of Family Medicine*. 2011; 9(3): 235–243.

52. Iglesias C, Nixon J, Cranny G, *et al.* 'Pressure relieving support surfaces (PRESSURE) trial: cost-effectiveness analysis'. *British Medical Journal*. 2006; 332(7555): 1416–1418.

53. Ryan AM. 'Will value-based purchasing increase disparities in care?' *New England Journal of Medicine*. 2013; 369(26): 2472–2474.

54. Ridge K. *Good for you, good for us, good for everybody: a plan to reduce overprescribing to make patient care better and safer, support the NHS, and reduce carbon emissions.* 52 September 2021. Available at: www.gov.uk/government/publications/national-overprescribing-review-report

55. Ayer AJ. *Language, Truth, and Logic*. 1936. Victor Gollancz.

56. Rosser R, Kind P. 'A scale of valuations of states of illness: is there a social consensus?' *International Journal of Epidemiology*. 1978. 7(4): 347–358.

57. Murray CJL, Lopez AD. *The Global Burden Of Disease*. 1996. World Health Organization.

58. Holmgren D. *Permaculture: Principles and Pathways Beyond Sustainability*. 2002. Holmgren Design Services, p. 5.

59. Wilson T, Bevan G, Gray M, et al. 'Developing a culture of stewardship: how to prevent the Tragedy of the Commons in universal health systems'. *Journal of the Royal Society of Medicine*. 2020; 113(7): 255–261.

60. Hardin G. 'The Tragedy of the Commons'. *Science*. 1968; 162(3859): 1243–1248.

61. Ostrom E. *Governing the Commons: The Evolution of Institutions for Collective Action*. 1990. Cambridge University Press, p. 2.

3

HELLISH DECISIONS IN HEALTHCARE

This chapter will:

- Explore the political perspective on resource allocation
- Clarify the aims of value improvement
- Highlight the ethical and technical aspects of decision-making.

By the end of this chapter you will have an understanding of:

- Donabedian's principle of optimality
- The flaw in utilitarianism
- The relationship between changes in resource investment and the balance of benefit and harm.

Hours of television drama set in emergency departments have familiarised – perhaps hardened – us to the hellish decisions that clinicians and patients face. Those who work in front-line clinical jobs have stressful and demanding lives that have become even more stressful as a result of the COVID-19 pandemic. Although the pressures differ, the jobs of those who pay for or manage healthcare are also stressful, and we want to emphasise here that the term 'people who manage healthcare' includes all clinicians, hence our preference for the term 'people who manage' rather than 'manager', which implies that clinicians plays no part in the allocation and use of resources unless they have explicit part- or full-time management responsibilities. The report on protecting resources by the UK Academy of Medical Royal Colleges[62] which we introduced in Chapter 1 as a beacon of light, emphasised strongly the need for every clinician to consider themselves responsible for these tasks just as they are responsible for the quality and safety of clinical care, 'because this process creates a higher value health care system where resources, cash, carbon and staff time, are released from some parts of the system to develop new services or support struggling services'.

There are, however, many decisions that have to be made and taken by politicians and people in leadership and management positions before an individual clinician can decide whether to use resources for an individual patient.

The politics of allocating public resources

Whilst it is easy for ministers and officials to create a policy which states that there will need to be an X% increase in efficiency each year, this is difficult to achieve in practice. By this we mean changing the service so it is X percent more efficient each year and not simply 'salami slicing', i.e. reducing every budget by X percent. Typically when governments require health services to become more efficient, they are not seeking financial savings, but rather that managers find ways of meeting the growth in need and demand from changes in demography and technology without additional resources.

The tensions between limits on finance and cost pressures on services play out differently in single-payer (Beveridge or tax-based) systems and multiple-payer (Bismarck or social insurance) systems. In a single-payer system it is easy to constrain the total budget; the pressure is then transmitted to hospitals, which find it difficult to manage within their allocated budgets. In multiple-payer systems hospitals are reimbursed for the services they provide and the cost pressures are transmitted upwards to generate financial crises of demands exceeding what has been planned for. 'Financial crises' thus play out differently in the two systems: single-payer systems can experience crises of 'underfunding' and multiple-payer systems crises of loss of control over escalating costs. Depending on the financial and payment system this pressure for efficiency is retained by the payer in an activity-based payment system or passed to the providers in a system with a capped budget.

One set of difficult decisions is what the total spend on healthcare – as opposed to spending on other services that affect health – ought to be. The opportunity cost of increasing spend on healthcare is that less is spent on other services that can improve health, for education or to relieve poverty, for example. Even before COVID-19 the NHS in England received more resource than education, with the amount doubling between 1997 and 2019, whereas education's allocation increased by much less.[63]

A second set of difficult decisions concerns how much to allocate, for example, to people with cancer versus people with respiratory disease, or elderly people with multiple morbidity, or any other of the 30 principal segments of the population defined by need. In times of austerity these kinds of decisions become more obvious and pressing, often with a view on immediate harm to patients. These are hellish decisions for those who make and take them.

Henry Kissinger, still writing good sense at the age of 98 in 2022, highlighted the distinction between decision-making and decision-taking. The process of decision-making is technical and is the responsibility of an 'official', someone appointed to perform a certain function, such as the head of an organisation responsible for allocating finance to different clinical needs. In making decisions about the allocation of resources, decision-making involves the assessment of, for example, benefits and costs (harm/risk in the short term is a lens) based on the best available evidence.[64] Decision-taking is the final step in the process, with decisions being both technical and ethical, as outlined by Nobel Prize-winning economist Herbert Simon:

> *In ordinary speech there is often confusion between the element of judgement in the decision and the ethical element. This confusion is enhanced by the fact that the further the means–end chain is followed, i.e. the greater the ethical element, the more doubtful are the steps in the chain, and the greater is the element of judgement involved in determining what means will contribute to what ends.*[65]

As there is an ethical element to decisions, politics becomes involved. Kenneth Arrow, who is famous for his 'Impossibility Theorem', argues that:

> *In a capitalist democracy there are essentially two methods by which social choices can be made: voting, typically used to make 'political' decisions, and the market mechanism, typically used to make 'economic' decisions.*[66]

Michael Moore argues that 'political' decisions are those where the market does not work because resources are public:

> *Politics is the answer that a liberal democratic society has given to the (analytically unsolvable) question of what things should be produced for collective purposes with public resource.*[67]

'Politics' in this context is not party politics, but the processes through which policies are agreed in ways that enable their successful implementation. This becomes difficult when resources are constrained and have to be re-allocated to improve value. Everyone would prefer to be involved in a decision-making process that results in more money being given to a service or a sub-group of the population. No-one likes to be involved in a decision that results in money being taken away from a service or population sub-group, but those hellish decisions to have to be taken, and there are two important facts that have to be borne in mind:

- There is no single formula or computer program that solves the problem
- There is no single ethical principle that solves the problem.

It is common for people to quote the principle of utilitarianism – doing the greatest good for the greatest number – as a justification for decisions taken about value. But, as John Rawls argued,[68] applying that principle creates two kinds of problems:

- How can the lesser life prospects for some be justified by an increase in the total sum of prospects?
- How is value to be assessed?

Rawls argues that utilitarianism does not take seriously distinction between persons and assumes that there is an impartial spectator who is capable of experiencing the desires of others as if they were their own, assigning to them appropriate weights to maximise the satisfaction of the group. As Ivan Karamazov pointed out to his idealistic younger brother:

> *Tell me frankly, I appeal to you – answer me: imagine that it is you yourself who are erecting the edifice of human destiny with the aim of making men happy in the end, of giving them peace and contentment at last, but that to do that it is absolutely necessary, and indeed quite inevitable, to torture to death only one tiny creature, the little girl who beat her breast with her little fist, and to found the edifice on her unavenged tears – would you consent to be the architect on those conditions? Tell me and do not lie!* [69]

Rawls argued for a different conception in which questions of distribution are resolved based on his principles of 'justice as fairness'. One of those principles concerns inequalities, which he argues can be justified on the grounds that they benefit the most disadvantaged.

Optimising value

It is common for people to state that they wish to maximise value, but in practice this is not possible because of 'bounded rationality' – the reality of decision-making using available data under strict time constraints, as described by John Sterman:

> *The capacity of the human mind for formulating and solving complex problems is very small compared with the size of the problem whose solution is required for objectively rational behaviour in the real world or even for a reasonable approximation to such objective rationality.*[70]

Herbert Simon suggests that given bounded rationality, we ought to aim not at maximising value but at 'satisficing', a term he invented. Simon challenged fellow academics for giving the impression that complex social problems could be solved by maximising value.

> *Whereas economic man supposedly maximizes – selects the best alternative from among all those available to him – his cousin, the administrator, satisfices – looks for a course of action that is satisfactory or 'good enough'. Because administrators satisfice rather than maximize, they can choose without first examining all possible behaviour alternatives and without ascertaining that these are in fact all the alternatives. Because they treat the world as rather empty and ignore the interrelatedness of all things (so stupefying to thought and action), they can make*

> *their decisions with relatively simple rules of thumb that do not make impossible demands upon their capacity for thought. Simplification may lead to error, but there is no realistic alternative in the face of the limits on human knowledge and reasoning.*[65]

We have to make decisions that are **good enough**, not perfect. Furthermore, the term maximise in this context implies that decision-making can have only beneficial results, whereas the term optimise reminds us that all decisions are a balance between benefits and harms. Our aim therefore should be to optimise value for both individuals and populations.

This use of the term 'optimising' was developed by Avedis Donabedian, who introduced the concept of quality assurance into healthcare in 1966 and is considered by many to be the founder of the quality movement in healthcare, writing two classic books on the subject:

- *Explorations in Quality Assessment and Monitoring*, published as three volumes in 1980[71]
- *An Introduction to Quality Assurance in Health Care*, a lifetime's work condensed into 200 pages[72]

In *Explorations in Quality Assessment and Monitoring*, Donabedian describes not only the concept of structure, process and outcome, first outlined by him in 1966, but also his 'unifying model of benefit, risk and cost', which we introduced in Chapter 2. The power of this model is that it describes for the first time the relationship between the level of resources invested in healthcare and the degree of benefit obtained from that level of investment. Donabedian showed that as healthcare resources are increased in any particular intervention the benefit increases initially but then flattens off, illustrating what some people have called the law of diminishing returns (Figure 3.1).

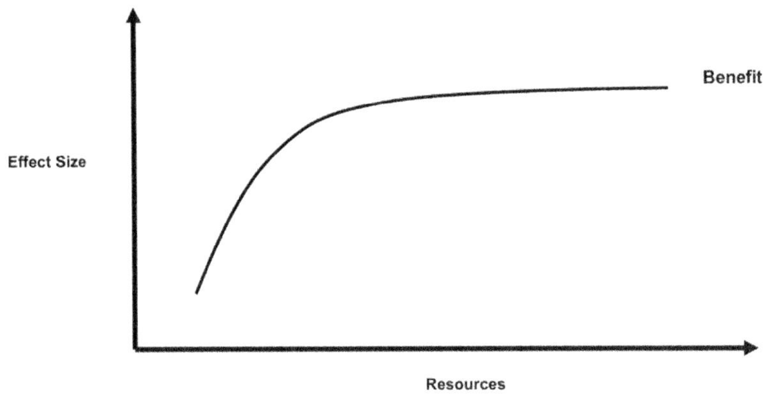

Figure 3.1: The law of diminishing benefit

In contrast to the trajectory of benefit obtained in relation to investment, the amount of harm done increases in direct proportion to the resources invested. For each unit increase in resource, there is a unit increase in the volume of care and a unit increase in the amount of harm done. In fact there may be a progressive increase in the amount of harm done if, with each unit increase in the availability of care, patients who are less fit and more at risk of harm are covered by a service (Figure 3.2). It is important to emphasise that the harm described in Donabedian's model is not the result of medical errors or safety problems: harm occurs in all health services, even those that are the safest and of the highest quality, as an inevitable consequence of the risks associated with interventions such as X-rays, drugs and anaesthetics.

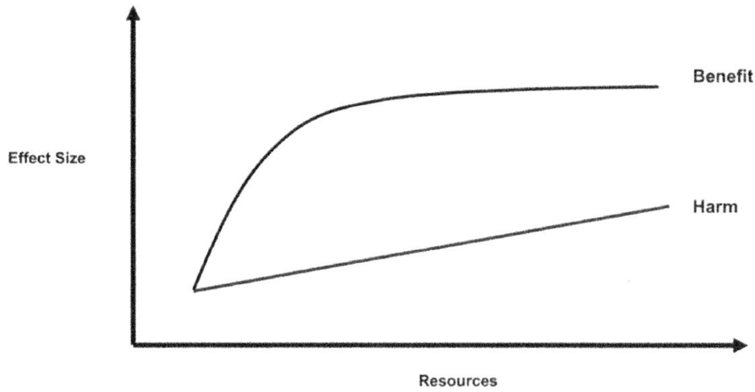

Figure 3.2: The law of undiminishing harm

As a consequence, there comes a point at which the investment of additional resources will lead to a reduction in net benefit, calculated by subtracting the harm from the benefit. We make no apology for reproducing this image, which we regard as the most important image in debates and decisions about value. Indeed when we show it in a lecture or workshop we propose to participants that they bring out their phones and photograph it (Figure 3.3)

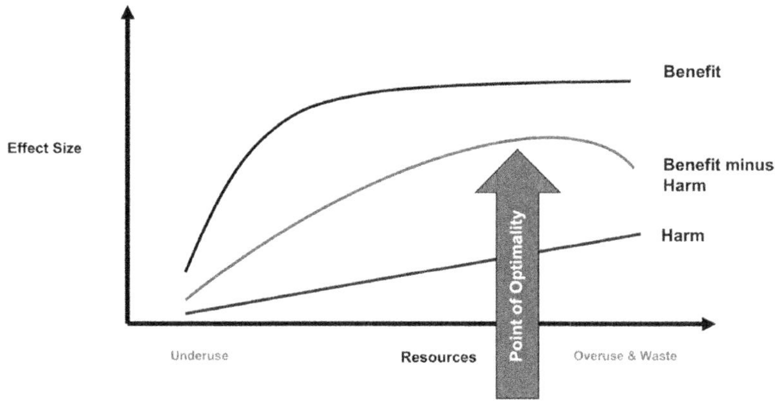

Figure 3.3: The optimal relationship between resources, benefit and harm

Below the 'point of optimality' there is underuse of an intervention, often complicated by inequity, while above the point of optimality there is overuse.

Donabedian's prose is crystal clear:

> *If benefits to health are used as the sole criterion of quality, there is no clear-cut level of service which corresponds to optimum care. One must presumably continue to add services until no measurable additional benefits accrue, but that is to proceed without considering the risk that is inherent to a greater or lesser degree in all health care. . . the services prescribe the use first of large benefits and small risk. Then, as services are added, each increment has progressively larger risks and smaller benefits. . . the curve of 'benefits against risks' rises to a peak.*[71]

Donabedian describes optimality explicitly as:

> *The balancing of improvements in health against the cost of such improvements. The definition implies there is a 'best' or 'optimum relationship' between costs and benefits of health care, a point below which more benefits could be obtained at costs that are low relative to benefits and above which additional benefits are obtained at costs too large relative to corresponding benefits.*[71]

Clinicians and patient groups often desire the provision of maximally effective healthcare, but **optimality** is a more appropriate objective when need and demand are greater than the resources available. Patient interest groups can also appreciate optimality, provided they are informed about the harms of treatment.

In summary, it is not only clinicians who have to make difficult decisions. People who pay for and manage health services also have to make hellish decisions about the allocation of resources, and it is essential to remember that clinicians are also included in this group – even if they do not have explicit managerial responsibilities in their job description. The people called patients and the public all need to understand value and that spending more on one intervention or group of people means spending less on some other intervention or group.

The 10 key value questions we all have to address

The European Union report on value-based healthcare showed the four aspects of healthcare as four pillars supporting universal healthcare, with the term 'value' chosen to recognise its double meaning as both an economic concept and a moral concept.[73]

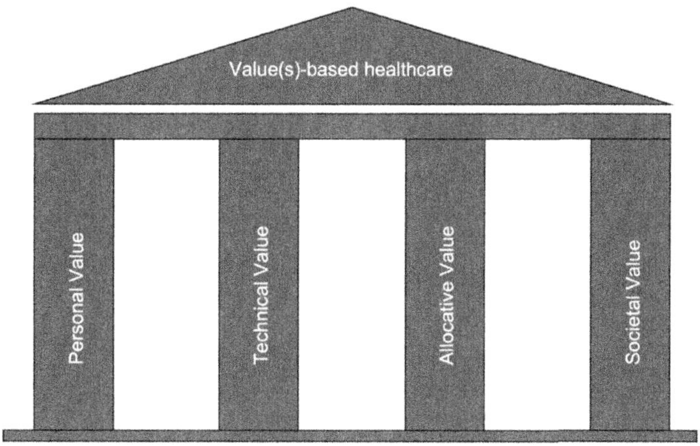

Figure 3.4: The four value pillars

These four perspectives are actually best not represented as separate entities; a Venn diagram or the arrow diagram we used in Chapter 2 would be a more accurate representation. Nevertheless, taking these four perspectives as the basis for future decision-making we can identify 10 key questions that every country needs to address. The first five focus on the allocation of resources; the first three of these need to be asked and answered nationally, while the remaining seven questions are the new agenda for integrated care systems.

Question 1: How much money should be spent on healthcare?

Question 2: How much money should be top-sliced for nationally organised services?

Question 3: Has the money for healthcare been distributed to different parts of the country by a method that recognises variation in need?

Question 4: Has money been allocated to different patient groups in a way that is equitable and that will optimise value for the whole population?

Question 5: Are the resources that have been allocated being used on the right interventions?

Question 6: Are all of the right patients, and only the right patients, being offered the high-value interventions?

Question 7: Are we sure that every individual patient is getting the right intervention in the way that is right for them?

Question 8: Is the quality of care as high as it can be with the resources available?

Question 9: Are clinical risks being minimised?

Question 10: Why not just get a grip, improve quality and safety, and reduce costs while you are at it?

Two chapters on concepts and language might give the impression that the creation of value-based healthcare is just an intellectual activity. Action is required to bring about the revolution that is needed, and that is the subject of the next chapter.

Questions for reflection when teaching or developing networks

If using these in network building or teaching, give one of the questions to the group and ask them to work in pairs to reflect on the question for 3 minutes; try to get people who do not know one another to work together. When taking feedback, let each pair make only one point. In the interests of equity, if you start with the pair on the left-hand side of the room for the first question, start with the pair on the right-hand side of the room for the second question.

- Which term – maximising, optimising or satisficing – do you think best describes what your health service is trying to achieve when it makes decisions?
- How could a population or clinical group be helped to understand that increasing the level of investment in a service might lead to a reduction in value for the population?
- How would you distinguish decision-makers from decision-takers in your health service?

References

62. Academy of Medical Royal Colleges. *Protecting Resources and Promoting Value: a Doctor's Guide to Cutting Waste in Clinical Care*. Published November 2014. Available at: www.aomrc.org.uk/wp-content/uploads/2016/05/Protecting_Resources_Promoting_Value_1114.pdf

63. Clark D. Public sector expenditure on education in the United Kingdom in 2021/22, by sub-function. Published 25 August 2022. Available at: www.statista.com/statistics/298910/united-kingdom-uk-public-sector-expenditure-education/#statisticContainer

64. Kissinger H. *Leadership: Six Studies in World Strategy*. 2022. Penguin.

65. Simon HA. *Administrative Behavior: A Study of Decision-Making Processes in Administrative Organizations*. 4th Edition. 1997. Free Press.

66. Arrow KJ. *Social Choice and Individual Values*. 1951. Wiley.

67. Moore MH. *Creating Public Value: Strategic Management in Government*. 1995. Harvard University Press.

68. Rawls J. *A Theory of Justice. Revised Edition*. 1999. Oxford University Press.

69. Dostoyevsky FM. *The Brothers Karamazov*. 1958. Penguin Books.

70. Sterman J. *Business Dynamics: Systems Thinking and Modeling for a Complex World*. 2000. McGraw Hill Education.

71. Donabedian A. *Explorations in Quality Assessment and Monitoring* (three volumes) 1980. Health Administration Press.

72. Donabedian A. *An Introduction to Quality Assurance in Health Care*. 2002. Oxford University Press.

73. European Commission. *Defining Value in Population-Based Healthcare*. Published November 2019. Available at: https://ec.europa.eu/health/sites/default/files/expert_panel/docs/2019_defining-value-vbhc_factsheet_en.pdf

4

TRANSFORMATION BY CHANGING THE STRUCTURE

This chapter will:

- Discuss the relative contribution of structure, systems and culture to organisational success
- Emphasise the benefits of bureaucracy, when used appropriately
- Discuss principles that may be helpful when thinking about changing structure with the aim of increasing value
- Define the contribution of leadership to increasing value
- Emphasise the need for transformation, not reorganisation.

By the end of this chapter you will understand:

- How to explain the merits of good bureaucracy
- That there is no ideal structure for a health service
- The importance of limiting the energy used on structural design and redesign
- The steps that a single organisation can take to promote and facilitate the development of value-based healthcare.

In this book so far we have:

- Argued that health services worldwide which are committed to universal healthcare will need to adopt value-based healthcare to ensure its sustainability

- Analysed and summarised the language used to define and explain value and stewardship
- Described the different types of decision-making that determine value.

This chapter describes the revolution that has to take place for a health service to become a value-based health service with a culture of stewardship. To bring about a successful revolution we have to understand the current structure and culture of health services and in addition their leadership and management, or, to use another term, governance.

The need for good governance

Governance is a relatively new term in public discourse. The word itself is not new but it is only in the past 20 years that governance has entered general use, somewhere between governmental and management. Here is one definition: 'An activity by organizations, and/or individuals, which is designed to exercise control, regulation, inducement, incentive or persuasive influence over the whole network.'[74] There are three inter-related factors involved in governance: structure, systems and culture.

The action taken by most countries that want to improve healthcare is to reorganise the structure, and structural causes of problems do have to be tackled.

The benefits of good structure

Good governance is essential and, as we have emphasised on a number of occasions, it is crucial for there to be effective and low-cost administration of health and social care. Without an openly transparent bureaucracy, all sorts of problems creep in, such as nepotism and corruption. Bureaucracy has had bad press since Franz Kafka but, as Charles Perrow highlights, many of those who complain about it have never experienced the capricious and partial environment of an organisation without rules. Here is his case for the defence:

> *'Bureaucracy' is a dirty word, both to the average person and to many specialists on organizations. It suggests rigid rules and regulations, a hierarchy of offices, narrow specialization of personnel, an abundance of offices or units which can hamstring those who want to get things done, impersonality, resistance to change. Yet every organization of any significant size is bureaucratized to some degree or, to put it differently, exhibits more or less stable patterns of behaviour based upon a structure of roles and specialized tasks. Bureaucracy, in this sense, is another word for structure.*[75]

Bureaucracies are very good at linear tasks, for example employing people and managing contracts. But health problems are non-linear or complex and require a different approach. Moreover, bureaucracy or structure is only one part of an organisation running a health service, as shown in Figure 4.1.

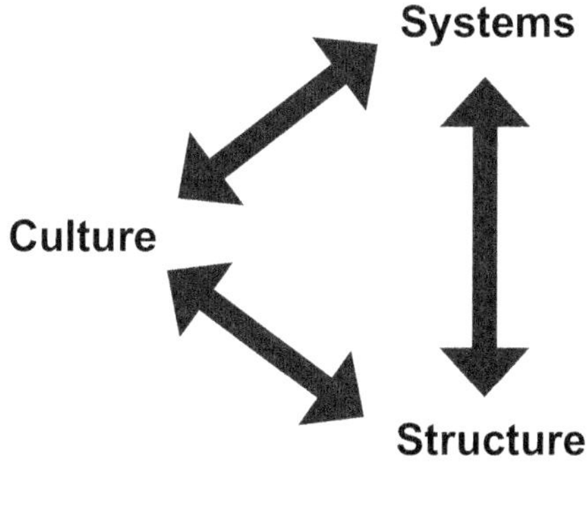

Figure 4.1: Health service overview

To maximize and optimize value, it is essential to create the right systems and the right culture. However, the best structure to obtain value from healthcare, or, to put it another way, the least worst structure, also needs to be considered. Karl Popper, the distinguished author of *The Open Society and Its Enemies*, emphasises that those who say they are working for 'the best' solution are at risk of developing hubris, which could cloud their judgement, and that it is much safer just to try to minimise harm and damage and develop the least worst solution.[76]

The failure of the preoccupation with structure

Comparisons of different health services have been undertaken, the most well-known being that of the Commonwealth Fund, which sets out a number of process and outcome criteria and relates them to the money spent. Obviously, the United States is an outlier with very high spending but poor outcomes at a population level, although of course some of its institutions are among the best in the world. When we compare similar countries, for example the Netherlands, Germany and the UK,[77] however, we can see differences in outcome, process and expenditure, as well as great similarities. We noted in the opening chapter that all health services and all populations give many examples of unwarranted variation, which in turn illustrate the existence of the two other problems that can be seen in every society and which are repeated, with no apologies because of their immense significance, below. They are:

Overuse, which leads to:

- Waste, that is, anything that does not add value to the outcome for patients or uses resources that would give greater value if used for another group of patients
- Patient harm, from over-diagnosis and over-treatment, even when the quality of care is high.

Underuse, which leads to:

- Failure to prevent the diseases that healthcare can prevent, stroke in atrial fibrillation for example
- Inequity from underuse by groups in high need.

There are no good randomised controlled trials comparing different types of bureaucracy, though it is possible to evaluate certain aspects of management in this way. The general consensus is that although bureaucracy has a certain number of important functions it is only a minor determinant of the effectiveness of an organisation. Of much greater importance are the organisation's systems and culture, with most authorities giving more weight to the latter. However, it is also important to think hard about structure: even if the most perfectly designed structure cannot deliver a good health service, a poorly designed one can inhibit the best efforts of those who work within it.

Promoting cost reduction is a poor way of motivating clinicians. Similarly, the term 'savings' implies cuts when in fact the aim of policy is to increase value. If a hospital is overspent then savings need to be made, but even if a service is overspending it needs to get more value from the resources available to meet rising need and demand in an era of zero growth. Cost reduction and all the other steps that need to be taken to increase value have to be promoted as a means of treating more patients to a higher standard. The key is cultural change – developing a culture of stewardship in which every professional feels it is their responsibility to optimise the use of the resources and is supported via key systems to enable this.

Equity, and its opposite inequity, are still confused by many with equality and inequality. Inequality is an objectively defined judgement, for example, health inequalities such as variation in mortality rates, or health service inequalities such as variation in the provision of services to different populations. There may be equality in the provision of health services that is iniquitous if one population has greater need than the others. Similarly, there may be unequal distribution of resources, with a higher amount of money per head allocated to a population with high levels of deprivation and need because it has been decided to do this in the interests of equity. There is, as such, a growing appreciation of the need for healthcare payers and providers to think about distributive justice, which Norman Daniels defined in his book *Just Health Care* as an obsession with 'who ought to get what'.[78]

In fact, the evidence that we have at present suggests that trying to motivate clinicians to get more value is unnecessary. What is needed is to prevent them becoming demotivated, for example by asking them to save money and then reducing their budget by the amount they have saved. Modern management theory emphasises the need to avoid demotivation rather than the need to motivate.

The new agenda for leadership and management committed to increasing value is clear:

1. Create a culture of stewardship, with a governance and value management process that promotes and supports collective responsibility
2. Define population sub-groups with a common need and allocate resources optimally
3. Design a system for each population sub-group
4. Deliver value equitably through networks
5. Understand the functional drivers of improving value
6. Ensure that each individual makes decisions to optimise personal value.

As the next chapter will describe, the best way to increase value is to design a system and deliver the outcomes through a network of all the organisations serving a population, but there are steps that each organisation can take to modify their structure to make it easier to develop systems and networks and to change to create the right culture:

- Identify one or two people on the senior management team to lead on value improvement
- Give responsibility for population healthcare to someone in each clinical service – support them with expertise and resources to manage change
- Align budgets to segments of the population as closely as possible
- Relate activity to the population served as well as to the patients treated – report to the stakeholders on the population served and value improvement.

Obviously there are different implications for primary care teams, which usually have a good understanding of their population, than for large providers of care such as hospitals or specialised mental health services. There are also differences for payers, but they too need to change from their usual preoccupation with cost and the treatment of the patients who access services to focus on all people in need in the populations they serve.

Identify one or two people on the senior management team to lead on value improvement

Because value is assessed by relating outcomes to resources used it may seem appropriate for someone who is clinically trained or a public health professional to be given the responsibility, but Directors of Finance also have a key role to play. First they need to change the way the budgets are organised and develop budgets for each system – which is called programme budgeting or service line accounting in industry. However they also usually manage the information and analytic services, and these need to change the way information is collated and presented, and implement the change required to collect outcome data across populations and pathways. The proposal has been made that Directors of Finance should henceforth be known as Directors of Finance and Value.

In a primary care team it would also be appropriate to have at least two people, such as a GP with an interest in outcomes and equity, and a practice manager who can ensure the data analysis always includes consideration of place of residence, which is the best marker of deprivation, who can develop local value and accountability.

At a payer organisation, whether public or insurance-based, the Director of Finance would be the key player because the system of classification used as the basis for programme budgeting and resource allocation would be either the ICD (International Classification of Diseases),[79] or the new 'Bridges to Health' taxonomy.[80] Payers also need to inform those organisations they fund that they will in future want to know not only about cost and quality but also about 1). outcomes and 2). equity, even if the latter is demonstrated only by awareness of variations in access within different geographical sub-groups of a population, with place of residence being the most feasible indicator of deprivation.

Give responsibility for population healthcare to a leader in each clinical service

We have already emphasised the need to do away with the sharp distinction between 'clinicians' and 'managers' – which allows clinicians to accuse colleagues who accept a formal position such as part-time clinical director of the musculoskeletal services of 'going over to the dark side'. Every clinician needs to recognise that they manage resources, as laid out in the Academy of Medical Colleges report on protecting resources and promoting value.[81] It is also important for these clinical services, including imaging and laboratory services, as well as those addressing disease areas, to have a population perspective.

What is emerging is a new type of special interest for clinicians.[1,2] It could be population medicine or population nursing, for example leading a population-based system for people with leg ulcers or people with depression, or population physiotherapy, leading a population-based system for people with back pain. The clinician who is also a population lead needs to be allocated half a day or a day a week for this task, and in this time – with appropriate support – could be expected to:

- Estimate the level of need in their population, for example by using the published literature on incidence and prevalence
- Prepare a review of the relationship between need and service use, for example by analysing variation in GP referral rates and differences in referral related to the areas of deprivation in the population
- Develop a network of key professional and patient representatives
- Develop and deliver support and training to GPs, pharmacists and other key professionals
- Ensure all the information for patients is unbiased and accurate
- Design integrated care pathways and standards/measures across these pathways that are clear and made available on the dedicated website for the network
- Identify and agree the top priorities for change in the programme area based on unwarranted variation
- Lead the delivery of changes to the way the programme is organised and accessed across specialist, treatment, diagnosis and preventive care that will improve value
- Ensure that research, change management support, financial modelling, workforce analysis, process re-engineering, analytic

decision support and indeed every function is mapped to population groups, with clinically led accountability for delivering improved value
- Produce an annual report on the service provided and improvements in value delivered.

Primary care teams are usually thinking about the whole population for which they are responsible, but it would be sensible to make this the responsibility of one person, perhaps changing the title of the practice manager to 'population and practice manager', and giving this person the task of monitoring referral patterns and analysing how they relate to different levels of deprivation as indicated by the geography of their population.

It is also important to give analytic teams explicit encouragement and permission to find and publish reports that will challenge the assumptions of people who believe that their mission is only to provide high-quality, evidence-based interventions to patients. Analysts need to become revolutionaries, not just reporters. Dr Tim Wilson, one of the Founding Directors of the Oxford Centre for Triple Value Healthcare, set out five 'commandments' for analytic staff:

1. Use a common taxonomy for population segmentation
2. Hunt for the inverse care law to reduce inequity
3. Compare total resource use
4. Use population-based variation to create discomfort and curiosity in equal measure
5. Report on health and well-being outcomes, or where unavailable, report on their absence.

Payers should, of course, be primarily focused on their populations, particularly if they have a public health professional in their team, but provider problems often claim most of their attention.

Align budgets to segments of the population as closely as possible

Systems need budgets, and the development of a budget that includes all the resources for a particular segment of the population helps to develop a culture of stewardship. In 2020 the payers in England still had a budget that related to either real estate or types of care, with the headings below indicating the categories in which a typical payer spent approximately £600 million.

Service	Annual budget in millions(£)
Acute care	329,920
Community health	63,360
Continuing care	31,196
Mental health and learning disability	62,815
Primary care	82,932
Other	26,956
TOTAL	**604,078**

Table 4.1: Example English NHS Commissioner (payer) budget breakdown

These are large and vague categories, however. What, for example, are the relationships between 'primary' and 'community' care? And how much of 'acute care' is spent on people with long-term conditions? Furthermore, conventional accounting systems can make it impossible to determine how much is spent, for example on people with musculoskeletal problems – thus this was not included in the annual report of the single biggest hospital, which simply noted the funding categories 'pay' and 'non-pay' on its home page.

To enable and encourage clinicians to increase and optimise value they need to have information about the total resources being spent on segments of the population in which they are most interested, as we will discuss in Questions 4 and 5.

Relate activity to population served as well as patients treated

To relate activity to the population served as well as patients treated, the denominators need to change. In the past, clinicians and providers used the number of patients treated as their denominator. Payers and public health professionals used the population – typically the whole population. Now both sets need to use the same denominator, namely, the number of people with a particular condition, such as atrial fibrillation, broken down in more detail by age, ethnicity and deprivation. Measures for outcomes and access across pathways and programmes also need to be agreed. For learning, we also need to be able to compare how different populations are being served and answer questions such as those below:

- Is the service for people with seizures and epilepsy in Bristol of higher value than the service in Liverpool?
- Is the service for people with inflammatory bowel disease in Somerset in the top quartile in England in terms of outcome?
- Which network for people in the last year of life in London provides the best value?
- Is the service for people with hip pain in Nottinghamshire of higher value than the service in Leicestershire and Rutland?
- How many networks are there for people with frailty in Greater Manchester, and which gives the best value?

Important though the structure of an organisation is, it has its limitations, one of which is the temptation to reorganise it in search of improvement, for example to answer questions such as those above. To answer these questions for any population in the world we need systems, such as a system for people with epilepsy, and although structure is less important than systems and culture, the organisation of bureaucracies in the ways outlined above makes it much easier for systems to develop and for the right culture to be created and sustained. So, next, let's consider how the development of systems plays its part in the transformation of healthcare.

Questions for reflection when teaching or developing networks

If using these in network building or teaching, give one of the questions to the group and ask them to work in pairs to reflect on the question for 3 minutes. Try to get people who do not know one another to work together. When taking feedback, let each pair make only one point. In the interests of equity, if you start with the pair on the left-hand side of the room for the first question, start with the pair on the right-hand side of the room for the second question.

- How would you describe the culture of your organisation?
- If you were to ban three terms that you believe to be counterproductive what would they be?
- How widely is programme budgeting used in your organisation?
- What are the disincentives to good practice and stewardship of resources that you would like to remove or reduce in the service in which you work?

References

74. Schein EH. *Organizational Culture and Leadership.* 3rd Edition. 2004. John Wiley & Sons Inc.

75. Perrow C. *Complex Organizations: A Critical Essay.* 2014. Echo Point Books and Media.

76. Popper K. *The Open Society and its Enemies.* 2002. Routledge.

77. Mossialos E, Wenzl M, Osborn R, Sarnak D (Eds). *International Profiles of Health Care Systems, 2015.* 2016. The Commonwealth Fund.

78. Daniels N. *Just Health Care.* 1985. Cambridge University Press.

79. World Health Organization. International Statistical Classification of Diseases and Related Health Problems (ICD). Available at: www.who.int/standards/classifications/classification-of-diseases

80. Lynn J, Straube BM, Bell KM, Jencks SF, Kambic RT. 'Using Population Segmentation to Provide Better Health Care for All: The "Bridges to Health" Model'. *Milbank Quarterly.* 2007; 85: 185–208.

81. Academy of Medical Royal Colleges. *Protecting Resources and Promoting Value: a Doctor's Guide to Cutting Waste in Clinical Care.* Published November 2014. Available at: www.aomrc.org.uk/wp-content/uploads/2016/05/Protecting_Resources_Promoting_Value_1114.pdf

5

TRANSFORMATION THROUGH SYSTEMS DEVELOPMENT

This chapter will:

- Define what is meant by the term system
- Describe the stages in developing a specification for a system for a sub-set of the population
- Describe how systems need to be delivered by networks.

By the end of this chapter you will understand:

- What is meant by the term system
- The relative importance of structure, systems and culture
- The steps that need to be taken to develop the specification for a system
- The importance of networks and how they relate to bureaucracies.

The three factors that determine the effectiveness of an organisation are shown in Figure 5.1 on the next page.

The 20th century was the century of bureaucracy and bureaucracies, both public and private, which developed and delivered the astonishing technological advances in diagnosis and treatment that were part of the Second Healthcare Revolution, ranging from imaging through to chemotherapy and transplantation. The 21st century has been called the century of the system and the network[74,75] – but what is a system?

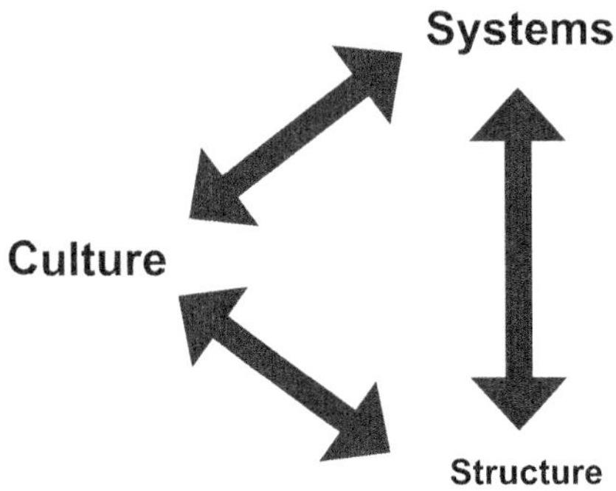

*Figure 5.1: Factors in organisational effectiveness**

**The size of the fonts reflects the relative unimportance of structure, and therefore of structural reorganisation, although it is important to ensure that structure does not interfere with systems or create the wrong culture.*

The term 'system' is widely used but often when people refer to a 'system of care', for example in the United States or in England, they are in fact referring not to a single system but to a set of structures. There are, it is true, a number of microsystems, such as payment systems or systems for procuring equipment openly and fairly, and certain clinical microsystems, like the microsystem for increasing safety in operating theatres. However, although they make a limited contribution to increasing value, these microsystems are not what is needed to transform a health service into one that increases value for both individuals and populations.

For the purposes of this book we define a system as a set of activities with a common aim and set of objectives for a defined segment of a population.

What is needed is a new perspective on healthcare systems, involving a move to 3D healthcare, as outlined in our previous book, *How to Design and Deliver Population Healthcare.*[76]

The need for 3D healthcare

To briefly recap, healthcare in almost every country is organised with respect to two dimensions, illustrated in Figure 5.2. The first is the traditional distinction of levels of care: primary, secondary and tertiary, also known as generalist, specialist and super-specialist. It is important to emphasise that there are two other important levels of care– self-care and informal care – which are often omitted from discussion. The second dimension is the bureaucracies, either public bureaucracies – which may be geographically defined or linked to a specific task such as the management of a hospital – or private companies that, in competition, develop the technological innovations needed.

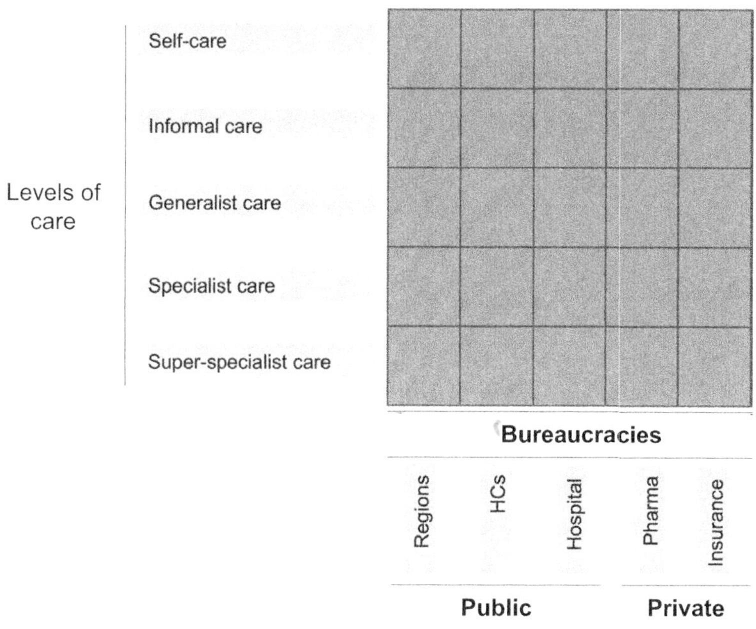

Figure 5.2: Two-dimensional healthcare

What is needed is a third dimension, defined by segments of the population with a common need, as shown in Figure 5.3.

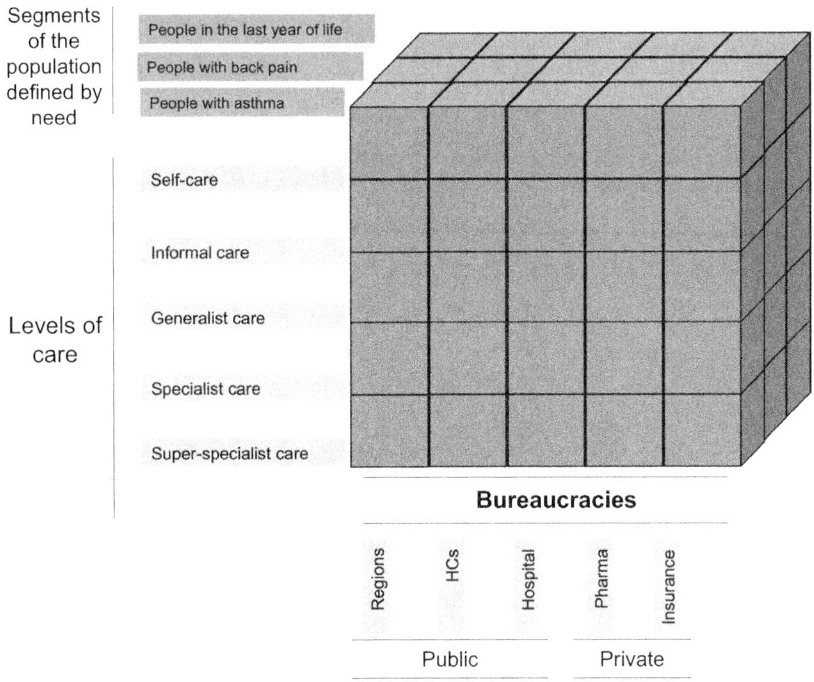

Figure 5.3: 3D Healthcare

This approach is of course common in industry, where what are called service lines dominate decision-making at the top level, whereas in the health service decision-making usually focuses on the two dimensions illustrated in Figure 5.2. Supermarket chains obviously have to have finance departments, procurement teams and real estate of different sizes, but the principal focus is on customers and their needs – meat, fish, vegetables, etcetera: these are the service lines for which management are held accountable for a 'return'.

It could be argued that a system, for example for people with epilepsy or headache, or in their last year of life, is a new type of structure, but this is not the case, and it is more important to think about the system as a new perspective – a third perspective. We need a new perspective in healthcare and that is offered by focusing primarily not on different levels of care or on the bureaucracies, which are essential, but on segments of the population defined by common need.

In the past the ICD was used to segment populations, but increasing use is now being made of a new taxonomy called Bridges to Health.[77] Its main advantage is that it allows people to be classified not only with respect to single conditions but also with respect to multimorbidity – an increasingly important issue as a result of population ageing.

Designing and developing a system

There are a number of steps involved in designing, developing and ultimately delivering the system's objectives, though delivery is primarily through networks rather than the system itself. The reason for this is that there should be a single system specification for a large population that can then be delivered to local populations by local networks. Not only is it obviously much more efficient to design a system specification for, to give an example, people with atrial fibrillation, once – it is also much more effective because if a number of networks serving a number of local populations are all using the same system specification they can compare their performance and learn from one another against agreed best practice models and standards. The principle is one of mutual learning, not competition. This is called learning through action or 'action learning'.[78]

When a number of organisations work together in this way, comparing their performance with respect to common sets of criteria and standards, they create a community of practice, and this is a much more effective way of improving performance than setting up yet another bureaucracy. The development of networks will be discussed in the next section of this chapter. In this section we are focusing on design and development, following the steps set out below.

1. Define the scope of the system
2. Define the population to be served
3. Reach agreement on the aims and objectives of the service
4. For each objective find one or more criteria
5. For each objective identify levels of performance that can be used as quality access and outcome standards
6. Identify all the resources used in the system, thus creating a system budget
7. Develop a network to deliver the system's objectives.

Defining the scope

Although it may seem fairly easy to define the scope of a system, for example 'people with atrial fibrillation', there are a small number of qualifications that always need to be borne in mind. First, is this a system for all people with atrial fibrillation, diagnosed or undiagnosed, or is it a system only for people who have been diagnosed with atrial fibrillation? The contribution that screening can make to improving population outcomes for people with atrial fibrillation is not clear but simply talking about 'people with atrial fibrillation' might lead some people to think about introducing screening in their practice or locality, which would divert resources, including the scarcest – their time.

In addition to deciding on whether a system should focus on people who have not yet been diagnosed – and this is an important issue because diagnosis almost always occurs later in subgroups of the population who are more deprived, and late diagnosis is another example of inequity in healthcare – it is also important to stipulate the age range for many conditions. Taking type 2 diabetes as an example, it is important to introduce a cut-off such as 'people with type 2 diabetes aged 18 and over' in light of the increasing incidence of type 2 diabetes in teenagers. It could be, of course, that the system should deal with people with type 2 diabetes across all age ranges, but usually what is called the Paediatric Diabetes Service is orientated to children and families and should probably take the lead in a system for improving care for people under the age of 18 with type 1 or type 2 diabetes.

Agreeing the population

One of the key moves in the transformation of a service that is focused on quality to a service that is focused on quality and value is the shift from using the number of patients treated as the denominator to using the number of people with a health problem as the denominator. An example would be switching from the percentage of people who have a hip replacement who report that they can walk more easily to the percentage of people in the whole population who have pain and difficulty in walking who report an improvement in their walking ability over the year.

Populations are defined in various ways in different countries. One approach is to use the boundary of a jurisdiction, a local authority or a health board for example, and sometimes these are the same. It may be appropriate to include all people covered by a particular health insurance company, which would be a distributed population, or it may be useful to build up a population by aggregating the populations of primary care teams.

What is important is that the population is clearly defined, and that people are given information about the age structure of the population and about different levels of deprivation, which can be defined because levels of deprivation are quite closely related to place of residence. It is good to express the population precisely even though the precise number of people will change from day to day, for example:

Box 5.1: Population definition in part of West Yorkshire
People registered in the 88 practices of Bradford, Airedale and Craven, with a total population size of 601,638: *Airedale, Wharfedale and Craven* 155,638 people registered with 17 practices *Bradford Districts* 328,000 people registered with 42 practices *Bradford City* 118,000 people registered with 29 practices

Setting the aim

The aim of a system should be encapsulated in a single, high-level statement, such as:

- 'Reducing mortality from breast cancer' – which was the aim of the UK breast cancer screening programme
- 'Enabling children with epilepsy to fulfil their potential'
- 'Increasing value for individuals and the population of people with type 2 diabetes'

The aim should be high-level and may be difficult to measure, but should have a degree of ambition, for example saving XX number of lives over YY time period. In having the aim of reducing the risk of dying from breast cancer in a population, and acknowledging that it might take 10 years for this to occur as a result of screening, the people designing the breast cancer screening system also had to take into account the fact that many other changes in treatment would take place in the coming decade, which would make it difficult to attribute any decline in breast cancer mortality to the screening programme. What was important, however, was to be clear that the aim was to reduce mortality from breast cancer, not to reduce overall mortality. Often even successful prevention programmes do not reduce overall mortality and people die of another cause, and for this reason it is important to be explicit about the aim and then set objectives.

Setting objectives

'A system is a set of activities with a common aim and set of objectives' is the definition we gave at the opening of this chapter, and objective setting is of vital importance. In setting objectives with clinical colleagues the first step is often relatively simple because they are used to setting clinical objectives, and set out below are the objectives a group of clinicians came up with when asked to define the objectives of an asthma control system:

- To prevent asthma
- To diagnose asthma quickly and accurately
- To slow the process of the disease by effective and safe treatment
- To help the individual afflicted adapt to the challenges of having asthma
- To involve patients, both individually and collectively, in their care

From population and value-based healthcare perspectives, however, we need to think much more broadly, and it is good to use an additional set of objectives as a stimulus, either before starting objective setting or after the clinicians and patients who will be affected have come up with the clinical objectives, adapted for the population. These additional objectives, which people need to consider to bring about the revolution, are set out below:

- To make optimal use of resources and minimise waste
- To reduce the carbon footprint of the service
- To mitigate inequity
- To promote and support research
- To support the development of staff and utilise the full scope of team capabilities
- To report annually to the population served.

Choosing criteria

Progress towards system objectives needs to be measured, and to do this it is essential to choose criteria to measure progress or the lack of it. The term 'criteria' is a generic term. Some people like to use the term 'measures' for data that accurately reflect the variable being studied, using, in contrast, the term 'indicator' for data that are less precise. For example:

- A survey of patient experience would provide a good measure of the ability of a service to meet its explicit objective 'to provide care in a way that is acceptable to patients' and the degree to which it was achieving this objective
- A count of the numbers of letters of complaint would be less valid, but could be used as an indicator of progress.

Almost always the validity of the criterion determines its cost, in that those which are less valid cost less, so a decision has to be made about how much resource is to be invested to set criteria and accordingly collect data to measure progress or the lack of it. Often it is helpful to involve researchers in this type of debate even if they have not worked directly on a particular health issue, because researchers think a lot about the validity of criteria.

Although the main mission of a system is to improve an outcome or outcomes, it may take years for these to change, for example to achieve a reduction in the level of frailty in a population. Therefore using the definitions first developed by Avedis Donabedian and reproduced below, it is sensible to include criteria that cover structure, process and outcome.

> *Structure*
>
> *... structure, although it may include administrative and related processes that support and direct the provision of care. It is concerned with such things as the adequacy of facilities and equipment; the qualifications of medical staff and their organization; the administrative structure and operations of programs and institutions providing care; fiscal organization and the like.*
>
> *Process*
>
> *... the process of care... based on considerations such as the appropriateness, completeness and redundancy of information obtained through clinical history, physical examination and diagnostic tests; justification of diagnosis and therapy; technical competence in the performance of diagnostic and therapeutic procedures, including surgery; evidence of preventive management in health and illness; coordination and continuity of care; acceptability of care to the recipient and so on.*
>
> *Outcome*
>
> *The outcome of medical care, in terms of recovery, restoration of function and of survival.*[79]

Setting standards

Donabedian once defined a standard in a lecture as a 'pre-set level of goodness', an imprecise but very clear definition. It is important to set standards to allow networks to compare their level of performance not only with other networks but also against these explicit standards.

Often three different levels of standard are set:

- A standard of excellence that is achieved by the best network
- A minimum acceptable standard below which no service should fall
- An achievable standard.

One reason for choosing an achievable standard in addition to the standard of excellence is that excellence is sometimes the result of a chance collection of individuals in a highly propitious environment, and all the other networks looking at this excellent service can find reasons why it is exceptional and not relevant to them. An achievable standard can be set by arbitrarily taking the cut-off point between the top quartile and the remainder of the services. Those which are in the top quartile can be encouraged to strive for excellence and those which are not in the top quartile can be encouraged to strive to reach it. Furthermore, there are often services in the top quartile supporting populations with major challenges of deprivation, giving those services serving similar populations motivation to strive to be in the top quartile. It is important to align internal and external accountability so that not only do people within the system know what is expected, but also that other people, outside the system but holding the various bureaucracies that make up the network to account, understand how the criteria were chosen and the standards set.

Developing a budget for the system

The term 'budget' usually implies finance, but in value-based healthcare the focus is on resources – finance, carbon and time, including the time of patients and their carers. The important thing is to write down all the resources that have been committed, including non-financial resources such as the contribution made by voluntary societies. Often a budget will initially represent the existing investment of resources in a population or programme, rather than the equitable budget required. Budgets will therefore vary by population and geography within a system and there may need to be movement between budgets to enable improved equity and meeting the standards of good care.

Creating networks

If the system specification is for a large population, a country or region for example, in which there will be many local networks, then each network will have to work out its own budget. This means that the last stage in the creation of a system specification, whether for one population or many, is to set up a network.

Systems of care are delivered by networks, not by single organisations, and the network has to include representatives of the key professional and patient organisations and the relevant institutions or bureaucracies that are responsible for the provision of health and social care.

It is important to emphasise that the fact that there is a system specification does not mean that the service will be delivered in exactly the same way in every population. There is an important difference between strategic and operational command, as the military call it. The strategy is set once, defining what is to be achieved, but it is left to local, operational commanders to decide how to achieve the aim, taking into account local history, geography and politics. In one part of the country it may be that the service is delivered with pharmacists playing a central role, whereas in another part of the country it may primarily be based in health centres. The precise configuration of the service depends upon local circumstances; for example, rural solutions are sometimes different from urban solutions and local history plays a part. There is, however, a need for a network group to co-ordinate the work.

Someone should be given lead responsibility for co-ordination and some recognised time within their job description to provide support, for example to manage co-ordination of the group and the community of practice website. This requires a set of skills related more to the person's personality than to their professional background or rank: the person developing the network needs empathy, the ability to understand what other people are thinking and to communicate this; and sympathy, the ability to feel for another person's emotional state, for example when caught in a difficult position between loyalty to their employing organisation and commitment to the objectives of the system.

Bureaucracies are essential and there will always be bureaucracies, both public and private, in healthcare for linear tasks such as the fair and open employment of staff. The relationship between networks and bureaucracies is best described by Nonaka and Takeuchi.

> *A business organisation should have a non-hierarchical, self-organising structure working in tandem with its hierarchical formal structure. As business organisations grow in scale and complexity they should simultaneously maximise both corporate level efficiency and local flexibility... The most appropriate name is the 'hypertext' organisation.*[80]

The relationship between a network and the hierarchy of a bureaucracy is best expressed pictorially, as shown in Figure 5.4.

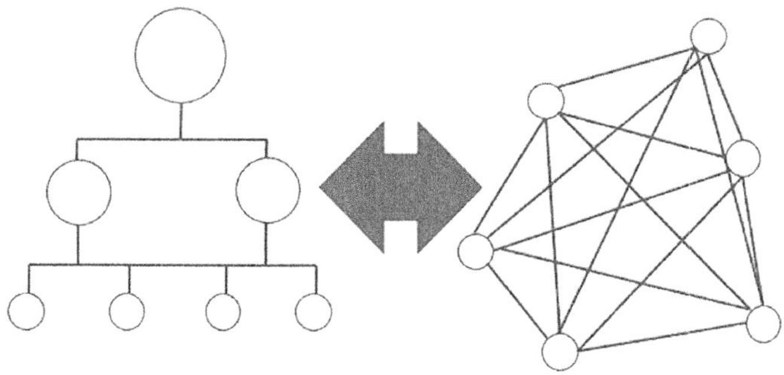

Figure 5.4: Relationship between a network and a hierarchy

An organisational governance structure and network structure can co-exist and be mutually reinforcing, for example medical directors at site level reporting to a system medical director for operational quality. The network takes a role in planning, designing and delivering more strategic value from improvements in the overall care pathway and care model offered to a population. The day a week allocated for the network co-ordinator and support for this person, for example from a librarian, are the highest priorities for any additional resources. The support that is equally balanced between the operational quality infrastructure and the network infrastructure is key. The network infrastructure, however, promotes greater understanding on research, change management, culture and stewardship.

The 1990 Health and Care Act in England introduced the principles, methods and, most important of all, the culture of the market to the NHS in England.[81] Healthcare organisations other than one's own were to be regarded as competitors and the term collaborators came to have the negative connotations that it had in wartime, i.e. that collaborators side with the enemy. In a healthcare network, however, there are no enemies other than epilepsy, dementia or any other disease. Everyone is in it together, working together in a collaborative culture. From the start of the book we have emphasised the need to develop a culture of stewardship, but to do this – whether our focus is on saving universal healthcare or saving the planet – we need a collaborative culture, because without a collaborative culture a system, no matter how well designed, will not deliver value to individuals or populations.

So culture is even more important than systems, and this is the focus of the next chapter.

Questions for reflection when teaching or developing networks:

If using these in network building or teaching, give one of the questions to the group and ask them to work in pairs to reflect on the question for 3 minutes. Try to get people who do not know one another to work together. When taking feedback, let each pair make only one point. In the interests of equity, if you start with the pair on the left-hand side of the room for the first question, start with the pair on the right-hand side of the room for the second question.

- Why is the development of systems rather than structural re-organisation a better way to transform healthcare?
- Which segment of the population, e.g. people with epilepsy or people with back pain, are most in need of a system?
- How could you ensure that the most deprived sections of the population you serve are involved in the network?

References

74. Castells M. *The Network Society: A Cross-Cultural Perspective.* 2004. Edward Elgar Publishing Ltd, pp. 42–43.

75. Benkler Y. *The Wealth of Networks: How Social Production Transforms Markets and Freedom.* 2006. Yale University Press, p. 472.

76. Gray JAM. *How to Design and Deliver Population Healthcare.* 2022. Offox Press.

77. Lynn J, Straube BM, Bell KM, Jencks SF, Kambic RT. 'Using Population Segmentation to Provide Better Health Care for All: The "Bridges to Health" Model'. *Milbank Quarterly.* 2007; 85: 185–208.

78. McGill I, Brockbank A. *The Action Learning Handbook.* 2004. RoutledgeFalmer.

79. Donabedian A. 'Evaluating the quality of medical care'. *Milbank Quarterly.* 2005; 83: 691–729.

80.Nonaka L, Takeuchi H. *The Knowledge-Creating Company: How Japanese Companies Create the Dynamics of Innovation.* 1995. Oxford University Press.

81. The National Archives. *National Health Service and Community Care Act 1990.* Available at: www.legislation.gov.uk/ukpga/1990/19/contents

6

TRANSFORMATION THROUGH CULTURAL REVOLUTION

This chapter will:

- Define the meaning of culture
- Describe the importance of culture and its relationship to structure and systems
- Discuss the relationship between culture and leadership
- List the phenomena that can be used to assess the culture of an organisation.

By the end of this chapter you will:

- Understand the importance of culture
- Understand the way that culture distinguishes leadership from management
- Be able to appraise the culture of your own and other organisations.

There is general agreement among those people who have studied how organisations change and improve that there are three components – structure, systems and culture – and that structure is the least important. Both systems and culture are regarded as being very important, but if pushed to a vote most experts would probably give culture priority over systems (as shown in Figure 6.1) since, for example, you could have the most elegantly designed systems but without a collaborative culture those systems would not work, so culture is key.

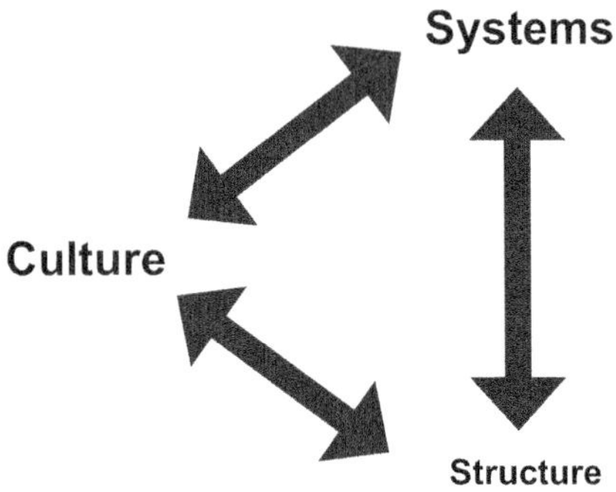

Figure 6.1: Factors in organisational effectiveness (where font size = importance)

There are very many definitions of culture of course, both in general dictionaries and in the leadership and management literature. Perhaps the most highly respected opinion is that of Edgar Schein, whose book on organisation and leadership clearly defines culture in the following way:

> *The culture of a group can now be defined as a pattern of shared basic assumptions that was learned by a group as it solved its problems of external adaptation and internal integration, that has worked well enough to be considered valid and, therefore, to be taught to new members as the correct way to perceive, think, and feel in relation to those problems.*[82]

Most people have a feel for the term 'culture', even if they could not give an exact definition or express it in everyday language as, for example, 'it's the way we do things around here', or 'we think we're different because. . .' However, culture does not develop by accident – it has to be created by the leadership of an organisation.

Leadership and culture

Again the experts in the study of organisations are generally agreed that what differentiates management from leadership is that leadership creates culture whereas management works within that culture. If, for example, it is regarded by the leadership as being acceptable to fiddle the codes related to patient diagnosis or treatment to extract a bit more money from the payers then management will get on and interpret the codes in this way. Here are examples of ways in which people describe their relationship with leadership and management. In their study of Toyota, Morgan and Liker came to a clear conclusion: 'Leadership and a company's culture are inextricably intertwined.'[83]

Schein captures the essence of the difference between leadership and management thus:

> *When we examine culture and leadership closely, we see that they are two sides of the same coin; neither can really be understood by itself. If one wishes to distinguish leadership from management or administration, one can argue that leadership creates and changes cultures, while management and administration act within a culture.*[82]

However, it is important to be clear about what is meant by the term 'leadership', which does not simply mean the head of an office, but involves many people at all different levels of an organisation.

Stimulating neuroplasticity and creating a new social reality

These terms may appear to be surprising in a book on value-based healthcare but they are of fundamental importance to anyone who wants to make a difference. We will start with neuroplasticity, and there are other related terms beginning with 'neuro', including neuro-imaging and neurolinguistics. We need to think about what happens in the brains of people as well as in their minds. Unfortunately most doctors who qualified before the year 2000 were taught the conventional wisdom of a very eminent neurologist, Professor Ramón y Cajal of Madrid, who won the Nobel Prize in 1906 for his elegant dissection and depiction of brains and neurons. However, Cajal said that from the end of childhood, no further development could take place in the brain; all that happened would be that brain cells would die off,[84] and this has been believed, accepted and taught to generations of doctors. Cajal was wrong.

It is now clearly established scientifically, using techniques such as neuro-imaging and related means of measuring the function of integrated neurons, which were unavailable to Cajal, that we can form new connections, new neural networks in our brains, at any age – and this is called neuroplasticity. These neural networks influence how we think, feel, behave and make decisions, and in bringing about a change in culture it is important to change the way people's brains think, and to tell them that your objective is to do just that, perhaps using the phrase 'rewiring the brain'. The importance of changing the way people think is not to make them compliant but because if a number of people think the same way and use the same language, for example using the terms 'value' and 'stewardship' in the same way, a new social reality is created. Language describes physical reality, for describing leopards and tables and bottles for example, but these would exist even if there was no such thing as language, whereas value, waste, stewardship and accountability exist only because language has created them. The leadership of an organisation has therefore to think about creating a new reality, not simply creating a new glossary or culture. Thus when we talk about creating a new culture we are actually talking about creating a new reality, in which:

- All health services work together for the benefit of individuals and populations

- There is keen interest not only in the quality of the service provided to patients but also in the benefits that everyone in need in the population receives from the use of resources
- Patients are fully engaged in helping to identify the measures and outcomes that are important to them
- Unwarranted variation is identified and investigated in debates about overuse and underuse
- Services seek to identify and minimise inequity by monitoring the population base and referral patterns to both primary and secondary care
- The service has jurisdictions responsible for regulation and funding, and different levels of care – primary, secondary and tertiary – but also population-based systems for segments of the population with a common need
- There is a single system specification [model] for a particular sub-segment of the population, such as people with rheumatoid arthritis or single homeless people, with local networks delivering the services to achieve the system's objectives
- There is transparency to patients and the public in general about the service models, agreed measures that matter and improvements (or not) in these measures each year, including comparison with the best performing systems. Where there is a lower achievement or unwarranted variation this is also published alongside the positive results – measurement, comparison and evidence are all part of the new culture.

This is the new reality that we are aiming for, but it requires a revolution, a cultural revolution including a linguistic revolution, and there are other steps the leadership must take.

Creating the culture of stewardship

Although 'culture' sounds like a vague, diffuse term, there are a number of clear strategies that leadership can implement to create the culture they want, and these include, not in order of importance, the following:

- Creating a glossary so the right terms are used with the same meaning throughout the organisation
- Making it clear which behaviours should be encouraged and which discouraged
- Developing what Edgar Schein calls 'artefacts' – visible manifestations of the new culture
- Training staff in the key concepts and terms
- Being explicit about cultural priorities on the organisation's website and in key documents.

Let us examine each of these in more detail.

Creating a glossary on value and stewardship

The glossary from the Oxford Value and Stewardship Programme at the end of this book can be used as a framework. This is a distillate of a glossary some 200,000 words long, covering a much wider territory than value and stewardship. However, a simple glossary can be very effective in supporting the creation of a new culture, particularly if steps are taken to ensure that people know about and use it. For example, making it clear that every member of staff, including the most senior, is expected to carry it with them to check the meaning of terms from time to time, thus making it an 'artefact' specific to the organisation. The more ceremony that can be attached to the production and handing over of a glossary to new members of staff and the more reminders that can be given, for example during annual appraisals, the better.

Encouraging the right behaviours to prevent waste

It is important for the leadership to make clear which behaviours they consider to be conducive to the culture they wish to create and which they do not. For example, in creating a culture of collaboration it is very important for the leadership to make clear that criticism of other organisations in the network made when they are not in the room is unacceptable. This is not to muzzle criticism but to ensure that in a collaborative culture these types of debate take place in the open with all the parties involved present.

In clinical practice it is possible to determine many ways in which clinical decisions and actions can be identified and either encouraged or discouraged. Obviously there is a need to discourage and discontinue interventions for which there is no proof of cost-effectiveness. A greater challenge is to tackle overuse of interventions for which there is evidence of cost-effectiveness. The report of the Academy of Medical Royal Colleges is very helpful in explaining to clinical staff how to think and behave differently in this regard, and so create a new reality.[85]

Creating artefacts

In summary, artefacts can include notices, maps and reports, particularly if these are prepared with inspiration, but it is also good to think of really practical symbols. For example, a hospital or health centre can make it clear that it is committed to greening its environment by planting trees and bushes, and then describing why this has been done on its website.

When launching a new culture it is vitally important for all the key people to be trained in the new way of thinking. This is not a tradition in healthcare, but if we are to increase value and develop a culture of stewardship, we need to ensure that people are trained, particularly people who have management and leadership responsibilities, very many of whom also continue to work as clinicians seeing individual patients.

These are the principal questions that key people need to be able to answer:

- What do you understand by the term complexity?
- What is meant by the term 'system' and how does it differ from a network?
- What is meant by population-based healthcare rather than bureaucracy-based care?
- What are the three meanings of the term 'value' in 21st century healthcare? Not 'values' as in 'we value diversity' but the economic meanings.
- What is the relationship between value and efficiency?
- What is meant by 'optimal use of resources'?
- What is meant by the term 'quality', and how does it relate to value?
- What is a 'standard'?
- How would you assess the culture of an organisation?
- How would you decide if an organisation had a strong culture of stewardship?

It is important for this training to reach the widest range of people possible and not just the senior management team: every clinician who has some management responsibility should be included.

Be explicit about the culture

It is essential to be explicit about the commitment to increasing value and reducing waste. Obviously this needs to go on the website as part of 'Our values' (the term value in the plural meaning principle). There may be a principle such as 'to provide better services of better value for patients' or 'to establish systems and processes that are sustainable' –

with the term sustainable capturing value and stewardship of shared environmental resources. Alternatively it is often possible to amend an existing value such as modifying 'Strive to be the best' to 'Strive to give best value for individuals and our population' or 'Strive to be the best at optimising value and minimising waste.'

It is necessary to promote this, to raise it at every board meeting, and to systemise it in the board agenda and papers that are presented, which must include reference to the impact on value-based care. Also give all employees a card with the values on it – another artefact. This requires an approach that could be called marketing but could also be called propaganda in the best, and original, meaning of the term.

Structure, process and culture all need to be focused on increasing value for both individuals and populations, and although we have given our judgement about their relative importance it is appropriate to indicate that they all need equal attention.

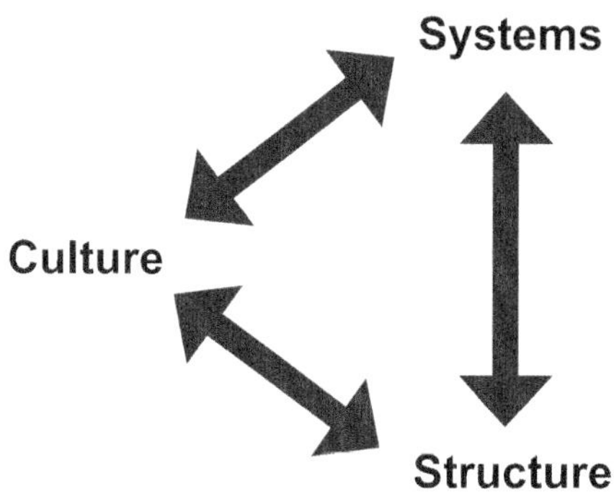

Figure 6.2: Factors in organisational effectiveness

Now we have established an organisation committed to value-based healthcare with a culture of stewardship we are able to address the top 10 questions that health services need to ask, but before doing this let us reflect on a topic which is rapidly rising up the health service agenda: the carbon footprint of healthcare. This is of vital importance in its own right but it is also centrally important to value-based healthcare for three reasons:

- If carbon is reduced financial expenditure is almost always reduced
- The culture of sustainability is a culture of stewardship
- Staff are highly motivated to work on carbon and climate change, including many who would not be motivated by appeals to save money

Questions for reflection when teaching or developing networks:

If using these in network building or teaching, give one of the questions to the group and ask them to work in pairs to reflect on the question for 3 minutes. Try to get people who do not know one another to work together. When taking feedback, let each pair make only one point. In the interests of equity, if you start with the pair on the left-hand side of the room for the first question, start with the pair on the right-hand side of the room for the second question.

- What does our website say about the culture of our organisation, how well known is that statement and how well does it reflect the actual culture?
- If we wanted to change one thing about our culture what would it be, and how would we do it?
- If we could change one thing about the culture of our national service what would it be?

References

82. Schein EH. *Organizational Culture and Leadership.* Third edition. 2004. Jossey-Bass.

83. Morgan JM, Liker JK. *The Toyota Product Development System: Integrating People, Process, and Technology.* 2006. Taylor & Francis.

84. Swanson L, Newman E, Araque A. *The Beautiful Brain: The Drawings of Santiago Ramón y Cajal.* 2017. Abrams.

85. Academy of Medical Royal Colleges. *Protecting Resources and Promoting Value: a Doctor's Guide to Cutting Waste in Clinical Care.* Published November 2014. Available at: www.aomrc.org.uk/wp-content/uploads/2016/05/Protecting_Resources_Promoting_Value_1114.pdf

7

THE NEXT PARADIGM: ZERO CARBON HEALTHCARE

This chapter will:

- Describe the principle sources of carbon use in healthcare
- Summarise the actions that can be taken to reduce carbon
- Suggest how carbon reduction can become a core theme in developing value-based healthcare and creating a culture of stewardship

By the end of this chapter you will:

- Understand the principle causes of carbon use in healthcare
- Be able to link discussions about finance to discussions about finance and carbon
- Be able to link carbon reduction work in your service to work on financial sustainability and value

Value is assessed by the relationship between outcomes achieved and resources made available, allocated and used. As described in Chapter 1, the focus regarding resources has shifted from solely financial to include recognition of professional time as a further constraint and valuable resource, thanks in no small part to the COVID-19 pandemic, which led to shortages of human resources when financial constraints were removed and money appeared to be unlimited. When considering resources, we must look beyond our immediate institutions and also consider the wider impacts on the environment and natural systems that support human life, and always include carbon in any discussion about resources.

There are nine planetary boundaries, describing environmental thresholds within which humanity can survive and thrive. We have already transgressed four of these: climate change, loss of biosphere integrity, land-system change and altered biogeochemical cycles (phosphorus and nitrogen),[86] largely as a result of human interference with the natural world. The 2021 Intergovernmental Panel on Climate Change concluded that anthropogenic (man-made) emissions of greenhouse gases (GHG) have unequivocally caused rapid global warming.[87] In addressing this, however, we must ensure that our collective action meets minimum social requirements, in line with the United Nations Sustainable Development Goals.[88] To maximise value, we must therefore seek to operate in the space between providing minimum social standards and the maximum ecological ceiling, a concept termed 'doughnut economics' (Figure 7.1).[89]

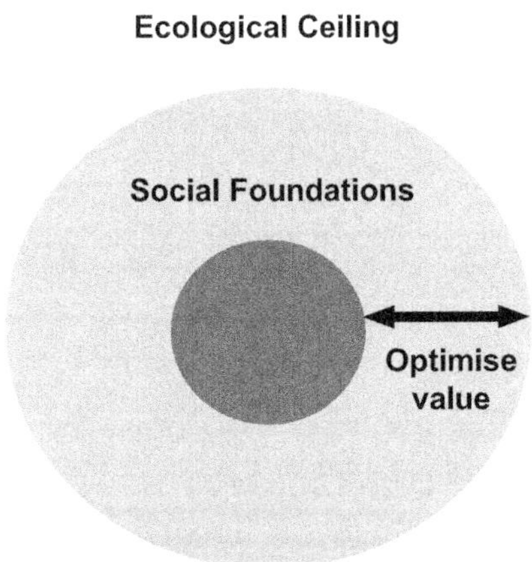

Figure 7.1: When improving value, in a healthcare setting or otherwise, we must operate in the space between the ecological ceiling – relating to our planetary boundaries within which human life is supported – and social foundations that allow humanity to thrive

Human and planetary health

Planetary health is intricately linked to human health, and climate change has been posed as the greatest threat to global public health of the 21st century.[90] The latest Lancet Countdown report signalled code red in relation to the global health crises emerging from climate change, including the health impacts of extreme heat, wildfires, transmission of climate-sensitive infectious diseases and extreme drought. Air pollution is the largest environmental cause of morbidity and premature death, with 3.3 million deaths attributable to anthropogenic air pollution in 2019, one-third relating to our burning of fossil fuels.[91] Vulnerable populations are at greatest risk of climate-related health impacts, including those with existing health conditions, the elderly and children. Health impacts of climate change also risk widening inequalities (and associated health gaps) and follow a social gradient, with those at lower levels of socioeconomic deprivation most likely to suffer from food and water insecurity, least able to adapt their homes or move, and suffering disproportionately from uninsured loses. For example, coastal communities (already experiencing higher levels of socioeconomic deprivation)[92] are at greatest risk of forced migration resulting from rising sea levels.[93]

The 26th United Nations Climate Change Conference (COP26, 2021), hosted by the UK in Glasgow in partnership with Italy, was the first ever COP to place health at the centre of climate negotiations. The WHO released a special report on climate change and health in advance of COP26, emphasising the need to place health and equity at the centre of climate action.[94] This called upon governments and policy-makers to rapidly bring about transformative change in order to protect both planetary and human health. The WHO special report was delivered to COP26 delegates at a Climate Action for Health event during the Science and Innovation day, alongside an open letter entitled 'Healthy Climate Prescription', signed by 600 organisations representing 46 million nurses, doctors and healthcare professionals globally. Signatories included the WHO Director, The Lancet and the World Medical Association, who called upon world leaders to 'to avert the impending health catastrophe by limiting global warming to 1.5 °C, and to make human health and equity central to all climate change mitigation and adaptation actions'.[95]

The carbon footprint of healthcare

The provision of healthcare itself paradoxically compounds this problem, with the healthcare sector contributing 4.4% of all GHG emissions globally, meaning that if the healthcare sector was a country it would be the fifth largest emitter.[96] An analysis of the carbon footprint of the NHS in England found that it generates around 25 megatonnes of CO2e (carbon dioxide equivalents) per year.[97] In 2020, NHS England launched the Greener NHS scheme and became the first national healthcare system to commit to meeting net zero carbon emissions (with targets of net zero for those within the direct control of the NHS by 2040, and for those upstream in the supply chain by 2045).[98] At COP26 all other UK nations joined this pledge, alongside other countries making net zero commitments, while 46 countries committed to developing low carbon, sustainable health systems.[99]

Surprisingly, breakdown of the NHS carbon footprint demonstrates areas typically associated with scope for improving sustainability, such as building energy, water and waste, are responsible for just 15% of the total.[100] Instead, the majority (two-thirds) of the NHS carbon footprint relates to its supply chain, including medical equipment and pharmaceuticals. Healthcare professionals are in a strong position to directly influence these areas, alongside other components such as patient travel.

Sustainable health and healthcare systems

In transitioning to sustainable health and healthcare systems, we can consider maximising sustainable value, using a framework devised at the Centre for Sustainable Healthcare in Oxford. This can be used whenever considering alternative options for maximising value within a healthcare setting, and encourages us to balance patient and population outcomes against the triple bottom line (environmental, social and financial sustainability) (Figure 10.2).[101]

$$\textbf{Sustainable value healthcare} = \frac{\textbf{Patient and population outcomes}}{\textbf{Environmental + Social + Financial impacts (The triple bottom line)}}$$

Figure 7.2: Sustainable value healthcare equation. Adapted from Mortimer et al. *(2018)*[101]

Strategies for mitigating the carbon footprint of healthcare can draw upon the four principles of sustainable healthcare:[101]

1. Disease prevention and health promotion: stopping individuals from becoming patients will have the greatest impact on reducing the healthcare carbon footprint. Many areas of disease prevention and optimisation confer co-benefits to both human and planetary health, including encouraging active transportation via walking or cycling, and reducing red and processed meat consumption.
2. Patient empowerment and self-care, supporting individuals to optimise their own health and make decisions about their healthcare that are right for them. In a medicalised world we often forget that just because we can do something (e.g. operating and 'fixing') means that doing so provides net positive value to the quality of life of an individual.

3. Developing lean models of care, ensuring that each step adds value to patients and reducing unnecessary consumption. This may include streamlining whole patient pathways and seeking to reduce unnecessary single-use products, such as rationalising glove use.
4. Seeking to use low-carbon alternatives. This might draw upon circular economy principles, opting for reusable alternatives, active maintenance and repair, remanufacture and recycling.

There are often financial savings associated with green models of care, as optimising resource use and improving efficiency is at the core of sustainable healthcare. Some interventions will require upfront investment and financial savings will be seen over longer time frames, and savings made from other green measures should be ringfenced for such interventions. Sustainable models of care also equate to better value healthcare: where we minimise unwarranted variation, divest from low-value interventions and focus resources on high-value care that is right for individual patients, we also reduce carbon use.

At COP26, 49 countries committed to developing climate-resilient health systems. Alongside strategies for mitigating the carbon footprint of healthcare, such as those as outlined above, we must also adapt to climate change, including developing systems that can meet surges in demand (due to the health impacts of climate change) and withstand extreme weather events.

Conclusion

Stewardship is defined as 'the careful and responsible management of something entrusted to one's care'. In the healthcare setting we have become used to the concept of antimicrobial stewardship in response to antimicrobial resistance, defined by the Academy of Medical Royal Colleges report on 'Protecting Resources and Promoting Value' as 'A coherent set of actions which promote the responsible use of antimicrobials. This definition can be applied to actions at the individual level as well as the national and global level, and across human health, animal health and the environment.'[102]

The model of healthcare developed during the 20th century is unsustainable both financially and in terms of its environmental impact. We must now extend the concept of stewardship to the natural world upon which we depend. As stewards of the planet and healthcare professionals we have a responsibility to current and future generations to develop sustainable health and healthcare systems. This is especially pertinent given the direct and indirect impacts of climate change on human health, making this our core business. Furthermore there is strong evidence, best summarised in the *Oxford Textbook of Nature and Public Health*,[103] that decay in the natural environment has a direct effect on health, principally by increasing inflammation, the precursor to a number of long-term conditions. The editors propose that we should move from thinking just about the prevention of individual diseases, for example, focusing on dietary change as a means of preventing type 2 diabetes, to thinking much more about the treatment of the underlying causal inflammation of this and other diseases by protecting and improving the natural, green environment in every city and healthcare facility. The need for reducing the carbon footprint of healthcare has long been recognised, with a BMJ editorial in 1989 having the simple title 'Greening the NHS'.[104] The mission now is clearer – zero-carbon healthcare is our future.[105]

The future is not a destination like the North Pole or the Cape of Good Hope, the future is something like a wind farm, which we have to imagine, design, plan and build. We all have a role to play in developing sustainable systems that maximise value within the constraints of our finite natural resources (Figure 7.3).

Better sustainable value healthcare = better for human health = better for planetary health = better for financial health.

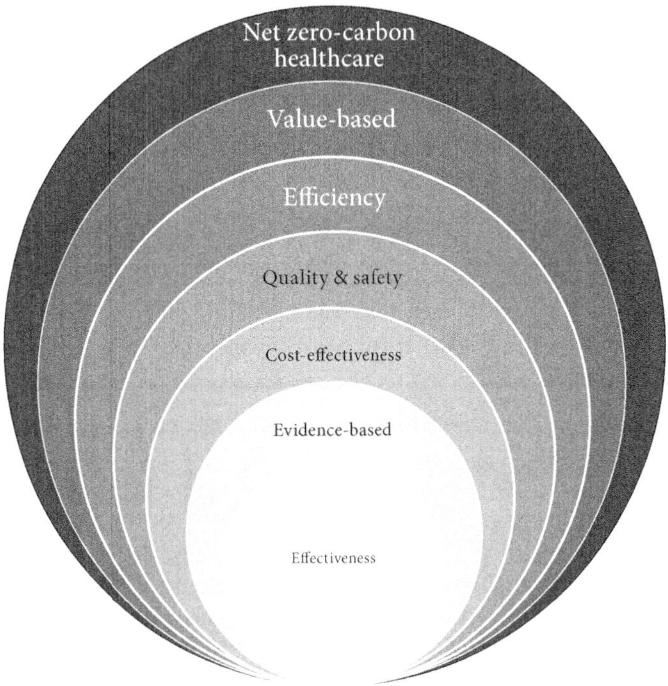

Figure 7.3. Net zero-carbon healthcare will be the new paradigm

Questions for reflection when teaching or developing networks:

If using these in network building or teaching, give one of the questions to the group and ask them to work in pairs to reflect on the question for 3 minutes. Try to get people who do not know one another to work together. When taking feedback, let each pair make only one point. In the interests of equity, if you start with the pair on the left-hand side of the room for the first question, start with the pair on the right-hand side of the room for the second question..

- Good work is being done by our engineers on core energy and carbon costs of the buildings but how could we reduce the carbon footprint of staff and patient travel?
- Good work is being done by our engineers on core energy and carbon costs of the buildings but how could we reduce the carbon footprint of low value clinical activity?
- Could we identify five types of waste that could be reduced?
- How could we make our buildings and estates greener?

References

86. Steffen W, Richardson K, Rockström J, *et al.* 'Planetary boundaries: guiding human development on a changing planet'. *Science*. 2015; 347: 1259855.

87. Working Group 1, Co-chairs V Masson-Delmotte V and P Zhai. *Climate Change 2021: The Physical Science Basis. Intergovernmental Panel on Climate Change*. Available at: www.ipcc.ch/report/ar6/wg1

88.United Nations. Sustainable Development Goals. Available at: https://sdgs.un.org/goals

89. Raworth K. *Doughnut Economics: Seven Ways to Think Like a 21st Century Economist*. 2017. Random House Business Books.

90. Costello A, Abbas M, Allen A, et al. 'Managing the health effects of climate change: Lancet and University College London Institute for Global Health Commission'. *The Lancet*. 2009; 373: 1693–1733.

91. Romanello M, McGushin A, Di Napoli C, *et al.* 'The 2021 report of the *Lancet* Countdown on health and climate change: code red for a healthy future'. *The Lancet.* 2021; 398: 1619–1662.

92. Asthana S, Gibson A. 'Averting a public health crisis in England's coastal communities: a call for public health research and policy'. *Journal of Public Health.* 2022; 44: 642–650.

93. Shukla JB, Arora MS, Verma M, Misra AK, Takeuchi Y. 'The impact of sea level rise due to global warming on the coastal population dynamics: a modeling study'. *Earth Systems and Environment.* 2021; 5: 909–926.

94. WHO. *COP26 Special Report on Climate Change and Health: The Health Argument for Climate Change.* Published 11 October 2021. Available at: www.who.int/publications/i/item/9789240036727

95. Healthy Climate Letter. Healthy Climate Prescription. Available at: https://healthyclimateletter.net

96. Health Care Without Harm, Arup. *Health Care's Climate Footprint: How the Health Sector Contributes to the Global Climate Crisis and Opportunities for Action.* Climate-smart health care series, Green Paper Number One. Published September 2019. Available at: https://noharm-global.org/sites/default/files/documents-files/5961/HealthCaresClimateFootprint_092319.pdf

97. Tennison I, Roschnik S, Ashby B, Boyd R, Hamilton I, Oreszczyn T. 'Health care's response to climate change: a carbon footprint assessment of the NHS in England'. *The Lancet Planetary Health.* 2021; 5: E84–E92.

98. NHS England. Greener NHS. Available at: www.england.nhs.uk/greenernhs

99. WHO. COP26 Health Programme: Country Commitments. Available at: www.who.int/initiatives/cop26-health-programme/country-commitments

100. HM Treasury. Public sector annual reports: sustainability reporting guidance 2019 to 2020: Guidance for government bodies on sustainability reporting. Published 19 September 2019. Available at: www.gov.uk/government/publications/public-sector-annual-reports-sustainability-reporting-guidance-2019-to-2020

101. Mortimer F, Isherwood J, Wilkinson A, Vaux E. 'Sustainability in quality improvement: redefining value'. *Future Healthcare Journal.* 2018; 5: 88–93.

102. Academy of Medical Royal Colleges. *Protecting Resources and Promoting Value: a Doctor's Guide to Cutting Waste in Clinical Care.* Published November 2014. Available at: www.aomrc.org.uk/wp-content/uploads/2016/05/Protecting_Resources_Promoting_Value_1114.pdf

103.van den Bosch M, Bird W (Eds). *Oxford Textbook of Nature and Public Health: The Role of Nature in Improving the Health of a Population.* 2018. Oxford University Press.

104. Gray M, Keeble B. 'Greening the NHS: A plan to make the NHS more environmentally friendly'. *British Medical Journal.* 1989; 299: 4–5.

105. Stancliffe R,Bansal A, Sowman G, Mortime F, Towards net zero healthcare, *British Medical Journal.* 2022; 379: 367-369

PART II

THE 10 KEY VALUE QUESTIONS HEALTH SERVICES NEED TO ASK

INTRODUCTION

Although we now have the appropriate organisational structure in place, our work is not yet done. Health services need to ask, and be able to answer, a series of questions to ensure the sustainability of universal healthcare for the decades to come. This needs a small and committed band of revolutionaries drawn from every department and discipline and given the time and authority to be radical, with their primary focus being on the networks developing systems for the first set of population segments. They need to be confident enough to say 'We need transformation, not reorganisation – in fact, we need a revolution that will not only affect the organisations in which we work but also how we think and feel as individuals. We need a cultural revolution.'

One way to ignite this revolution is to publish an 'atlas of variation', modelled on Jack Wennberg's revolutionary *Dartmouth Atlas of Health Care*, first published in 1996.[1] Another, complementary, way is to ask a set of awkward questions, and these form the second part of this book. The first is: How much money should be spent on healthcare? This is a high-level strategic question, and the subsequent questions get into more detail and relate to shorter timescales. Presenting them as a numbered list implies a hierarchy and gives the impression of different tribes of decision-makers working in isolation though in a co-ordinated way. The reality is much more complex than this and needs discussion before moving on to the questions.

Decision-making for better value – tactical, operational and strategic

> Muir Gray to a GP: *'What would you define as your five-year objective?'*
>
> GP: *'Five o'clock this afternoon – that's my only bloody objective!'*

Most clinicians feel under such pressure that discussions about the longer term seems irrelevant but it is essential to try to engage all staff in thinking about the year ahead and 5 years ahead, thinking about operational and strategic issues to use military language. Here are the 10 questions that need to be addressed to optimise value, and indeed to ensure the sustainability of universal healthcare, arranged in order from the most strategic to the tactical.

Question 1: How much money should be spent on healthcare?

Question 2: How much money should be top-sliced for nationally organised services?

Question 3: Has the money for healthcare been distributed to different parts of the country by a method that recognises variation in need?

Question 4: Has money been allocated to different patient groups in a way that is equitable and that will optimise value for the whole population?

Question 5: Are the resources that have been allocated being used on the right interventions?

Question 6: Are all of the right patients, and only the right patients, being offered the high-value interventions?

Question 7: Are we sure that every individual patient is getting the right intervention in the way that is right for them?

Question 8: Is the quality of care as high as it can be with the resources available?

Question 9: Are clinical risks being minimised?

Question 10: Why not just get a grip, improve quality and safety, and reduce costs while you are at it?

The sequence in which we address these questions appears logical, moving from national decisions about the value of the whole of healthcare to questions that could be addressed and answered straight away. However, they could be set out in the reverse sequence, determined not by the size of potential impact but by the speeds with which benefits could be realised, tackling technical before allocative value:

Question 1: Why not just get a grip, improve quality and safety, and reduce costs while you are at it?

Question 2: Are clinical risks being minimised?

Question 3: Is the quality of care as high as it can be with the resources available?

Question 4: Are we sure that every individual patient is getting the right intervention in the way that is right for them?

Question 5: Are all of the right patients, and only the right patients, being offered the high-value interventions?

Question 6: Are the resources that have been allocated being used on the right interventions?

Question 7: Has money been allocated to different patient groups in a way that is equitable and that will optimise value for the whole population?

Question 8: Has the money for healthcare been distributed to different parts of the country by a method that recognises variation in need?

Question 9: How much money should be top-sliced for nationally organised services?

Question 10: How much money should be spent on healthcare?

If we classify the decisions that a clinician makes with, or about, individual patients as tactical decisions, using the military classification of decisions as being tactical, operational or strategic, then Questions 1 to 6 in the above reversed list could be regarded as decisions made by people in operational command posts, to continue with the military analogy. Many of these people will also be clinicians, for example a GP with responsibilities for their practice organisation, working with the practice manager, or a specialist in respiratory medicine paid to be the clinical director of a hospital respiratory service for two sessions a week while continuing their clinical duties on the other four days. Questions 8 to 10 are clearly strategic, with Question 7 being part strategic and part operational – a strategic decision being made on how much to allocate to people with respiratory problems, as distinct from other sub-groups of the population such as people with cardiovascular problems or people in the last year of life, and an operational decision then being made as to how much of that budget should be allocated for people with asthma and how much for people with chronic obstructive pulmonary disease (COPD), etc. This can be set out in a table (see other page):

	Level of decision-making		
	Tactical	Operational	Strategic
Who is involved	Clinicians and patients	People who manage services and budgets, including clinicians and patients and population representatives	Policy-makers, planners and politicians
Time frame	This day, this week, this year	This year and the next 1-2 years	This year, the next 10 years and onwards
Focus	This patient	This local population with a defined need, e.g., people with type 2 diabetes	All geographical population and all population segments with differing needs

Managing the three levels of decision making

Healthcare is more complex even than warfare, however, and probably the most complex business on Earth. One reason for this is that it is the clinicians, the front-line soldiers, who determine the total amount of resource committed and the balance of resources. If the orthopaedic surgeons are better organised and keener than the ophthalmologists, expenditure on people with bone and joint problems will increase faster than expenditure on services for people with visual problems – remembering that it could be the other way round in the neighbouring population served by the general hospital 20 miles down the road. What we need is for everyone, including clinicians, to feel concern about the sustainability of universal healthcare and to recognise that their behaviour as individuals has an influence on sustainability. If resources are wasted at their present level universal healthcare is unsustainable.

But before analysing decision-making it is essential to reflect on the difficulty of these decisions.

It would be nice to think that we live in a world of complete rationality, a world in which a decision led to maximum value being obtained from the resources available, but we do not live in that type of world. We live in a world in which decisions have to be made using bounded rationality, namely under time pressure and without all the data we would necessarily like. In such a situation all we can seek to do is to make the best use of resources we can – which may well not be the best possible use of resources - an approach called 'satisficing' by Economics Nobel Prize winner, Herbert Simon.[2]

We often seem to be trying to maximise value from the resources available, but it is much more realistic to adopt the principle developed by Simon of making decisions that are good enough rather than trying to achieve the best possible outcome.

It is important to be honest and to recognise that:

- We do not have all the data we need
- We are making decisions under terrific time pressure
- There is no computer that can make these decisions for us.

We have to operate within what Simon called 'bounded rationality', and any decision-making that is official, or decision-making by a politician, requires that we are satisficing and not maximising value.

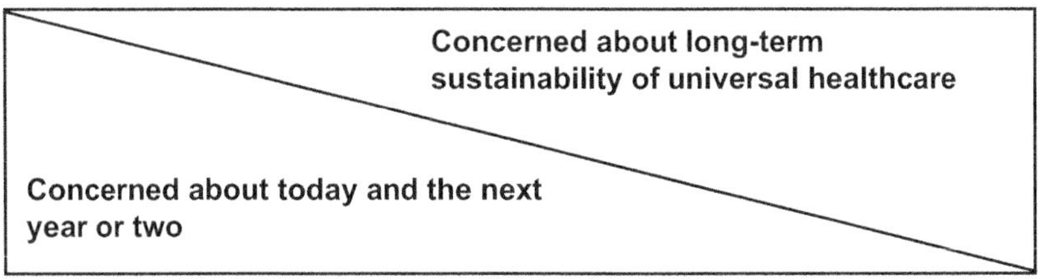

Conflicting healthcare spending concerns

This is not to say that clinicians should be calculating the cost of every single test and treatment, but they should be thinking about whether that test or treatment is really going to add value for an individual.

So, let's start by asking our original Question 1: How much money should we as a society spend on healthcare?

References

1. Wennberg JE, Cooper M. *The Dartmouth Atlas of Health Care*. 1996. AHA Press.

2. Simon HA. *Administrative Behavior: A Study of Decision-Making Processes in Administrative Organizations*. 4th Edition. 1997. Free Press.

QUESTION 1

HOW MUCH MONEY SHOULD BE SPENT ON HEALTHCARE

This section will:

- Examine the choices faced by a government that has to consider investment in healthcare in competition with all other bids for public sector funding
- Review the different aspects of this choice, which depend on the way healthcare is funded.

By the end of this section you will have an understanding of:

- The arguments against increasing investment in healthcare
- How this question is relevant to both tax-based and insurance-based systems of healthcare.

There appears to be no limit to the amount of money that could be spent on healthcare, but what became apparent during the COVID-19 pandemic was the fact that the term 'resources' means much more than money, and when money appeared to be unlimited the constraints were intensive care beds, oxygen, personal protective equipment and, scarcest of all, the time of clinicians.

The job of government is prioritisation

Governments have to decide how much to spend on healthcare compared with their expenditure on other types of service for the citizenry. A few of the areas in need of financing are shown in Figure Q1.1 but there are of course many more.

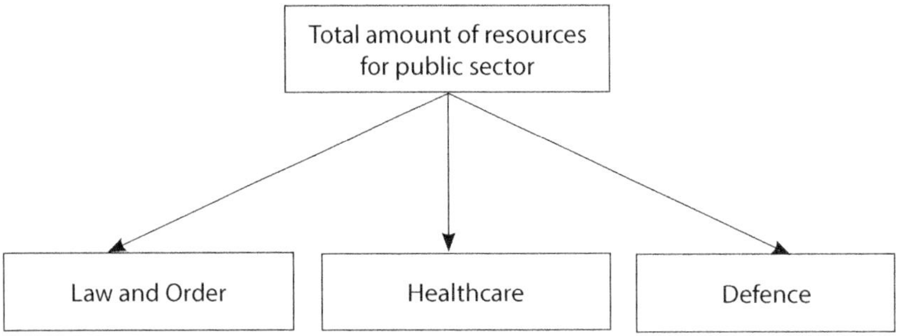

Figure Q1.1: Government allocation of resources

It is also important to recognise that each person in the population could have their own personal physician and still want a second opinion. At the time of writing, the record for the highest level of expenditure on healthcare is held by the USA, which spends more on healthcare as a proportion of gross national product (GNP) than any other country with a developed economy, with the worst return on investment.

It could be argued that it does not matter what proportion of GNP is spent on healthcare because people might as well spend money on healthcare as on holidays, cars or any other type of conspicuous consumption. Expenditure on healthcare does, however, depend on how the money allocated to healthcare is raised. If, as in the USA, healthcare insurance is part of employment costs, an increase in the cost of this affects the cost of American consumer goods.

The amount spent on healthcare is a value judgement based on several different criteria, such as those outlined in Box Q1.1.

Box Q1.1: Criteria by which to judge the level of expenditure on healthcare

- The proportion of GNP spent on healthcare in other comparable countries
- The opportunity costs, namely the value that would be obtained if this resource was used for some other purpose, of increasing spending on healthcare in comparison with all the other demands on government funds, such as education, defence or law enforcement. Every unit of expenditure on healthcare is a unit that cannot be spent on education, defence or law enforcement, and that is a value decision.
- The relationship between the capacity of the health service and public concern about shortfalls in service provision. For instance, concern about waiting times in many countries has been the driver to increase investment in healthcare, but this type of decision-making may simply lead to a diversion of resources to a particular service highlighted by the media, rather than increasing the amount of GNP allocated to healthcare.

The COVID-19 pandemic saw an era in which the financial cost of healthcare was not the focus of debate and there was increased investment in health services without detailed consideration of the opportunity cost, but this question will resurface.

This debate involves macro-economic decisions. In countries like the UK in which expenditure is principally public, the decision of those who distribute the public purse is relatively simple, based first on a decision about the proportion of the GNP that is to be public expenditure, and then the proportion of that expenditure that is to be allocated to healthcare. In many of those countries in which the proportion of GNP spent on healthcare is greater than 10% the options are more complex. This is because much of this spending is not from private citizens making a decision to invest in healthcare rather than another holiday, but from insurance schemes subsidised or underwritten by the government, and this also affects the size of public sector spending.

Even in insurance-based health services the government has to be involved. In a country where insurance schemes are not supported by public sector spending they are usually supported by that country's employers, and this affects the price of goods and services produced by the country. In the 1970s, the cost of healthcare insurance to Chrysler as an employer became greater than the cost of steel in the cars the company produced. This was not the only problem faced by Chrysler – the quality of their cars was much worse than the quality of those from their Japanese rivals – and the combination of cost and quality dealt a heavy blow to Chrysler and to all American car companies.[3] This issue is still very much alive, and an article in the New England Journal of Medicine, one of the top two medical journals in the USA, in 2020 described how healthcare spending had risen by 2.2% annually in the USA over the past 20 years, compared with an annul increase of 1.1% in other developed countries.[4] The impact of this is huge.

> *Research has demonstrated that nearly all wage and salary increases between 1999 and 2009 for the median-income American worker were absorbed by increases in health care premiums, out-of-pocket expenses, and taxes to fund Medicare and Medicaid, which has resulted in little left over for discretionary purchases or savings.*[4]

Furthermore…

> *There is also no evidence that life expectancy has improved more rapidly among Americans than among people in comparable countries, despite higher health care expenditures in the United States.*[4]

And, if the growth could be constrained to 1.1% it would liberate:

> *$3 trillion—money that could instead be spent on addressing social determinants of health by means of investments in education, social services, and improved living standards.*[4]

Some economists think that increases in public sector spending and increases in the cost of goods and services due to increases in health insurance costs harm a country's economy and, therefore, impair the health of the population in the long term. A ministry of finance or treasury can, as such, argue that it is of greater value to population health to control investment in healthcare rather than to allow expenditure to be uncontrolled, because increasing wealth by limiting expenditure on public services will itself improve health. In most developed countries, the ministry of finance/treasury, and not the health ministry, has decided that not much more than 10% of GNP should be spent on healthcare.

Following the global COVID-19 pandemic governments have recognised the need to invest in public health infrastructure, and to rebrand it as investment for 'security' because of the acceptance that more careful planning is needed in case another pandemic arises.

The job of national government is to maximise what Mark Moore has called 'public value' by the way it allocates resources to these different uses[5] and one line of argument about investing in healthcare which is now emerging is that increasing investment in healthcare will increase wealth in the local population, for example by increasing employment, and therefore reduce one of the social causes of ill health – deprivation – and that it will have other economic benefits.

An analysis of this issue titled *From Safety Net To Springboard*, by Michael Wood and Ilse Bosch was published in 2023 by the NHS Confederation and the healthcare consulting company CF (Carnall

Farrars). It concluded that *"every pound invested in the NHS results in around £4 back to the economy through gross value added (GVA)"*. The report also reported their estimates of the differential effects of investing in different types of care. The return on investment is greater from investment in primary care or community care than from investment in acute care. Furthermore, the authors estimate that if £1Billion were to have been invested *"in community, primary or acute care the additional economic growth created would have returned more than this amount back into the national NHS budget, thus paying for itself"*

This is another way of expressing social value and goes against the widespread belief that an increase in public spending is bad for the economy and may gain more influence in the years to come, particularly as the population ages and as AI and other technical developments reduce the need for labour in the private sector but of course a government would need to consider not only the Return on Investment, from investing in healthcare but also the return from investing in other sectors such as education and schools. This is an example of what is meant by the term Social Value.

How to get better national value

Value is subjective, and therefore relative. The best way to consider value is not in isolation but in comparison. It is certainly appropriate for a national service to bid for another £8 billion and to estimate what benefit the population would get for that additional resource. However, from the point of view of the UK population as a whole, a better question would be: what would give greater value – the investment of £8 billion in the NHS or in the education and support of children under the age of 10?

Alternatively, the value of different allocations could be estimated, for example by asking: what would be the difference in the health of the population from investing either:

- £8 billion in healthcare?
- £6 billion in healthcare and £2 billion in the education and support of children under the age of 10?
- £4 billion in healthcare and £4 billion in the education and support of children under the age of 10

The aim is to achieve optimal allocative efficiency, to use the economists' term. Thomas Rice, basing his work on the thinking and writing of Alain Enthoven,[6] makes this point nicely, writing:

> An efficient allocation of health care resources to and within the health care sector is one that minimizes the social cost of illness, including its treatment. This is achieved when the marginal dollar spent on health care produces the same value to society as the marginal dollar spent on education, defense, personal consumption, and other uses. Relevant costs include the suffering and inconvenience of patients, as well as the resources used in producing health care. This goal should not be confused with minimizing or containing health care services, often as a share of gross national product (GNP). But, a lower percentage of GNP spent on health care does not necessarily mean greater efficiency. If the reduced share of GNP is achieved by denial or postponement of services that consumers would value at more than their marginal cost, then efficiency is not achieved or enhanced by the cut in spending.[7]

The continuing increase in need and demand for healthcare mean that this question will continue to challenge governments for years to come. Moreover, once this decision has been made those making decisions about healthcare will have to address other questions, the first of which is to ask how much money they need to retain or 'top-slice' for nationally organised services.

Questions for reflection when teaching or developing networks:

If using these in network building or teaching, give one of the questions to the group and ask them to work in pairs to reflect on the question for 3 minutes. Try to get people who do not know one another to work together. When taking feedback, let each pair make only one point. In the interests of equity, if you start with the pair on the left-hand side of the room for the first question, start with the pair on the right-hand side of the room for the second question.

- What is the evidence that investment in public services other than healthcare would have a greater benefit for the health of the population than increased investment in healthcare?
- What might happen if people in their twenties were allowed to opt out of paying for the health service?
- What, if any, would be the benefits of funding healthcare by insurance rather than taxation if insurance funding were not able to increase the proportion of the national wealth invested in healthcare because of the impact that higher insurance premiums would have on industry?

References

3. Halberstam D. *The Reckoning.* 1986. William Morrow and Company, Inc.

4. Skinner J, Cahan E, Fuchs VR. 'Stabilizing health care's share of the GDP'. *New England Journal of Medicine.* 2022; 386: 709–711.

5. Moore MH. *Creating Public Value: Strategic Management in Government.* 1995. Harvard University Press.

6. Enthoven AC, Smith KW. *How Much is Enough? Shaping the Defense Program, 1961–1969.* 1971. Harper & Row.

7. Rice T. *The Economics of Health Reconsidered.* 1998. Health Administration Press.

QUESTION 2

HOW MUCH MONEY SHOULD BE TOP-SLICED FOR NATIONALLY ORGANISED SERVICES?

This section will:

- Review the principal expenditures that do not directly serve the needs of patients
- Examine the arguments used to justify the investment in top-sliced activities in terms of the value produced
- Explain the problems encountered when trying to measure the value of those activities.

By the end of this section you will have an understanding of:

- The reasons why health service funds should be invested in research
- The difficulty in deciding how much investment in information technology adds value
- Why a health service should invest in the education of the professionals it needs
- How to justify some investment in management and the arguments used to determine the proportion of resources that should be invested.

Eyeball to eyeball, clinician and patient, the consultation is at the heart of patients' experience of healthcare. About 20,000 consultations occur every day in a population of one million and many decisions are reached in a consultation by the principal, the person called the patient, with the agent, the person called the doctor – probably around 100,000 decisions a day for every million population. Many clinicians also make decisions without directly engaging with the patient, either by providing knowledge from their laboratory or radiology service, or by contributing their expertise in a multidisciplinary team meeting to which another clinician has brought the patient's records but not the patient.

These clinical services are of direct value to patients, provided that they are doing the right things to the right patients, and not only doing them right – to adapt the old proverb about the need to do the right things right – but also doing them better, more safely, more environmentally aware and less expensively every year.

Imagine you are responsible for paying for or managing the health services for half a million people. You would be expected to work out what resources you would need to manage the common health problems of that population – broken legs, asthma, maternity services and end-of-life care, for example. Yet some needs are less common and require more highly specialised services that should not be provided in every hospital, such as transplantation, treating acute paediatric leukaemia or radiotherapy. There are also support services that are not clinical, such as education and research, and, more recently, control of the COVID-19 pandemic. Decisions have to be made about how much money should be allocated for these purposes, as outlined in Figure Q2.1.

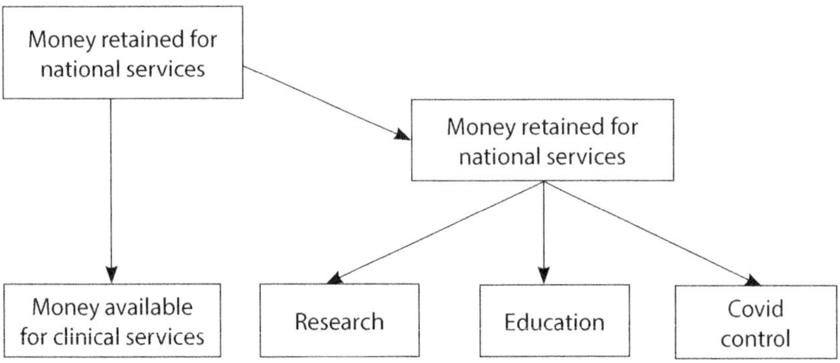

Figure Q2.1: 'Top-slicing' money before the funding of clinical care

An analogous decision takes place once money has been allocated to a local population, which we will address in Question 3, but here we will continue to consider the whole of the spend on management, both national and local, because the principles are the same. Decisions also have to be made about how much money to allocate to managing a health service, though this decision is rarely as explicit as the decision on how much to allocate to research. Of course someone has to pay clinicians, buy the equipment they use and carry out a myriad of activities, such as organising the car parking (someone recently defined a modern hospital as a set of departments united only by complaints about car parking!). Resources have to be invested in management or administration – the term varies from one service to another – but how much of the resources? The answer is: as little as necessary for the effective administration of the service – but there is no evidence-based formula that can be used to answer this question.

There are no randomised trials of health services with 5% management costs compared with health services with 10% management costs, in part because of the difficulty in defining what is meant by a 'management cost'. It has been argued that healthcare management illustrates Parkinson's Law perfectly – management tasks increase in direct proportion to the amount of management time available to tackle them.[8] The logical conclusion of this principle, a hospital fully staffed with administrators but without a single patient, was compellingly portrayed in the BBC television series *Yes, Minister!* The cost of management increases as the amount of regulation increases. If, for example, it is mandated that clinicians must have an externally validated appraisal of their competence each year, a system has to be set up to manage this process and management costs increase as a consequence, so managers cannot be blamed for all the increase in the costs of management.

Whatever the proportion of resources spent on management, nobody argues with the fact that some investment is necessary. If all management costs were cut, a service would grind to a halt very quickly. Just how quickly depends on how much stock is available, but in a hospital working on 'lean' principles, with very little stock in the pharmacy, laboratories or linen store, the service would grind to a halt within a week. The same cannot be said for investment in education or research: if such investment were cut, the impact would take longer to manifest.

An analysis of the value of management is very difficult, as is evaluation of the marginal benefit of increasing investment in management or the marginal cost of cutting management. A simpler approach, with no evidence that it is any less effective, is just to assume that bureaucracy inevitably grows in size, and simply impose a cut, the size of which has been decided arbitrarily.

What is the value of education?

The clinical staff of a health service is the resource which delivers that service to patients. They need buildings and equipment and management support, and they are also of central importance in realising the potential benefit that investment in equipment and buildings offers, but where do staff come from?

Health service staff are recruited as a result of investing in advertisements, but to ensure that there are sufficient trained staff to recruit, a health service has to address a standard business question: 'make or buy?'

The attraction of 'buying' staff is obvious. The service only has to pay the salaries of the staff it employs, and not meet the costs of training. A service can invest a significant sum in the training of clinicians, or it can buy the clinical staff produced by another country. There is, however, a moral issue when developed countries buy the professional staff trained by poor countries. The costs of the education could of course be met by the higher education sector, but that too would require government investment, so a decision has to be made about the numbers of staff that will be required in 10 years' time and, of course, a huge investment is needed in the training that many clinicians require after university.

Within education lurks a resource whose value is often underused – the library service. Knowledge is the enemy of disease. The application of what we know will have a bigger impact on health and disease than any drug or technology likely to be introduced in the next decade. By managing knowledge better the eight major problems of healthcare can be minimised:

- Errors
- Poor quality care delivery
- Poor experience of patients
- Waste
- Unknown variations in policy and practice
- Failure to introduce high-value interventions
- Uncritical adoption of low-value interventions
- Failure to recognise uncertainty and ignorance.

Most organisations could increase value significantly by recognising that the most valuable resource in their library is the librarian and ensuring that librarians are as active in the clinic and the boardroom as in library real estate. This may mean that they need to reduce the hours that the library is open to allow librarians to be where decisions are made.

What is the value of research?

The value of investment in research is more complicated than that of investment in education. Again, a health service could answer the make or buy question by 'buying' research outputs from other countries, subscribing to journals or to the Cochrane Library, or simply using the free services of PubMed from the National Library of Medicine in the USA or Google Scholar.

There are, however, a number of reasons why health services would be ill-advised not to invest in the support of research. If decisions are to be evidence-based and the health service does not invest in research, the evidence base will be increasingly stocked with research funded by industry, and there will be increased investment in drugs simply because the evidence base, for example, for non-drug therapies, such as walking therapy for arterial disease (which creates no commercial profit) or psychological therapy for depression, will be much weaker without health service investment.

There is, however, another factor that has to be taken into consideration when deciding how much to invest in research, and this is the value that such investment has for the economy of the country as a whole (Figure Q2.2 on the following page):

If an improvement in the health of the population is regarded as an economic good, as it should be, the return for society from investment in research can be shown to be high. A major review of the economic benefits of investing in the US National Institutes of Health (NIH) concluded that 'the public return on investment has been substantial. Although results have led to increases in healthcare expenditures, health gains were large and valuable.'[9]

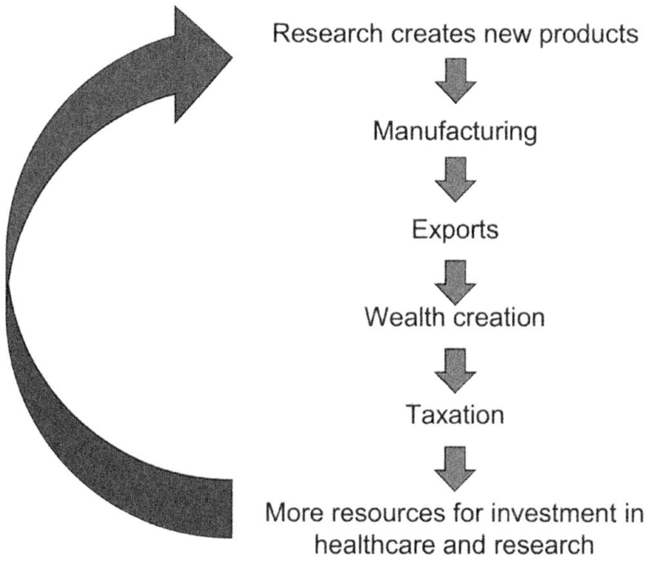

Figure Q2.2: The benefits of research to the economy

If investment in research can be justified, the next question to ask is: how much? The NHS Research and Development programme was set up on the recommendation of a House of Lords Committee, with the aim of investing 1.5% of NHS resources in the direct costs of research and 'support of research'. This support is needed to meet the extra costs in a clinical service in which clinicians are carrying out research.[10–12] This policy was a necessary consequence of the introduction of the healthcare market because the total cost of care in a hospital with a large research programme was often greater than the cost of care in a hospital with no research.

In England in 2012 a decision was made to set up Academic Health Science networks, designed to bring together the NHS, universities and industry to improve healthcare and create wealth by fostering innovations, but 2014 may be seen as the year in which the need for better value research was finally recognised. There had been individual papers of great importance, such as that of the late, great Doug Altman on 'The Scandal of Poor Medical Research' in 1994,[13] but in 2014 *The Lancet* published two editorials and five articles with titles that summarised everything that needed to be done:

- Chalmers I, *et al.* 'How to increase value and reduce waste when research priorities are set'. *The Lancet.* 2014; 383: 156–165.
- Loannidis JP, *et al.* 'Increasing value and reducing waste in research design, conduct, and analysis.' *The Lancet.* 2014; 383: 166–175.
- Al-Shahi Salman R, *et al.* 'Increasing value and reducing waste in biomedical research regulation and management'. *The Lancet.* 2014; 383: 176–185.
- Chan AW, *et al.* 'Increasing value and reducing waste: addressing inaccessible research'. *The Lancet.* 2014; 383: 257–266.
- Glasziou P, *et al.* 'Reducing waste from incomplete or unusable reports of biomedical research'. *The Lancet.* 2014; 383: 267–276.

Then, in December 2014, *The Lancet* published a trenchant editorial on the need to envisage that research was not only based on a systematic review of existing evidence but also needed to incorporate the findings in an updated systematic review, and emphasised the risks of relying on research that resulted in single papers focused on one intervention.[14]

The value of research to patients

Research results are often of value to patients, in that they can help to progress disease treatment immeasurably. The involvement of children in leukaemia research, for instance, has helped transform that disease from a certain killer to one that is often cured. However, the immediate value to patients of being involved in research is less clear. It is true that it can give patients the opportunity of a new treatment not routinely available, but those new treatments on trial may be ineffective. It is also true that patients in research are looked after very carefully, according to strict protocols. Accordingly, if a patient is offered a choice of two services and only one of them is active in research, it would be wise for them to choose that service because the clinicians will be accustomed to working to a clearly defined care pathway.

For many patients, however, the value of involvement in research is a sense of altruism. The Million Women Collaborative Study in England, fully open to the public at www.millionwomenstudy.org, recruited more than a million women as they attended breast cancer screening, and the women felt that they were not research subjects but partners in the battle against breast cancer[15]

What is the value of IT?

A modern health service cannot run without computing. Some investment is therefore necessary, but how much? There is no simple answer.

The cost of the investment is usually easy to estimate, although the history of IT investment in both industry and the public sector is that, unless the contracts are very carefully drafted, the actual cost often exceeds the planned cost. The administrative benefits are easier to describe, but more difficult to measure in financial terms. Thus IT reduces the staffing costs of healthcare administration, but the magnitude of these management savings has never been clearly estimated because computerisation has crept into hospitals piecemeal, and at the same time, administration has become more complex.

There is, however, another benefit from IT investment: a clinical benefit for patients.[16,17] There is good enough evidence that such investment:

- Reduces clinical errors
- Increases the effectiveness of healthcare by allowing the faster uptake of high-value interventions
- Reduces the harmful effects of healthcare by preventing unknowing prescribing of drugs that interact with one another.

More evidence is needed, particularly about the contribution of clinical decision support systems – software that reminds and alerts both clinicians and patients about clinical actions that should or should not be considered – but the evidence that some investment will produce clinical benefit is 'good enough'.[18]

Putting a computer system unthinkingly into an unstructured mess of consultations and clinical encounters will not, by itself, transform the mess, and may instead increase confusion. One study showed that mortality increased following the introduction of computerised prescribing.[19] On the other hand, the introduction of technology as part of a process of transformation can be revolutionary. The benefits of IT are not simply a reduction in administrative costs; they result from its revolutionary, disruptive impact. The adjective 'disruptive' became famous as a result of Clayton Christensen's book *The Innovator's Dilemma*, subtitled *When New Technologies Cause Great Firms to Fail*.[20] In it, Christensen describes how innovations can be disruptive and paradigm-changing, and how those companies that are complacent or do not appreciate this become extinct. He then turned his attention to healthcare and with two medical co-authors published *The Innovator's Prescription*, subtitled *A Disruptive Solution for Health Care*.[21] The disruptive technology is the internet, and all that flows from it – including patient power.

The appropriate use of technology will transform healthcare. The focus on big IT projects distracts attention from a multitude of smaller changes initiated and enabled by technology. Sometimes the technology has direct financial costs, while other initiatives use the web, e-mails or open source software, which often have service implications and costs. The result of those forces - sometimes called eHealth – is best defined by examples such as:

- The development of networks
- E-mail consultations by patients
- Telecare support of disabled people in their own homes
- Explicit descriptions of care pathways
- The delivery of community care by professionals using robust tablet devices to record and communicate key information about patients
- Sending laboratory results directly to patients.

It is important to appreciate that the impact of computing and IT will come not only from big projects approved by hospital and health service boards and implemented using the best principles of project management, but also from public engagement. Decisions about the contribution of the internet have passed out of the hands of the boards of the big bureaucracies and much more into the hands of citizens as part of the Third Healthcare Revolution.

How to get better value from research, education and IT infrastructure

There is value for health services from investing in research, education and IT infrastructure, but for each there is a need to decide 1). how much to invest, and 2). how to minimise waste. This needs to be addressed for each of these investments.

Investing in research

For research, some investment is essential to meet what are called the excess treatment costs of research in hospitals that carry out research, otherwise the populations they serve will be unfairly disadvantaged because they will get less healthcare. There is also a need for health services to invest in research for areas that industry will not fund, health services research for example, but it is unclear how much to invest. To compare investment in research with investment in treatment is not very helpful, but it could be useful to compare investment in research with investment in education because both have long-term benefits.

To get better value from the resources invested in research it is essential to ensure that the lessons from the papers of Chalmers and Glasziou are put into practice.[22,23] The only research that a health service should fund, or for which it should allow researchers access to patients if the service is not funding the research, is that which:

- Addresses questions that patients have agreed as being of high priority
- Is based on a systematic review of all the available evidence
- Is designed and managed using methods that will minimise financial and carbon costs
- Publishes the results, preferably also incorporated into an update of the systematic review.

Investing in education

For education, the level of investment should be sufficient to meet the future manpower needs of the health service, but these are difficult to estimate accurately. Both emigration and immigration affect the need, as well as technical developments in healthcare and political developments like Brexit, so there is no easy way to decide how much or how little to invest in education. In such cases the easiest step to take is simply to reduce expenditure and estimate what the effect would be of reducing spend by 5% or 10%. When the value of an investment is uncertain, either compare it with investment in another comparable service – in the case of education that would be research – or analyse the marginal effects of either increasing or decreasing the level of investment and then estimate the effects of change at the margin, a process called marginal analysis.

Having decided how much to invest in education, how best to optimise value? This is a hot debate, not only in healthcare. It depends on the outcomes desired, and there is by no means agreement on those outcomes. In fact, there is considerable disagreement in the health service between those whose funds are top-sliced, and the educators, usually university departments, who spend those funds. Health services want people trained, universities want them educated, and the outcomes of the two processes are different, with professional bodies caught in the middle. In nursing, for example, the move to make nursing a profession requiring a university degree has been criticised not only for its cost but also for its contribution to what is seen as decreased compassion in care. Part of the challenge for people investing in healthcare is that many of the professions are still in their 19th century or early 20th century configurations – medicine and nursing, physiotherapy and occupational therapy, psychiatry and specialities to treat physical systems, to give only a few examples. To change the boundaries of all these profession or guilds is an impossible task. It is simpler to make them focus on the challenges they all face in meeting rising need in an era of constrained resources.

Investing in digital services – welcome to the Third Healthcare Revolution

It is increasingly important that local organisations invest in digital services that support service transformation and deliver tangible returns on investment, particularly from the perspective of the person called the patient.

The First Healthcare Revolution was based on empiricism, exemplified by the need for pure water being agreed 30 years before bacteria were discovered and supported by strong government. The Second Healthcare Revolution gathered strength in the 20th century, and may be called the high-tech revolution, in which big bureaucracies developed and delivered high-tech healthcare like MRI, hip replacement and transplantation. In addition the doctor replaced the priest, in terms of charismatic and sapiential authority, namely, the authority that comes from medical knowledge imbued in the doctors during their training but hidden from the public behind the locked doors of university and hospital libraries, along with a new type of authority – Aesculapian authority:

> *In his theory of administration, Paterson originally hypothesized five kinds of authority: sapiential, moral, personal, charismatic, and structural. However while investigating problems of hospital administration at Weyburn, Saskatchewan, in 1957, he found that none of his existing types of authority described that of the doctor accurately. He eventually added a new type of authority, which appeared to be three of his previously described types, sapiential, moral and charismatic, combined in a particular manner. This he called Aesculapian authority.*[24]

The COVID-19 pandemic demonstrates that both revolutions are continuing. As well as representing a considerable public health challenge, with 'the air' being much more difficult to deal with than water, it requires high-tech solutions such as genome-based testing and vaccine development, not to mention –70 °C refrigeration. One of the reasons we have not dealt well with the COVID-19 pandemic is that we have failed to recognise that we are now in the midst of the Third Healthcare Revolution – one driven by *citizens*, *knowledge* and the *internet*. Be it someone's iPhone or a Zoom meeting or consultation, the internet has made possible our response to the coronavirus, and it is inconceivable to think what life would be like without these tools.

Another reason we have not managed the pandemic well, however, is the failure to understand the implications of the Third Healthcare Revolution, namely it is not just internet technology but universally available knowledge, both true and false, which has put powerful weapons in the hands of citizens.

The Third Healthcare Revolution has also provided opportunities for individual clinicians and people who understand the new world of digital technology into which we have moved. Indeed a myriad of small projects using machine learning or AI are now being used for multiple tasks, having crept in without the need for significant financial investment – and therefore without formal appraisal and approval – as part of this new revolution. This includes their application in areas such as diagnosis, the interpretation of images and the choice of best treatment. It is, however, important to remember that although AI usually stands for artificial intelligence there is another widely used interpretation: augmented intelligence, i.e. how technology can augment and support human intelligence.[25]

Having decided how much is available after top-slicing, the next question covers regional variation in need.

Questions for reflection when teaching or developing networks:

If using these in network building or teaching, give one of the questions to the group and ask them to work in pairs to reflect on the question for 3 minutes. Try to get people who do not know one another to work together. When taking feedback, let each pair make only one point. In the interests of equity, if you start with the pair on the left-hand side of the room for the first question, start with the pair on the right hand side of the room for the second question.

- How could a population be helped to understand that increasing the level of investment in a service might lead to a reduction in value for the population?
- Can you identify a service that has passed the point of optimality, or will do so if growth is not slowed or stopped?
- How would you explain the quotation 'more is not necessarily better' if you were given 2 minutes on local radio?

References

8. Parkinson CNC. *Parkinson's Law, or The Pursuit of Progress*. 1958. John Murray.

9. Claiborne Johnston S, Rootenberg JD, Katrak S, *et al.* 'Effect of a US National Institutes of Health programme of clinical trials on public health and costs'. *The Lancet*. 2006; 367: 1319–1327.

10. Horton R. 'Health research in the UK; the price of success'. The Lancet. 2006; 368: 93–97.

11. Rothwell PM. 'Funding for practice-orientated clinical research'. *The Lancet*. 2006; 368: 262–266.

12. The National Heart, Lung, and Blood Institute Acute Respiratory Distress Syndrome (ARDS) Clinical Trials Network. 'Pulmonary-artery versus central venous catheter to guide treatment of acute lung injury'. *The New England Journal of Medicine*. 2006; 354: 2213–2224.

13. Altman DG. 'The scandal of poor medical research'. *British Medical Journal*. 1994; 308: 283.

14. *The Lancet*. 'Consequences of a competitive research culture'. *The Lancet*. 2014; 384: 2084.

15. University of Oxford. The Million Women Study. Available at: www.millionwomenstudy.org/introduction

16. Greenes RA. *Clinical Decision Support: The Road Ahead*. 2006. Elsevier Science.

17. Osheroff JA, Teich JM, Levick D, *et al. Improving Health Outcomes with Clinical Decision Support: An Implementer's Guide*. 2005. HIMMS Publishing.

18. Halamka JD. 'Health information technology: shall we wait for the evidence?' *Annals of Internal Medicine*. 2006; 144: 775–776.

19. Han YY, Carcillo JA, Venkataraman ST, *et al.* 'Unexpected increased mortality after implementation of a commercially sold computerized physician order entry system'. *Paediatrics*. 2005; 116: 1506–1512.

20. Christensen CM. *The Innovator's Dilemma: When New Technologies Cause Great Firms to Fail*. 1997. Harvard Business Review Press.

21. Christensen CM, Grossman JH, Hwang J. *The Innovator's Prescription: A Disruptive Solution for Health Care*. 2008. McGraw-Hill Education.

22. Chalmers I, Bracken MB, Djulbegovic B, *et al.* 'How to increase value and reduce waste when research priorities are set'. *The Lancet*. 2014; 383: 156–165.

23. Glasziou P, Altman DG, Bossuyt P, *et al.* 'Reducing waste from incomplete or unusable reports of biomedical research'. *The Lancet*. 2014; 383: 267–276.

24. Siegler M, Osmond H. 'Aesculapian authority'. *The Hastings Center Studies*. 1973; 1: 41–52.

25. Tarassenko L, Watkinson P. 'Artificial intelligence in health care: enabling informed care'. *The Lancet*. 2018; 391: 1260.

QUESTION 3

HAS THE MONEY FOR HEALTHCARE BEEN DISTRIBUTED TO DIFFERENT PARTS OF THE COUNTRY BY A METHOD THAT RECOGNISES VARIATION IN NEED?

This section will:

- Explain the methods that can be used to allocate resources to different populations
- Highlight the difficulty of doing this to the satisfaction of all parts of a community.

By the end of this section you will have an understanding of:

- The limits of epidemiology and the need for judgement in decision-making
- The tensions inherent in any system for allocating finite resources to populations with different levels of need
- The system used by the NHS for resource allocation.

Question 3 has both technical and political aspects that are interwoven like weft and woof.

The mission of government-funded healthcare is to provide equal access to care. The Inverse Care Law, first formulated in the UK in 1971 by Dr Julian Tudor,[26] appears to hold true in every country: '. . .the amount of care provided is inversely related to the need for care.'

Reviewing variation in activity in relation to variation in need can highlight inequities in the provision of healthcare. Thus, for example, in a 2010 study of joint replacement in England, Judge *et al.* found that the most deprived populations had the lowest rates of hip and knee replacement, and concluded that 'people in affluent areas get most provision relative to need' (see Figure Q3.1).[27]

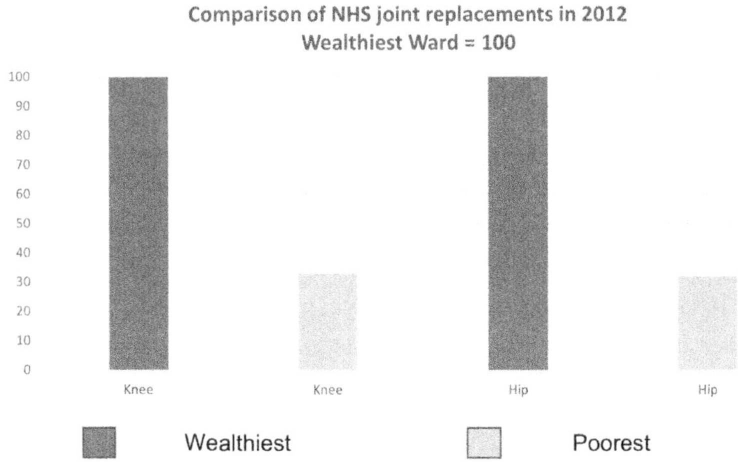

Figure Q3.1: Hip and knee replacements in deprived populations

The Inverse Care Law is difficult to overcome for a multitude of reasons, not all of which can be addressed by increased investment in healthcare. For countries that allocate resources to geographically defined populations, it is accepted that the formula used for the allocation of health service resources should reflect variations in need. However, how this should best be done is by no means agreed.

Technical issues in the allocation of resources

There is no consensus on the optimal criteria for resource allocation. Although publicly funded healthcare is designed to meet need, and resources are allocated on the basis of need, the definition of need is not always straightforward, and the quantification of need in different populations is complicated. If the aim is to maximise value by matching resources to need, there are two principal determinants in accounting for geographical variations in the need of a population.

1. Demography – the differences in the age and sex structures of populations. Age differences are the more material as most diseases are more common in older people.
2. Socioeconomic status – since almost all diseases are more common in people on low incomes who tend to have both lower life expectancy and lower healthy life expectancy due to the earlier onset of disabling disease. There is a question over the extent to which this is a direct consequence of material deprivation or primarily caused by social determinants such as a sense of alienation and low worth. Towards the end of the 20th century there was recognition in many countries of the need to tackle the social determinants of disease and inequity, and in the UK this culminated in a major project led by Sir Michael Marmot.[28] There is the related question as to whether poverty is defined in absolute terms, with respect to a certain level of income, or in relative terms, with respect to the distribution of income in the population.

There is agreement that formulae for resource allocation which aim to estimate fair allocations to areas using data on their populations ought to take account of the population size and age profile. There is continuing controversy, however, over how best to take account of the additional needs of a population that are due to deprivation. It is a riddle that cannot be resolved for two reasons. First, we lack reliable data, collected routinely, that can produce estimates of the relative needs of populations. Hence, all measures we use are proxies, but we cannot decide which proxy is best by looking at true measures of need because these are not available. Second, even if we had true measures of need, we lack the evidence necessary to estimate directly how these ought to translate into relative needs for resources. We can illustrate this by looking at the English experience in developing and revising formulae since the 1976 report of the Resource Allocation Working Party (RAWP).[29] In England, the formula for resource allocation has been, and continues to be, a subject for debate.

The RAWP report recommended taking account of demography using national average spend by age and sex, and this principle has been applied without controversy since. Figure Q3.2 shows data for what is described as the age–cost curve. This shows a relatively high need for primary care in children under 5, a typical pattern of low need until age 40, and a tendency for need to increase with age after that, and to increase dramatically for those over 70.

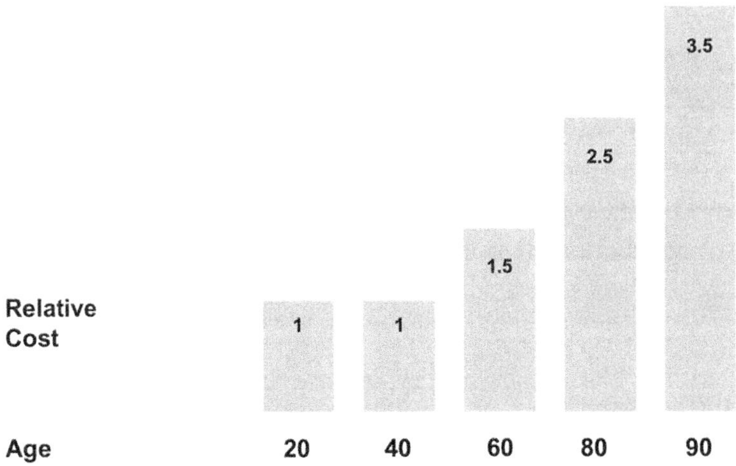

Figure Q3.2: Age–cost estimates used in the formula for England in 2009

The RAWP report, in looking for ways to take account of additional need, rejected measures based on the utilisation of services on the grounds that, although these data did reflect need, they were contaminated by the inequitable distribution of supply. Instead, the RAWP approach used the index of standardised mortality ratios (SMRs), which are the ratios of actual to expected mortality for all ages – and made heroic assumptions, such as that an area with 10% higher (or lower) mortality than expected ought to receive 10% more (or less) resources.

The justification for the RAWP report's use of mortality data as a measure of relative need is that these are independent of supply of, and access to, services. They are also a good measure of the cumulative social and health experience of people living in an area, and a sensitive indicator of general healthcare needs – reliable, accurate, routinely available, and providing a more timely indicator of relative need than indices derived from census data.

The second problem is illustrated in assuming that mortality is a good source of data for relative need, then asking: 'How ought we use these data in a formula to allocate resources?'[30] This raises three further questions:

- What index should we use?
- What age range should we use?
- What weight should be used for the chosen mortality index and age range?

What has happened since the 1990s is that heroic assumptions relating the need for resources to SMRs have been replaced by the application of a series of complex statistical models giving estimates of how various measures of need translate into resources. However, all these models employ data on the utilisation of services, and so are open to the criticism that they are contaminated by inequities in the distribution of, and access to, supply.[31,32]

Political issues in the allocation of resources

There is no ideal way to allocate resources. Every solution creates problems and tension between those who see themselves as losers and those who are seen as winners, even though the 'winners' rarely feel that their needs have been adequately met.

It is also important to try to mitigate the enthusiasm for delegation so that not all healthcare resources are allocated to the smallest population size. In most countries, specialist services such as transplantation and cardiothoracic surgery are managed on a larger population scale, whereas funding for common problems tends to be delegated to a smaller population size. There is a trend towards the devolution of budgets in many countries, but before praising this trend unreservedly it would do us well to remember what one wise observer said about decision-making: 'centralise praise, decentralise blame'. When resources are constrained it is easier for people in the centre to delegate tough, unpopular decisions.

The topic of decision-making was addressed in some detail in Chapter 3. Leading US economist Kenneth Arrow was clear that decision-making, if not guided by a market economy, is always political. In his view, all decisions about the allocation of resources should be classified as political even if politicians are not directly involved.[33]

Occasionally party politics can play a part. In Italy, for example, decisions about the closure of hospitals are heavily influenced by local mayors, who are often the drivers of investing a significant proportion of resources in hospital care or, to be more precise, hospital infrastructure costs, and to maintain much-loved local hospitals on their own terms, in part because these are such important employers and contributors to the local economy. In England, there is a different political complexion. A formula that gives more weighting to population ageing will favour those populations with a higher proportion of older people who traditionally vote Conservative. Similarly, a formula that gives greater weighting to deprivation as a measure of need will shift resources to parts of the country where levels of deprivation are higher, which traditionally have voted Labour.

There is no simple resolution to this problem. Judgement is needed at all stages during allocative decision-making, as well as transparency of the process by which decisions are reached.

The challenges of social health insurance-based systems

The above issues of course relate to tax-based health services, and social health insurance-based systems, also termed the Bismarckian model, present a different set of challenges because there is no single fixed amount of money to be allocated with spend in a population being determined by clinical activity, recharged to a number of insurance funds. The challenges vary depending on the type of insurance in place, and there are usually a number of insurance companies covering the population of a jurisdiction, i.e. a politically defined population of a city, region or province. There may be a few big companies and a number of smaller companies, the latter often linked to particular trades, and both usually national organisations. Governments depend on competition between the insurance companies to keep healthcare costs down, and there is no mechanism for geographical allocation.

How to get better value

We believe that the only way to get better value from geographical allocation is to move away from focusing solely on inputs towards focusing on outcomes. If two candidate formulae are being considered, the impact that each will have on the health of the populations that benefit and lose should be calculated.

Having divided the national resource equitably, the local service needs to slice that cake optimally, and Question 4 addresses this next step.

Questions for reflection when teaching or developing networks:

If using these in network building or teaching, give one of the questions to the group and ask them to work in pairs to reflect on the question for 3 minutes. Try to get people who do not know one another to work together. When taking feedback, let each pair make only one point. In the interests of equity, if you start with the pair on the left-hand side of the room for the first question, start with the pair on the right hand side of the room for the second question.

- Is it better to think of 'the best' way of allocating resources or the way that is 'least worst'?
- What measures could be used to assess the degree to which a policy of allocating resources in proportion to need had been successful?
- What is the case for allocating resources not only according to differences in the incidence of disease and mortality among different populations, but also taking into account the levels of poverty in those populations?

References

26. Tudor Hart J. 'The Inverse Care Law'. *The Lancet.* 1971; 297: 405–412.

27. Judge A, Welton NJ, Sandhu J, Ben-Shlomo Y. 'Equity in access to total joint replacement of the hip and knee in England: cross sectional study'. *British Medical Journal.* 2010; 341: c4092.

28. Institute of Health Equity. *Fair Society, Healthy Lives (The Marmot Report).* Published February 2010. Available at: www.instituteofhealthequity.org/resources-reports/fair-society-healthy-lives-the-marmot-review

29. Department of Health and Social Security. *Sharing Resources for Health in England: Report of the Resource Allocation Working Party (The RAWP Report).* 1976. Her Majesty's Stationery Office (HMSO).

30. Bevan G. 'The search for a proportionate care law by formula funding in the English NHS'. *Financial Accountability & Management.* 2009; 25: 391–410.

31. Morgan M, Mays, N, Holland WW. 'Can hospital use be a measure of need for health care?' *Journal of Epidemiology and Community Health.* 1987; 41: 269–274.

32. Sheldon TA, Smith GD, Bevan G. 'Weighting in the dark: Resource allocation in the new NHS'. *British Medical Journal.* 1993; 306: 835.

33. Arrow KJ. *Social Choice and Individual Values.* 1963. Wiley.

QUESTION 4

HAS MONEY BEEN ALLOCATED TO DIFFERENT PATIENT GROUPS IN A WAY THAT IS EQUITABLE AND THAT WILL OPTIMISE VALUE FOR THE WHOLE POPULATION?

This section will:

- Explain programme budgeting
- Give an account of the processes of marginal analysis and the assessment of allocative efficiency
- Review the issues relating to equity and fairness.

By the end of this section you will have an understanding of:

- The strengths and limitations of programme budgeting
- The difference between technical and allocative value
- The concept of equity

Apart from its colloquial use, the word 'mess' is used in the context of management to describe a problem for which there is no ideal solution and every solution that is generated is likely to create further problems. Another term for such a challenge is 'wicked problem'. In most countries with developed economies, a person who takes up a job in managing or paying for healthcare in all likelihood knows that they are going to inherit a 'mess' – the result of years, sometimes decades, of unplanned growth in spending on healthcare.

There are rare situations in small but very rich states where people are asked to design a health service from scratch, based on plans for an unusually large increase in investment. Although such a task would be relatively straightforward, the difficult decisions about the allocation of resources to different patient groups would still remain. For instance, how much money should be allocated to patients with cancer and how much to people with mental health problems?

Allocation by real estate

The categories of expenditure on healthcare budget sheets are usually presented according to:

- Institutions, such as 'secondary care', 'hospitals' or 'community services'
- Broad divisions within a hospital, such as the 'surgical division' or the 'medical division.'

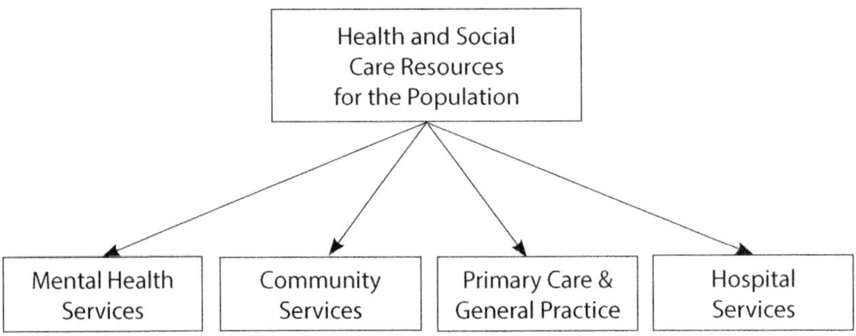

Figure Q4.1: The traditional pattern of allocation

Neither of these categorisations have much relevance to the experience of patients suffering from a specific health problem. Thus, to be able to answer Question 4 with any validity, it is necessary to organise the healthcare expenditure budgets according to the different types of need in the population.

Allocation by need

The need to organise healthcare budgets according to expenditure on subgroups of the population defined by need is increasingly being recognised. The Department of Health in England has defined a set of programme budget categories (PBCs),[34] based on the WHO's ICD, to accelerate this trend. The 23 categories are shown in Table Q4.1:

Number	Programme Budget Category
1	Infectious Diseases
2	Cancers & Tumours
3	Blood Disorders
4	Endocrine, Nutritional and Metabolic Problems
5	Mental Health Problems
6	Learning Disability Problems
7	Neurological System Problems
8	Eye/Vision Problems
9	Hearing Problems
10	Circulation Problems
11	Respiratory System Problems
12	Dental Problems
13	Gastrointestinal System Problems
14	Skin Problems (Including Burns)
15	Musculoskeletal System Problems (Excluding Trauma)
16	Trauma & Injuries
17	Genitourinary System Disorders (Except Infertility)
18	Maternity & Reproductive Health

Number	Programme Budget Category
19	Neonates
20	Poisoning
21	Healthy Individuals
22	Social Care Needs
23	Other

Table Q4.1: Department of Health (England) programme budget categories

This system of classification has many weaknesses, especially because some people have more than one condition. For this reason there is increasing interest in the Bridges to Health taxonomy, which has eight categories,[35] shown in Table Q4.2.

Population characteristic	Priority concerns of this population	Goals for healthcare
1. Healthy	Staying healthy by preventing accidents, illness and progression of early stages of disease	Staying healthy
2. Maternal and infant health	Healthy babies, low maternal risk, control of fertility	Staying healthy
3. Acutely ill, with likely return to health	Return to healthy state with minimal suffering and disruption	Getting well
4. Chronic conditions, with generally 'normal' function	Longevity, limiting disease progression, accommodating environment	Living with illness or disability

Population characteristic	Priority concerns of this population	Goals for healthcare
5. Significant but relatively stable disability, including mental disability	Autonomy, rehabilitation, limiting progression, accommodating environment, caregiver support	Living with illness or disability
6. 'Dying' with short decline	Comfort, dignity, life closure, caregiver support, planning ahead	Coping with illness at the end of life
7. Limited reserve and serious exacerbations	Avoiding exacerbations, maintaining function and specific advance planning	Coping with illness at the end of life
8. Long course of decline, from dementia and/or frailty	Support for caregivers, maintaining function, skin integrity, mobility and specific advance planning	Coping with illness at the end of life

Table Q4.2: Bridges to Health taxonomy

Category 4 in the Bridges to Health does include the ICD degree of granularity, with individual conditions such as 'epilepsy' and groups of conditions such as 'respiratory'.

Recognising multi-morbidity

There is growing interest in the limitations of the way in which the medical profession in every country has evolved into distinct tribes of 'generalists' and 'specialists' and, more recently, 'super-specialists'. For example, the first editorial in the *British Medical Journal* in 2020, which is always a signal of a journal's view of significant trends of the decade to come, was written by the four Chief Medical Officers of the United

Kingdom and the Presidents of all the Royal Colleges, and titled 'Rising to the Challenge of Multimorbidity'.[36]

> *Treating each disease in a patient as if it exists in isolation will lead to less good outcomes and complicate and duplicate interactions with the healthcare system. Training from medical school onwards, clinical teams, and clinical guidelines, however, all tend to be organised along single disease or single organ lines. As a result, a single patient may take multiple drugs recommended by different guidelines and see several specialists treating subcomponents of their overall health problem in isolation. Medical science is also disease based. Clinical trials still often exclude people who have more than one condition. Good vertical integration exists from bench to bedside for a single condition or disease, but there is little or no horizontal integration between diseases that often coexist. This will require an intellectual shift and rethinking some elements of our research, training, and practice in virtually every discipline.*

They suggest the focus should be on a new way of thinking, which they called 'cluster medicine': '. . .moving from thinking about multimorbidity as a random assortment of individual conditions to recognising it as a series of largely predictable clusters of disease in the same person'.[36]

Interestingly the first leader in the *Journal of the American Medical Association* in 2020, titled 'A Prescription for Longevity in the 21st Century', and written by a highly respected scientist, was subtitled 'Renewing Purpose, Building and Sustaining Social Engagement, and Embracing a Positive Lifestyle'.[37]

Delivering population healthcare

Although healthcare is very complex – perhaps the most complex challenge that a society has to tackle – it is important not to be overwhelmed by the scale of the challenge, but rather to focus on subgroups of the population defined by need, 'segments of the population' as the Bridges to Health call them. We need to recognise that if you take a segment of the population such as people with asthma, or a more complex condition such as dementia or frailty, large amounts of resources are being invested but no one has any idea how much is being spent or how the value realised from what they have invested compares with what is realised in other similar populations. Before describing the need to focus on segments it is important to clarify the language and to distinguish population segmentation from population stratification, which can be described as the horizontal division of the population by levels of risk, as distinct from vertical segmentation by need. The terms 'population healthcare' and 'population health management' are used for these two approaches:

- 'Population health' means the health status of a defined group of people
- 'Population health management' is a method that stratifies the population by levels of risk, allowing resources to be focused on those sub-groups at highest risk
- 'Population healthcare' focuses primarily on segments of the whole population defined by a common need, which may be a symptom such as breathlessness, a condition such as arthritis or a common characteristic such as frailty in old age, and does not involve institutions, specialities or technologies.

Population healthcare is the approach needed to allow a proper debate on allocative value.

Allocating resources to different segments of the population

In an analysis of the reasons why competition has failed to deliver high-quality healthcare in the USA, Porter and Teisberg argued that it is essential to set budgets at the level of a specific health problem and to encourage competition between 'Integrated Patient Units' that deliver care to patients with specific conditions.[38] In their view, competition between hospitals or insurance companies is too broad to have any meaning, but this is in the context of a society in which there is no finite population budget for healthcare.

Where there is a finite budget it has to be allocated to different groups defined by need to optimise what is termed allocative efficiency by economists, or allocative value to use the term from value-based healthcare.

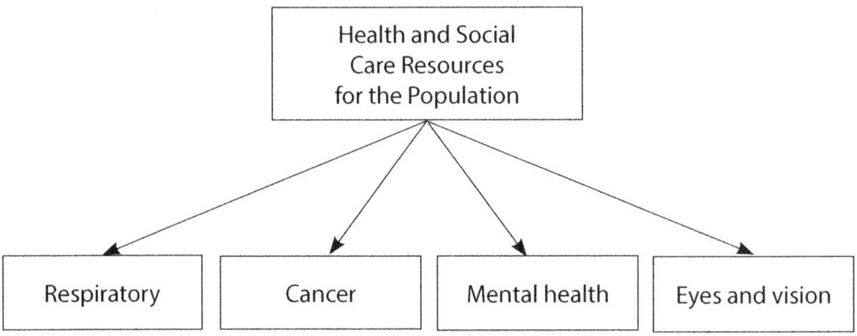

Figure Q4.2: Allocation of resources to patient groups

Allocative efficiency is maximised when resources are allocated to the various budgets for different segments of the population in such a way that it is not possible to increase harm, increase benefit or decrease harm by moving a single pound from one budget to another. This is sometimes referred to as the 'point of indifference' or the point of Pareto optimality:

> *When the consumption and production markets are in equilibrium, and when consumers' rates of indifference are equal to the economy's ability to transform one good into the others, we are in a position called Pareto optimality, named after economist Vilfredo Pareto. In an economy that is in a Pareto-optimal state, it is impossible to make someone better off (that is, increase that person's welfare) without making someone else worse off. Under such a situation, the economy has reached a state of allocative efficiency, although... this rests on a number of assumptions.*[39]

The aim is to create: 'A situation in which it is not possible to improve the welfare of one person in an economy without making someone else worse off.'[40]

To optimise allocative value, budgets need to be expressed not in terms of institutions, such as hospitals and community services, but as they relate to segments of the population.

> *The principle underlying programme budgeting is very simple. If decisions are to be made about broadly defined healthcare objectives and priorities – for example, what are the objectives associated with care of the elderly? What relative priorities are attached to the treatment of cancer compared with the prevention of heart disease? – then data should be provided in similarly broad terms to match the nature of the choices.*[41]

Allocating resources to different sub-segments of each segment

Once it has been decided how much to allocate to each programme budget, such as 'Problems of the Respiratory System' or 'Problems of Vision', it is necessary to ask how resources should be allocated within each budget. For instance, within the healthcare budget for 'Problems of the Respiratory System' it is necessary to reach a decision about the optimal allocation of resources for each of the major respiratory conditions and cost centres, such as:

- Asthma
- COPD
- Sleep apnoea
- Smoking cessation.

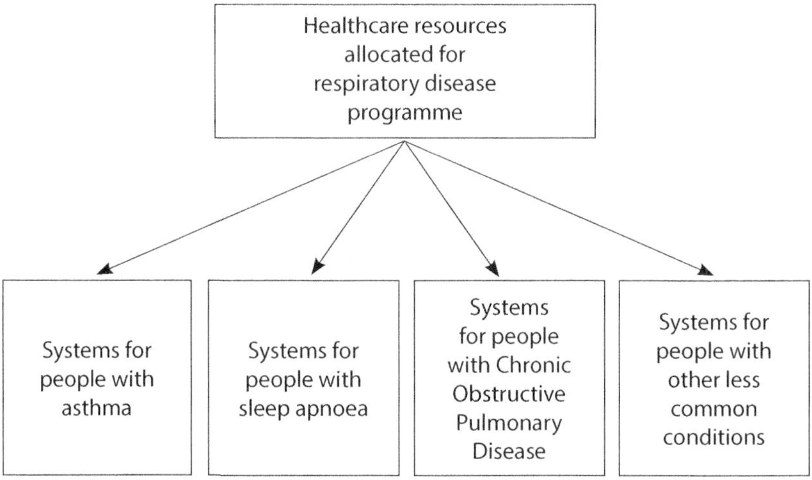

Figure Q4.3: Allocating resources within a segment of the population

Those who pay for healthcare have traditionally left the decisions about resource allocation within programme budgets to the providers of healthcare. However, there are also important allocation decisions to be taken within each programme budget that have hitherto been ignored but which are becoming increasingly necessary. Within each programme there are a small number of common problems and a larger number of rare problems that consume less of the budget overall but may have a higher cost. Thus, when a new effective treatment is introduced for a rare condition the cost per case may be very high because the company developing the drug has to recoup the costs invested in its development – which may be no less than the costs of developing a drug for a common disease – from a much smaller number of patients.

Making and taking decisions

A number of decision-making tools are being used and developed to appraise the impact of different resource allocation options, using metrics such as:

- Cost per quality-adjusted life year (QALY)
- Cost per disability-adjusted life year (DALY)

Other criteria that have been developed to help those who pay for or manage healthcare to make decisions about resource allocation include:

- The disease impact number (DIN), which is the number of people with a disease of whom one would benefit if an intervention were to be offered to all patients
- The population impact number (PIN), which is the number of people in a particular population who would benefit if an intervention were to be introduced to that population

As mentioned in Chapter 2, the aim of the person responsible for the allocation of resources is to reach the point of indifference or optimal allocative efficiency, known as Pareto optimality – the point at which it is not possible to increase value by moving a single unit of expenditure from one programme budget to another.

To date, there are no recorded examples of the point of indifference having been reached in healthcare resource allocation.

In situations where additional resources are available for allocation, cuts are required or there is a need to consider increasing expenditure in one programme budget by reducing that of another, a technique known as marginal analysis is used. This 'involves starting with a particular mix of services and analysing changes in that mix. If resources can be shifted to produce greater benefit then this should be done.'[42] In this description of marginal analysis, it is assumed that all decision-making leading up to the current expenditure status of programme budgets is explicit, evidence-based and logical – which is extremely unlikely in healthcare. For years health economists have wrestled with the problems of eliciting preferences, making choices equitably and maximising value. In allocating or shifting resources it would, of course, be ideal either to have a mathematical formula that could be used or a single ethical principle. Unfortunately, these do not exist.

There is no formula for allocating resources optimally

It might have been thought that in the era of super-computing there would be a program that could be used to estimate the best allocation of resources, but this is not the case. Thus Nobel Prize winner Amartya Sen describes the limitations of 'Arrow's Impossibility Theorem' (Ken Arrow himself gave it the more cheerful name of 'General Possibility Theorem'):

> *This is a mathematical result of remarkable elegance and power, which shows that even some very mild conditions of reasonable sensitivity of social decisions to what the members of a society want cannot be simultaneously satisfied by any social choice procedure that can be described as rational and democratic (as Arrow characterized these requirements, with some plausibility).*[43]

Arrow, himself a Nobel Prize winner, emphasised that: 'There exists no social welfare function satisfying a set of conditions necessary for democratic legitimacy and informational efficiency.'[44]

So, there is no simple formula to resolve the dilemma that decision-takers face in the allocation of finite resources. Arrow has been criticised for being anti-democratic, though his theorem in fact emphasises the importance of democracy, of people rather than computers making these decisions. But how are they to do it?

There is no principle for allocating resources optimally

Just as there is no formula for allocating resources optimally, neither is there a single ethical principle that can be used. Utilitarianism, developed by Jeremy Bentham and described as proposing: 'in its simplest formulation, claims that the morally right act or policy is that which produces the greatest happiness for the members of society'[45] – popularly known as 'the greatest good for the greatest number' – sounds attractive, but it mitigates against people with rare diseases so is not generally used.

Ultimately, decisions about resource allocation are made according to public values.[46] As there is neither a precise formula nor a single ethical principle to determine the allocation of resources that would result in perfect equity, the process by which decisions about allocation are made takes on great importance, for instance, establishing methods of ensuring that the decision-makers adhere to previously agreed principles. The test that is gaining popularity is whether decision-makers can give an account of the reasonableness with which they have undertaken their task:

> *Accountability for reasonableness is the idea that the reasons or rationales for important limit-setting decisions should be publicly available. In addition, these reasons must be ones*

> *that 'fair-minded' people can agree are relevant to pursuing appropriate patient care under necessary resource constraints. This is our central thesis, and it needs some explanation.*
>
> *By 'fair-minded,' we do not simply mean our friends or people who just happen to agree with us. We mean people who in principle seek to cooperate with others on terms they can justify to each other. Indeed, fair-minded people accept rules of the game – or sometimes seek rule changes – that promote the game's essential skills and the excitement their use produces.*[47]

Fortunately these authors also describe four conditions that can be used to assess the reasonableness of the decision-making process about the allocation of resources, namely that there should be:

1. Openness to the public, in particular ensuring that:
    - those groups least likely to press their claim and most likely to be overlooked need to be involved, and
    - no particular interest or lobby group is allowed an advantage to press their case or influence decisions
2. Objectivity and logic of the principles and criteria used to compare competing bids
3. The existence of an appeal process
4. Some form of regulation to make sure that conditions 1–3 are met.

Maximising value equitably

Programme budgeting based on the WHO ICD creates what sociologists would call a medical construct of healthcare, that is, the classification of health services through a medical lens or perspective. If instead the classification was based on sex, age, ethnic group or socio-economic group, a completely different budget structure would be developed that would also alter the nature of the decisions that have to be taken about resource allocation. Instead of asking the question, 'Has money been distributed equitably to different patient groups, such as people with cancer or with mental health problems?,' decision-makers would be asking questions such as:

- Has money been distributed equitably to different age groups, e.g. children, adults and elderly people?
- Has money been distributed equitably to meet the different needs of men and women?
- Has money been distributed equitably to different ethnic groups, e.g. people from South Asia or from Africa?
- Has money been distributed equitably to different socio-economic groups?
- Are the needs of people with rare diseases being overlooked?

To complicate the issue further, many people have more than one of these characteristics, a phenomenon known as intersectionality, since if a Venn diagram is drawn there are many overlaps. There is evidence that if these questions are asked, many health services appear to devote fewer resources relative to the needs of ethnic minority groups, women, older people, poor people and less well-educated people.

It could be argued that this is the result of issues unrelated to values, for example, the literacy of people with low levels of education. However, this ducks the issue. The decision-maker needs to form a judgement about whether healthcare resources should be invested in group-specific services, for example for sickle cell disease in people of Afro-Caribbean origin, or ancillary services, such as the provision of interpreters, which could increase utilisation.

The allocation of money to services for children poses a particular challenge, but the amount of resources actually spent is difficult to assess because although children are treated by every service except geriatrics, the only programme budget heading is 'Neonates'. When investing resources to improve the health of children, it is important to take into account:

- The present health and healthcare needs of children
- The value we place on children and their future contribution to society.

Using bounded rationality

At present programme budgeting and marginal analysis are impossible for most decision-makers. Not only are they subject to pressures to pay for some new drug or procedure but also, if they are fortunate enough to be given information about the cost-effectiveness (cost per QALY) of this new technology, this does not help them to decide whether investing resources in it will increase or decrease the health of a particular patient group, taking into account the fact that a decision to invest will result in the same amount of money being diverted from another use.

Those making the decisions are not able to do so as an academic exercise. They have to make and take decisions with limited time and deadlines; without all the knowledge they need; and without a computer program that can make the calculation for them.

Decision-makers therefore have to use 'bounded rationality' and good judgement.[48] These judgements are 'social value judgements', and NICE principles, drawn up with wide stakeholder involvement, are publicly expressed in a document with that title.[49] This document covers a range of issues, including difficult problems such as distributive justice and the tension between maximising value for society as a whole and responding to the needs of an individual in desperate circumstances, known as the 'rule of rescue'.

The population receiving healthcare services must accept that not all needs can be met. Indeed all that can be done is to make decisions openly and fairly. In itself this is a value judgement that can be challenged.

Being accountable for decisions

Increasingly the decisions made by those who are responsible for the allocation of resources are being challenged either by groups of patients or by individuals. Whereas the public – the entire population – can accept that difficult decisions have to be made that do not allow every patient group to obtain all the resources they want, pressure groups that represent people with one condition are less tolerant. Pressure groups campaign for more resources for the people who form their constituency, using both the press and the courts to do so.

How to get better value

At present most health services allocate money to the traditional bureaucracies. Here is an example from a typical jurisdiction in England, which we discussed in Chapter 4 (Table Q4.3). This table gives an account to the population served about how the money has been spent with respect to conventional service delivery organisations.

Service Area	Budget
Acute care	£329.9 million
Primary care	£89.8 million
Community health	£63.4 million
Mental health and learning disability	£62.8 million
Continuing care	£31.2 million
Other	£26.9 million

Service Area	Budget
Running costs	£16.6 million
Contingency	£7.0 million
Surplus	£3.7 million
TOTAL	£630.6 million

Table Q4.3: Budget breakdown by service area for an English health authority

Getting better value requires a different approach. Here are some practical suggestions that a population-based payer can consider:

- If such financial information is not available, start by using the ICD or Bridges to Health headings and describe the amount of resources used, for example bed days or clinic appointments
- Do not use only the ICD or Bridges to Health approach to classifying programmes – use the age distribution of the population as well
- Ensure all decision-makers understand key terms such as value and opportunity cost
- Model the effects of shifting resources from one budget to another.

This is the future, but of course the responsibility of an organisation allocating resources does not stop with their efforts to optimise allocative value: they have to ask the organisations to which they have allocated resources a set of questions to ensure that they are optimising technical value and hold them to account for answering these questions:

Question 5: Are the resources that have been allocated being used on the right interventions?

Question 6: Are all of the right patients, and only the right patients, being offered the high-value interventions?

Question 7: Are we sure that every individual patient is getting the right intervention in the way that is right for them?

Question 8: Is the quality of care as high as it can be with the resources available?

Question 9: Are clinical risks being minimised?

Question 10: Why not just get a grip, improve quality and safety, and reduce costs while you are at it?

Questions for reflection when teaching or developing networks:

If using these in network building or teaching, give one of the questions to the group and ask them to work in pairs to reflect on the question for 3 minutes. Try to get people who do not know one another to work together. When taking feedback, let each pair make only one point. In the interests of equity, if you start with the pair on the left-hand side of the room for the first question, start with the pair on the right hand side of the room for the second question.

- What are the principal weaknesses in managing the allocation of resources based on programme budgets that reflect the disease groupings of the ICD?
- Should disease prevention have its own programme budget or be included in the relevant disease-specific programme budget?
- What is the best way to describe the difference between equity and equality when under pressure during an interview on a local radio station?

References

34. NHS. Programme budgeting. Available at: www.england.nhs.uk/prog-budgeting

35. Lynn J, Straube BM, Bell KM, Jencks SF, Kambic RT. 'Using Population Segmentation to Provide Better Health Care for All: The "Bridges to Health" Model'. *Milbank Quarterly.* 2007; 85: 185–208.

36. Whitty CJM, MacEwen C, Goddard A, et al. 'Rising to the challenge of multimorbidity'. *British Medical Journal.* 2020; 368: l6964.

37. Pizzo PA. 'A prescription for longevity in the 21st century: Renewing purpose, building and sustaining social engagement, and embracing a positive lifestyle. *Journal of the Americal Medical Association.* 2020; 323: 415–416.

38. Porter ME, Olmsted Teisberg E. *Redefining Healthcare: Creating Value-based Competition on Results.* 2006. Harvard Business School Press.

39. Rice TH. *The Economics of Health Reconsidered.* 1998. Health Administration Press, pp. 19–20.

40. Wonderling D, Gruen R, Black N. *Introduction to Health Economics: Understanding Public Health.* 2005. Open University Press, p. 7.

41. Enthoven AC, Smith KW. *How Much is Enough? Shaping the Defense Program, 1961–1969.* 1971. Harper & Row.

42. Mitton C, Donaldson C. *Priority Setting Toolkit: Guide to the Use of Economics in Healthcare Decision Making.* 2004. Wiley.

43. Sen AK. *Choice, Welfare and Measurement.* 1982. Blackwell.

44. Arrow KJ, Sen AK, Suzumura K (Eds). *Handbook of Social Choice and Welfare, Volume 1.* 2002. Elsevier Science, p. 11.

45. Kymlicka W. Contemporary Political Philosophy: An Introduction. Second Edition. 2002. Oxford University Press, p. 10.

46. Moore MH. *Creating Public Value: Strategic Management in Government.* 1995. Harvard University Press.

47. Daniels N, Sabin JE. *Setting Limits Fairly: Learning to Share Resources for Health.* 2008. Oxford University Press.

48. Simon HA. *Administrative Behavior: A Study of Decision-Making Processes in Administrative Organizations.* 4th Edition. 1997. Free Press.

49. NICE. Our principles. Available at: www.nice.org.uk/about/who-we-are/our-principles

QUESTION 5

ARE THE RESOURCES THAT HAVE BEEN ALLOCATED BEING USED ON THE RIGHT INTERVENTIONS?

This section will:

- Explain the difference between absolute and relative benefits and the impact the method of presentation has on decisions-makers
- Discuss the use of the terms effective, cost-effectiveness and value
- Review how the QALY and incremental cost-effectiveness ratio (ICER) are being used to assess costs and benefits
- Introduce the concept of over-diagnosis and over-treatment.

By the end of this section you will have an understanding of:

- What is meant by framing and how to prevent bias caused by framing
- The difference between QALY and ICER
- The need to have different methods for appraising diagnostic tests and treatments
- How to discuss new tests and treatments without using the term 'effective'.

Having sliced the pie into wedges for segments such as people with musculoskeletal problems, people with cancer or people with respiratory disease, and then having taken the knife again to each slice to divide the resources fairly between sub-segments within each segment, the next step is to ensure that all resources that have been allocated to a particular sub-group of the population are used optimally. It is essential to ensure that:

- All interventions being offered are of high value
- The balance between the different types of intervention, and prevention, diagnosis, treatment, rehabilitation and long-term support, is optimal.

Appraising the value of interventions

The questions used to appraise new treatments, tests or services have evolved over the past 50 years.

The first era of effectiveness – producing evidence of benefit

Few people had more influence on healthcare in the last 50 years of the 20th century than Archie Cochrane, first due to his insistence on the importance of the randomised controlled trial (RCT) and the systematic review, and second through his challenge to the medical and research establishments that they should organise all relevant knowledge properly, leading to the creation of the Cochrane Collaboration. Cochrane launched the second revolution in healthcare in 1972 with the publication of *Effectiveness and Efficiency: Random Reflections on Health Services*,[50] and thus effectiveness became the focus of healthcare for the last three decades of the 20th century.

'All effective treatments must be free' was the declaration on Cochrane's banner carried at a communist rally in the 1930s. It was written after considerable thought but apparently made no impact on the communists on the march. However, it did have a profound influence on Cochrane himself, who remained obsessed with the need to demonstrate the effectiveness of treatments and, if treatments were found to be effective, for those treatments to be made available through a national health service. For Cochrane it was clear that the single best method for demonstrating the effectiveness of a treatment was the RCT, and he promoted the importance of such trials with commitment, energy, intelligence and a considerable degree of cunning throughout the rest of his professional career. As a result, the term 'effectiveness' entered the general vocabulary not only of the research worker, but also of all those who manage and pay for healthcare. The test for effectiveness has evolved and now, thanks to the work of the Cochrane Collaboration, is accepted as being a systematic review of all RCTs, published and unpublished, of that treatment.

Doing the right thing does not only mean choosing the right treatment, however. It also means getting the diagnosis right before starting treatment. In part owing to the greater availability of money for pharmaceutical rather than diagnostic research, the evidence base for diagnostic interventions is less strong than that for therapeutic interventions. The appraisal of screening tests and programmes are relatively simple because there are defined populations and any screening programme has a single aim.[51] When tests are used for diagnosis in routine clinical practice, however, appraisal becomes more difficult because different clinicians use the same test for different reasons. Furthermore, criteria applied to the introduction of new laboratory or imaging diagnostic tests may be less rigorous than those applied to the introduction of new drugs. An alternative approach to appraisal of the value of new diagnostic tests is described in the book *Patient-Centred Diagnosis*.[52] The author suggests that investment in technological methods of diagnosis should be appraised not only with respect to cost-effectiveness criteria but also by drawing a comparison with the outcomes of investing the same resource into releasing more time for clinicians to listen to patients and examine them properly.

The limitations of 'effectiveness'

After 35 years in common use, the term 'effective' is now used much more loosely and therefore has many different meanings. Some people still use it to convey the original meaning. For some clinicians, however, 'effective' is used to mean that, in their experience, patients appear to have got better, or even a single patient got better while using the treatment.

The people who argued for the adoption of Cochrane's definition of effectiveness also pointed out, fairly, that 'absence of evidence of effectiveness is not proof of absence of effect.' The application of this premise enables people to argue that the absence of evidence of effect is due to the design of a trial. For instance, it was argued that the absence of evidence of effectiveness of prostate cancer screening was due to the fact that reported trials were too small, and that the proposition that 'screening for prostate cancer is ineffective' was a statement made according to the rules laid down by those who funded research and healthcare.

We also now recognise that there is 'optimism bias' in research,[53] namely, that for a number of reasons research has given the impression that treatments are more effective than is actually the case. Another reason why the term 'effective' needs to be used with caution is that treatments have both beneficial and harmful effects, whereas the word 'effective' has come to be synonymous with beneficial effects.

The second era of effectiveness – balancing benefit and harm

In the 1990s, concern about the adverse effects of healthcare interventions became much more prominent. The adverse effects causing concern were not those arising from medical errors but those inherent in the interventions themselves. The effect of thalidomide is still the most powerful image of the adverse effects of a therapeutic intervention, but other examples exist. For instance, Thomas J. Moore documented the adverse effects of drugs to control minor arrhythmias after myocardial infarction (MI) in his book *Deadly Medicine: Why Tens of Thousands of Heart Patients Died in America's Worst Drug Disaster.*[54] Many people experience minor arrhythmias after an MI, and their risk of death increases if this arrhythmia becomes more severe. Drugs were developed to control some of these arrhythmias, and the case for introducing them was based on a plausible theory and some experimental evidence. The drugs became popular and were widely used. The evidence of benefit was not strong, however, and because the researchers' study design was focused on identifying the benefits, the evidence of harm was very weak and was ignored. By the late 1980s, these pharmaceuticals were said to be killing as many as 70,000 people every year in the USA – more than died in the Vietnam War. As a consequence, the key question for appraising value during the 1990s became: 'What are the benefits *and harms* of this intervention?'

Evidence about the harms of interventions is less plentiful than evidence about benefits because harms are less common than benefits, and research studies designed to demonstrate the benefits of a new treatment are often not large enough to provide strong evidence of any harm it may cause. This observation led Vandenbroucke and Psaty to the conclusion that:

> *. . .for a future that combines benefit and harms assessment, systematic reviews will need to incorporate and integrate the best information from both randomised trial and observational studies.*[55]

During the 1990s, it also became clear that the magnitude of both benefits and harms needed to be expressed in terms that were clear to clinicians and patients. Therefore, instead of expressing the results of a trial of a new treatment in relative terms (for example, that the new treatment doubled the cure rate with only a 10% harm rate), it was clearer if the number of patients receiving benefit and the number being harmed were described in absolute terms or numbers and not in percentages (Table Q5.1).

	Relative Terms	Absolute Terms
Benefits	100% improvement in cure rate	1 in 2,000 patients will be cured instead of 1 in 4,000
Harms	50% reduction in the rate of serious adverse effects	1 patient in every 10,000 dies of adverse effects instead of 2

Table Q5.1: Expressing benefits and harms in absolute and relative terms

This led to the development of two criteria – NNT and NNH:

- NNT: the number needed to be treated for one person to benefit
- NNH: the number needed to be treated for one person to be harmed

There is evidence to show that if a patient, doctor or payer is given information in relative terms, they are keener to use a new treatment than if the same data are presented in absolute terms.[56-58] This phenomenon, known as 'framing', is well known among those who wish to promote new tests and treatments.

By the late 1990s, as the cost of interventions had become a pressing issue for all services, the key question for appraising the value of interventions developed further, into: 'Does this intervention do more good than harm and add as much value as possible?' To answer this question information is needed on benefit, harm and cost.

The era of cost-effectiveness and NICE

The National Institute for Clinical Excellence, NICE, became a legal entity in 1999 but its impact is now greater because of the understanding that even high-quality care delivered safely will not increase value if the intervention is not of proven cost-effectiveness. NICE, now the National Institute for Health and Care Excellence, has had an increasingly important cultural impact (not just in England and Wales) and its methods and guidance are central to the development and dominance of the value-based healthcare paradigm.

The mission of NICE, which was restated in the 2012 Health and Social Act and reinforced as a commitment under the NHS Constitution, was to balance benefits and costs to provide 'the best value for taxpayers' money and the most effective, fair and sustainable use of finite resources'. How it does this is described in the following way:

> *23. If possible, NICE considers value for money by calculating the incremental cost-effectiveness ratio (ICER). This is based on an assessment of the intervention's costs and how much benefit it produces compared with the next best alternative. It is expressed as the 'cost (in £) per quality-adjusted life year (QALY) gained'. This takes into account the 'opportunity cost' of recommending one intervention instead of another, highlighting that there would have been other potential uses of the resource. It includes the needs of other people using services now or in the future who are not known and not represented. The primary consideration underpinning our guidance and standards is the overall population need. This means that sometimes we do not recommend an intervention because it does not provide enough benefit to justify its cost. It also means that we cannot apply the 'rule of rescue', which refers to the desire to help an*

> *identifiable person whose life is in danger no matter how much it costs. Sometimes NICE uses other methods if they are more suitable for the evidence available, for example when looking at interventions in public health and social care.*
>
> *24. Interventions with an ICER of less than £20,000 per QALY gained are generally considered to be cost-effective. Our methods manuals explain when it might be acceptable to recommend an intervention with a higher cost-effectiveness estimate. A different threshold is applied for interventions that meet the criteria to be assessed as a 'highly specialised technology'.*

The decision was made at NICE to use the QALY as an outcome measure because this metric combines the increased life expectancy from an intervention with the quality of life of the increased years. Assessing cost in relation to QALYs is referred to as cost–utility analysis. In addition to recognising that much of healthcare is concerned with improving people's quality of life, the QALY also reflects the value judgement that survival is an insufficient measure of benefit and that there is a need to consider expected quality of life years.

The use of QALYs allows the cost and benefit of different interventions to be expressed in the same currency, allowing different interventions to be compared for different conditions, and services to be compared not only with one another but also with designated thresholds above which interventions are regarded as not cost-effective. This approach has been very helpful and is widely used (such as by NICE in England, and by the Australian Drugs Reimbursement Committee) in assessing the cost-effectiveness of a diagnostic test or treatment[59,60]– in turn enabling decisions that are consistent, transparent and fair.

This is the way NICE explains how it realises principle number 7 in its set of 13 principles:

Box Q5.1: NICE Principles	
Principle 1:	Prepare guidance and standards on topics that reflect national priorities for health and care
Principle 2:	Describe our approach in process and methods manuals, and review them regularly
Principle 3:	Use independent advisory committees to develop recommendations
Principle 4:	Take into account the advice and experience of people using services and their carers or advocates, health and social care professionals, commissioners, providers and the public
Principle 5:	Offer people interested in the topic the opportunity to comment on and influence our recommendations
What we take into account	
Principle 6:	Use evidence that is relevant, reliable and robust
Principle 7:	Base our recommendations on an assessment of population benefits and value for money
What our guidance aims to achieve	
Principle 8:	Support innovation in the provision and organisation of health and social care services
Principle 9:	Aim to reduce health inequalities
Types of recommendation	
Principle 10:	Consider whether it is appropriate to make different recommendations for different groups of people
Principle 11:	Propose new research questions and data collection to resolve uncertainties in the evidence
What we do after making recommendations	
Principle 12:	Publish and disseminate our recommendations and provide support to encourage their adoption
Principle 13:	Assess the need to update our recommendations in line with new evidence

Obviously NICE has had a huge impact on the NHS, as have similar health technology assessment agencies (many based on the NICE model) in other countries on their own health services, but it has also had a big impact on the industries that supply the NHS because they have had to learn new ways of measuring and expressing the value of their innovations.

The changing perspective of industry on value

Health services stimulate and support pharmaceutical, medical equipment, diagnostic and IT industries, and the developers of products or services are sometimes disappointed by the lack of enthusiasm generated by their latest creation. The reason for this is not simply the added cost incurred by any new technology, at least in the short term, but the failure to appreciate the different meanings given to the term 'value'. This is further complicated by the fact that many health services are financially hard-pressed and unable to create an 'invest-to-save' fund that would allow investment in the short term to increase value in the long term.

For the past two decades, industry has recognised the need to present health service payers and providers with evidence of effectiveness and cost-effectiveness associated with new products or services, and NICE has played a very important part in this revolution. In some cases this has led to differences of opinion between industry and those who pay for healthcare regarding the strength of evidence used by industry. For instance, to generate evidence the pharmaceutical industry has been criticised for comparing a new drug against a placebo rather than the best existing treatment. Nevertheless, there has been a perception in industry that if they could demonstrate effectiveness and cost-effectiveness funds should flow.

In a period of financial constraint, when health service funds are not increasing – and may even be decreasing – the payer's interest is in how much value is added to the service for a particular group of patients, not just whether the treatment is effective. Effectiveness and cost-effectiveness will be taken for granted by health services but they will need to see, or be convinced, that value will be increased.

Some principles have been discussed with industry as examples of new types of skills that people need to acquire, not only in industry but also in start-up businesses, taking an idea or innovation on the long journey from bench to bedside. Listed below are five skills that people need in addition to being able to demonstrate effectiveness and cost-effectiveness:

- Explaining how a particular drug or technology increases value for individual patients
- Explaining how a drug or technology increases value for the population served
- Describing the system that can be created using the drug or technology as the catalyst for change
- Demonstrating that a technology is of higher value than some other intervention for the same condition, and how it could be funded by reducing investment in that intervention
- Demonstrating that a drug or technology is of higher value than interventions for other conditions covered by the same programme budget, and how it could be funded by switching resources from those interventions.

As described in Chapter 2, the introduction of value-based pricing in the NHS in England was challenging for the pharmaceutical industry.[61] It is worth repeating, however, that within this industry there are two different types of company: the big-name R&D firms and generics manufacturers.[61] The former type know that when they produce a new treatment that is more cost-effective than existing treatments, as approved by NICE, the NHS will need to find the money to pay for this new and better treatment. They understand that one source of this money is the money being spent on drugs of little or no value, which was discussed in the 2021 report by the Chief Pharmaceutical Officer titled *Good for you, good for us, good for everybody.*[62]

The R&D pharmaceutical companies know that the test of effectiveness that will be used is the RCT, or, even better, a systematic review of all available RCTs. Other industries, imaging for example, face a more difficult task because it may not be possible to organise an RCT and the developer will have to argue their case in a different way. However they too now appreciate that health services who have to pay for innovation will want to know the impact of the innovation on the outcomes and costs of a service, and they will not be satisfied with data that demonstrates only improved accuracy of measurement.

Ensuring the optimal balance between different interventions

The key issue for the 21st century is whether an innovation will produce more value for the population group to which it is expected to be applied. The increase in value is determined not only by the cost per QALY and the ICER of the individual intervention but also by the opportunity cost of the innovation. This has also been referred to as the 'opportunity value', that is, the value that could be realised by using the same amount of resource to invest in another type of service for the same group of patients.[63]

It is not sufficient, therefore, simply to assess the value of individual interventions. It is essential to assess the value of the balance of interventions provided within a system. This, chiefly, is assessing the value of the balance among interventions for prevention, screening, diagnosis, treatment and long-term care for a particular sub-segment of a population.

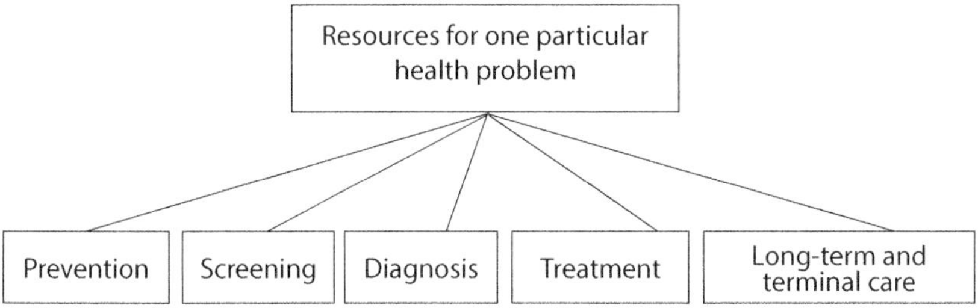

Figure Q5.1: Balancing the value of interventions

For instance, within the amount of money committed to COPD, it is possible to consider the relative benefits and harms of switching resources between smoking cessation to prevent COPD, telephone support for people with COPD and triple drug therapy (Figure Q5.2).

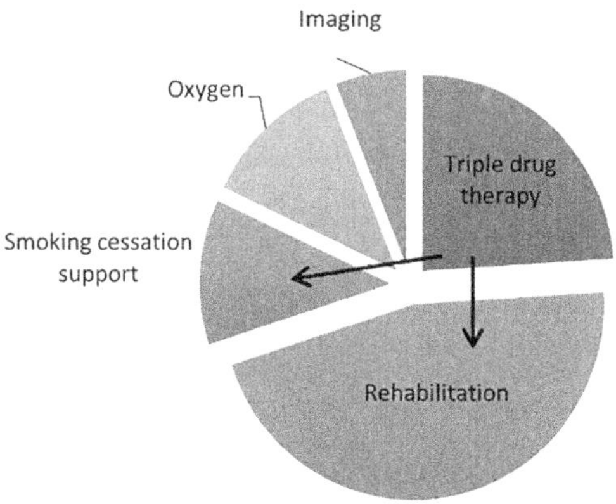

Figure Q5.2: Switching resources between different budgets funding different parts of the care pathway for COPD

By developing budgets for segments of the population defined by need, and not by primary and secondary care or hospitals and health centres, clinicians are given the opportunity to become stewards of the pooled resources for that population segment. They can fight for more resources for their segment, but they will be expected to be accountable both to people in that segment and to the entire population for the value derived from resources allocated to that population segment. They become the stewards.

To make this task more scientific, open and accountable, a tool has been developed called the Socio-Technical Allocation of Resources (STAR) tool.[64]

When using the STAR tool, it is essential to engage not only clinicians but also patients because the values of both groups need to be incorporated into the decision-making process. All the interventions for a particular sub-segment of the population are assessed and illustrated with respect to:

- The number of people treated
- The number who benefit
- The size of the benefit measured using QALYs.

All interventions are considered in the context of all financial resources available for a particular condition so that a judgement can be made about switching resources from interventions of lower value to interventions of higher value.

How to get better value

Many possible interventions could be provided for any group of patients, and these vary in their level of value to those patients. In most services it is usually possible to classify these interventions into four main categories (see Table Q5.2):

A. Interventions of high value that are provided
B. Interventions of low value that are provided

C. Interventions of high value that are not provided
D. Interventions of low value that are not provided

	High value	Low value
Provided	A	B
Not provided	C	D

Table Q5.2: The imperfect relationship between provision and benefit

The perfect high-value service would be one in which only high-value interventions are provided, i.e. only Category A interventions, with no interventions falling into Categories B or C. However, this situation is not common!

To increase the level of value in a service, those responsible for paying for healthcare and the provider must have a strategy for each of the four intervention categories:

A. Maintain provision and improve the quality of intervention year on year – 'keep them going, and do them better each year'
B. Initiate the decommissioning of these interventions – 'start them stopping'
C. Initiate the commissioning of high-value innovation – 'start them starting'
D. Prevent the interventions from entering the service – 'stop them starting'

When the process of value improvement starts, the focus of the debate is usually on the introduction of new interventions and the increased provision of certain interventions proposed by clinicians and patients, and the reduction or cessation of certain interventions proposed by payers. This, of course, is a recipe for argument and disagreement.

What is needed is for everyone to agree that within the budget available there needs to be a concerted effort to increase the proportion of interventions provided that are of higher value, and decrease the number of interventions provided that are of lower value.

There are a number of steps that can be taken to optimise value by ensuring that only the right interventions are implemented:

- Promote and support the concepts of evidence-based decision-making to ensure that any innovations adopted, managerial changes proposed and services provided are based on best current evidence
- Ensure that the cost-effectiveness of innovations is assessed as well as their effectiveness. The work of NICE and similar bodies in other countries is of central importance in this aspect of a programme to optimise value.
- Promote the culture of resource stewardship and reinforce it by introducing programme budgeting so that clinicians are responsible for optimising value from the resources allocated to their sub-group of a population
- Promote prevention, the best value service, through every service within every programme budget
- Promote innovations of high value or the need to increase the number of interventions that all clinicians agree to be of high value, district nursing for example, to be funded by reducing spending on lower-value activities
- Do not appeal to clinicians to find 'savings', which they often regard as being resources that will be taken from them and given to someone else who is inefficient or simply vanish into a black hole

These are key techniques that need to be adopted by all health services. Once this is achieved, we can move on to the next question: Are the right patients being offered the high-value interventions?

Questions for reflection when teaching or engaged in professional and organisational development

If using these questions in network building or teaching, give one of the questions to the group and ask them to work in pairs to reflect on it for 3 minutes. Try to get people who do not know one another to work together. When taking feedback, let each pair make only one point. In the interests of equity, if you start with the pair on the left-hand side of the room for the first question, start with the pair on the right-hand side of the room for the second question.

- If an innovation has been shown to produce more benefit than harm at reasonable cost, is it not reasonable to say that the funding required for it should come from the budget that already exists for that disease?
- On what grounds could a patient group challenge a decision by a health service not to provide a treatment?
- Preventive services are often claimed to reduce cost, but does this mean they are cash-releasing?

References

50. Cochrane AL. *Effectiveness and Efficiency: Random Reflections on Health Services.* 1972. Nuffield Provincial Hospitals Trust.

51. Raffle A, Gray M. *Screening: Evidence and Practice.* 2007. Oxford University Press.

52. Summerton N. *Patient-Centred Diagnosis.* 2007. Radcliffe Publishing.

53. Gray JAM. *The Resourceful Patient.* 2002. eRosetta Press.

54. Moore TJ. *Deadly Medicine: Why Tens of Thousands of Heart Patients Died in America's Worst Drug Disaster.* 1995. Simon & Schuster.

55. Vandenbroucke JP, Psaty BM. 'Benefits and risks of drug treatment: How to combine the best evidence on benefits with the best data about adverse effects'. *Journal of the Americal Medical Association.* 2008; 300: 2417–2419.

56. Hux JE, Naylor CD. 'Communicating the benefits of chronic preventive therapy: Does the format of efficacy data determine patients' acceptance of treatment?' *Medical Decision Making.* 1995; 15: 152–157.

57. Malenka DJ, Baron JA, Johansen S, et al. 'The framing effects of absolute and relative risk'. *Journal of General Internal Medicine.* 1993; 8: 543–548.

58. Fahey T, Griffiths S, Peters TJ. 'Evidence based purchasing: understanding results of clinical trials and systematic reviews'. *British Medical Journal.* 1995; 311: 1056.

59. Pearson SD, Rawlins MD. 'Quality, innovation, and value for money: NICE and the British National Health Service'. *Journal of the Americal Medical Association.* 2005; 294: 2618–2622.

60. Henry DA, Hill SR, Harris A. 'Drug prices and value for money: the Australian Pharmaceutical Benefits Scheme'. *Journal of the Americal Medical Association.* 2005; 294: 2630–2632.

61. Claxton K, Sculpher M, Carroll S. 'Value-based pricing for pharmaceuticals: Its role, specification and prospects in a newly devolved NHS'. 2011. Working Papers 060cherp, Centre for Health Economics, University of York.

62. Ridge K. Good for you, good for us, good for everybody: a plan to reduce overprescribing to make patient care better and safer, support the NHS, and reduce carbon emissions. Published 22 September 2021. Available at: www.gov.uk/government/publications/national-overprescribing-review-report

63. Gray M, Porter T. 'Opportunity value'. *Journal of Health Services Research & Policy.* 2009; 14: 129–130.

64. Airoldi M, Morton A, Smith JAE. 'STAR—People-powered prioritization: a 21st-century solution to allocation headaches'. *Medical Decision Making.* 2014; 34; 965–975.

QUESTION 6

ARE ALL OF THE RIGHT PATIENTS, AND ONLY THE RIGHT PATIENTS, BEING OFFERED HIGH-VALUE INTERVENTIONS?

This section will:

- Explain how patients seen by a clinical service often have different characteristics from patients treated in research studies
- Introduce the concept that cost-effectiveness is reduced as the threshold for treatment changes
- Consider the role of the clinician in personalising evidence.

By the end of this section you will have an understanding of:

- The different factors that result in an intervention shown to do more good than harm for one group of patients being offered to other patient groups
- How to describe the law of diminishing returns
- What is meant by overuse of a technology
- How to describe personalised medicine, and how to distinguish it from precision medicine.

In a world in which the evidence of effectiveness of most common interventions is clearly summarised in systematic reviews such as the accessible excellent Cochrane Reviews, and in which the evidence of cost-effectiveness is calculated and promoted by organisations like NICE and similar bodies in other countries, it might seem self-evident that, having made an evidence-based decision about the right treatments to offer a population, the right patients would receive the right treatment – after all, the evidence about drug X and operation Y usually specifies clearly the clinical condition of patients who have benefited in RCTs that tested the interventions. Unfortunately, that is often not the case, and there can be underuse of effective interventions, often complicated by inequity, or overuse and waste.

Why are evidence-based treatments not deployed correctly?

There are three principal reasons why this is so:

- Absence of a system
- Unwarranted variation due to local clinical cultures
- Drift from evidence-based criteria over time

Absence of a system

Broken legs in young men present a simple challenge to the health service: 100% of young people with a fractured tibia reach the right specialist service. They need neither health literacy nor good quality primary care physicians; they will all quickly reach the right service and the treatment they receive will not differ much from one country to another. The same is not the case for older people with fractured neck of femur. In developed countries, 100% will reach the accident and emergency service, but this is not the case in many poor countries, where no more than 80% will do so. Even in developed countries, not all get the right treatment. It may not matter too much which of the many screws are used, but it does make a difference whether the operation is carried out quickly after geriatric assessment, and whether there is follow-up in which the skills of rehabilitation specialists are centrally involved – and this requires a system for managing fractured neck of femur in which orthopaedic surgeons and geriatricians work as a team.

Unwarranted variation due to local clinical cultures

Even high-quality services can vary widely. There is, for example, a 50-fold variation in the rate of operating on the ligaments and cartilages of the knees of young people. This is by no means the biggest variation published in the first *NHS Atlas of Variation*.[65] Examples of other variations are shown below, chosen not to shock but to demonstrate that even the clinical care of common conditions – for which there is good evidence about the principal treatments and clear guidelines about the organisation of pathways – can differ widely in different populations (Table Q6.1).

Variable	Ratio of the lowest to the highest rate after the 5 highest and 5 lowest are excluded
Endovascular aneurysm repair (EVAR) for aortic aneurysm/100,000	4.3
DEXA scans/1,000	6
Free thyroxine T4 tests/1,000 ordered by GP	16
Prostate-specific antigen (PSA) tests/1000	4.7
Percentage of deaths in hospital	1.73
Cruciate ligament reconstruction	50
Folate testing	14
Rheumatoid factor testing	107

*Table Q6.1: Significant unwarranted variations in healthcare**

**The table shows the ratio of highest and lowest activity in NHS population-based organisations that were unaware of how they compared with other similar organisations, having excluded the five highest and the five lowest returns to exclude the possibility of the extremes being the results of coding errors*

Sometimes the variation is warranted by variations in need, but much of the variation is unwarranted, defined by Jack Wennberg as variation warranted neither by specific evidence of variation in need nor by a conscious and explicit decision that this variation is justified having been made.[66]

When it is clear that someone needs an intervention – to have their blood pressure measured, for example – then everyone knows what to do. As soon as judgement is required, however – about, say, which people with moderately raised blood pressure should be treated – then culture becomes important. Obviously one doctor's interpretation of the evidence can vary from another's, which explains variation between clinicians, but Wennberg found that different cultures could be felt in different clinical communities. Thus in some communities of practice, surgery for back pain is viewed as the right intervention to offer early, while in others it is regarded as a last resort. Wennberg demonstrated that there was a certain way of working that he called a 'signature', which determined the rate of intervention in a population:

> *Surgical signatures reflect the practice patterns of individual physicians and local medical culture, rather than differences in need – or even differences in the local supply of surgeons.*

The development of a culture takes time, and endures because the community of practice often relates to one medical school that plays an important role in the development of the culture by ensuring that new entrants to the specialist training programmes acquire the signature of that programme. Then, when a community needs to recruit a new specialist, they choose the applicant from a shortlist of maybe four, all of whom have been trained and inculcated in the style of practice promoted by the training programme they all came from. The individual who is chosen is chosen because they are closest to the preferred local variant of the style of practice.

Thanks to the excellent Getting It Right First Time (GIRFT) programme,[67] which is described in more detail in Question 10, many clinicians in England are now aware of variations in quality. However, most clinicians are unaware of how they compare with other clinicians in terms of value. This requires performance to be related to the population served as the denominator and not to the number of patients treated, which measures quality rather than value.

We must also be mindful that unwarranted variation, and in particular overuse of low-value care (which at worst confers negative health impacts where unnecessary investigations, procedures and operations result in complications), holds a carbon cost as well as an opportunity cost. This constitutes a waste of resources, both tangible and intangible (including patient and staff costs), and adds to the carbon footprint of healthcare, which in itself has ramifications for human and planetary health.

It is important to emphasise that, although some variation results from financial incentives in health services that have fee-for-service payment of doctors, unwarranted variation is equally found in services that have doctors paid by capitation or salary with no financial incentive to do more.

Drift from evidence-based criteria over time

The wish to do good and the belief that more is better can also lead to drifts in the threshold at which interventions are offered. The patients most likely to benefit from an intervention are those whose clinical condition is exactly the same as that of patients in the research study which produced the evidence leading to the decision to introduce the treatment. For instance, abatacept was found to be an effective drug in patients with rheumatoid arthritis who had an 'inadequate response to methotrexate'.[68] Thus, according to the evidence, only patients with an inadequate response to methotrexate should be given abatacept. Once the drug entered clinical practice, however, adherence to this criterion was not always strictly observed, leading to drift and wider use of the drug. Drift may be driven by one or more of clinicians, patients or the healthcare industry.

Clinician-driven drift

Although an intervention is often introduced with strict criteria about which patients should be treated, clinicians can gradually drift away from these initial limitations and extend the indications for intervention, with the result that patients are treated who do not match the original criteria. Clinician-driven drift in the use of an intervention occurs when there is increased acceptability of the intervention and/or a reduction in the risks associated with it.

Acceptability can be defined as the willingness of the public or patient to be treated in a particular way. As diagnostic and therapeutic interventions become less uncomfortable, they are used on a greater number of patients. In addition, as the adverse effects of interventions diminish, the level of acceptability increases. For example, a greater number of clinicians may find it acceptable to recommend, and a greater number of patients may find it acceptable to agree to, an operation for the removal of the gall bladder when the development of laparoscopic (otherwise known as 'keyhole') surgery reaches the point at which it can replace open surgery. As the risk of surgery decreases, a greater number of people are judged to be 'fit for surgery', and therefore the number of operations undertaken with a lower relative risk increases. The absolute number of deaths, however, remains constant (Figure Q6.1).

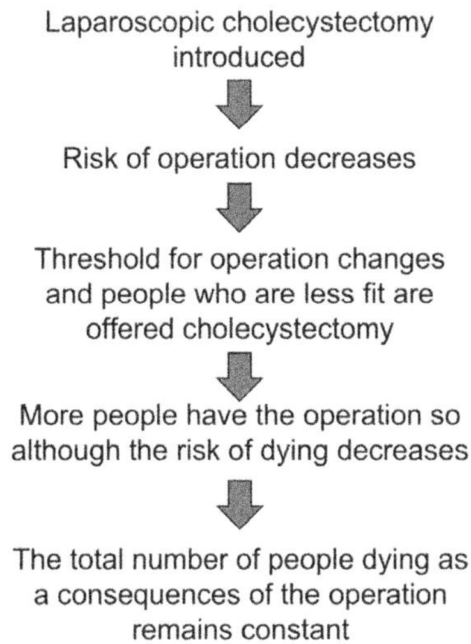

Figure Q6.1: The consequences of an improvement in technology

As the organisation of a health service increases and quality improves, often as a result of the development of specialist centres, the risks associated with treatment are reduced, and the types of patients previously considered to be too unwell for treatment are reclassified as eligible for treatment.

Patient-driven drift

I operated on the cataract of the retired professor of pathology. He was delighted. His golf handicap dropped by 2. In the following 2 months, five other members of his golf club were referred for cataract surgery.

Consultant ophthalmologist

When cataract surgery was first introduced, people with very little vision, some of whom were registered blind, received the operation and the results were amazing. As the capacity for cataract surgery increased, the criteria for undergoing the operation changed and people with less severe visual loss had their cataracts removed. Knowledge of the operation and its effects grew and, among older people, demand for operation increased. The initial strict criteria started to drift. Patient demands increase as interventions become less unpleasant or less risky.

Industry-driven drift

Individual healthcare companies try to increase market share, but the healthcare industry as a whole may lobby for a particular condition or treatment to be given priority. Direct advertising of a drug or product is one obvious method. In countries where 'direct-to-consumer' advertising of drugs is not allowed, healthcare companies, either alone or in concert, have started to fund patient groups that campaign for more resources for a particular health need. In addition, celebrities who have personal experience of a disease, either as patients or carers, may be recruited to act as figureheads, thus attracting media interest.

As a consequence of these three types of drift there may be underuse or overuse of technologies.

Overuse and waste

Obviously it is necessary to start stopping and to stop starting interventions for which there is no evidence of effectiveness, but there is also significant overuse of existing interventions for which there is no evidence of effectiveness. The 2021 Ridge report analysed the causes and consequences of overprescribing and polypharmacy, as well as their economic impact. Here is the summary:

> *The review has found that overprescribing is a serious problem in health systems internationally that has grown dramatically over the last 25 years. It has two main causes:*

- *Systemic: Key factors are single-condition clinical guidelines, a lack of alternatives to prescribing a medicine, a need for on-going review and deprescribing to be built into the process of prescribing, inability to access comprehensive patient records, the lack of digital interoperability, and pressure of time.*
- *Cultural: A healthcare culture that favours medicines over alternatives and in which some patients struggle to be heard.*

> *Overprescribing may disproportionately affect Black, Asian and Minority Ethnic communities and those who are more vulnerable, such as the elderly and those with disabilities.*
>
> *Recent initiatives by the NHS have helped stem the growth rate of overprescribing but it remains at unacceptable levels. Evidence is limited, but the review estimates that it is possible that at least 10% of the total number of prescription items in primary care need not have been issued.*
>
> *We know what will reduce overprescribing: shared decision-making with patients; better guidance and support for clinicians; more alternatives to medicines, such as physical and social activities and talking therapies; and more Structured Medication Reviews (SMR) for those with long-term health conditions.*[69]

This is a very important report, which is relevant worldwide, and it is important to remember that the cost is not only financial but also includes a carbon cost, which results from researching and manufacturing drugs and equipment.

Too Much Medicine is the name of a *British Medical Journal* campaign against over-treatment, often a consequence of over-diagnosis, which can do harm as well as good. With respect to diagnostic tests, the harm arises:

- As a direct result of tests, for example, exposure to radiation during computed tomography (CT) scanning
- As a result of over-diagnosis, one of the key issues of this decade.

Over-diagnosis leads to an increase in the number of people who become patients, and an increase in the likelihood of over-treatment. The reasons for over-diagnosis are shown in Box Q6.1.

Box Q6.1: Reasons for over-diagnosis

- A change in the threshold for defining a disease, e.g. type 2 diabetes
- A change in the criteria for defining a disease and its severity by a recognised authority, e.g. the WHO
- The provision of a screening service, or 'case finding', in the absence of strong evidence of a favourable balance of benefit versus harm
- The introduction of new tests and technologies that have increased sensitivity
- The introduction of new technologies that have the ability to identify lesions and other functional abnormalities that will not develop into harmful disease within the patient's lifespan
- The practice of ordering a battery of tests 'just in case' – particularly pertinent when the tests being requested are perceived to have negligible cost, e.g. biochemical laboratory tests.

The overuse of resources results not only in the waste of money, staff time and patient time, but also the unnecessary use of carbon - and this may be a motivator for action that is more powerful than appealing to clinicians to make better use of their financial budget.

Underuse and inequity

Although the focus of this question has been on the drift to over-treatment of people who will not receive as much value from an intervention as was promised by the research findings, the other risk is that there will be people who are exactly the right type for an innovation but who do not receive it.

Under-treatment is sometimes compounded by inequity, and it is important at this point to distinguish between two concepts, inequity and inequality:

- **Inequality** is an objective difference in mortality, morbidity or service provision
- **Inequity** is a difference in service access or use that is deemed unfair.

This was eloquently described by Julian Tudor Hart in his 'Inverse Care Law' thus: 'The availability of good medical care tends to vary inversely with the need for it in the population served.'[70]

There are a number of sub-groups in society in which this can be observed – people from certain ethnic groups, particularly if language is a problem, older people and people in the most deprived sub-groups of the population – and, of course, these groups sometimes overlap, a phenomenon called intersectionality. People in the most deprived sub-groups of society have a life expectancy of about 10 years less than those in the least deprived sub-groups and develop disabling disease about 10 years earlier.

One of the aims of universal healthcare is to mitigate inequity, and health services have a particularly important opportunity and responsibility. It is not uncommon to hear health service professionals speak out strongly about inequality although there is relatively little they can do about it; however, they can make a significant impact on inequity.

The first step in reducing underuse related to inequity is to increase awareness of inequity and its difference from inequality. The second is to start collecting and analysing data about the use of services related to the degree of deprivation, as shown in the diagram previously seen in Question 3, below.

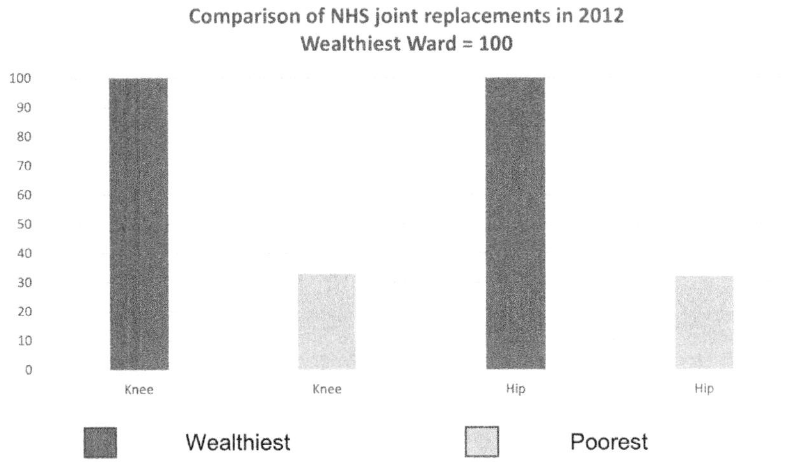

Figure Q6.2: Hip and knee replacements in deprived populations

The importance of the distinction between inequality and inequity is that a health service can do something about inequity, notably by:

- Explicitly stating that one of its aims is to mitigate inequity in its policy documents and websites

- Ensuring that all members of staff, and not just clinicians, understand the meaning and causes of inequity
- Measuring performance with the population as the denominator, and relating rates of activity and clinical issues, such as the stage of cancer at presentation, to place of residence, the best available indicator of deprivation
- Having within each clinical service a person specifically given responsibility for focusing on the population served by the service to complement the traditional focus on service quality
- Undertaking activities designed to mitigate the effects of deprivation, such as the support of voluntary groups that have as their aim health improvement in those deprived populations.

All health services need to adopt the principle that one of their aims is equal access and outcomes for all and that they need to take steps to mitigate the effects of deprivation and minimise inequity.

How to get better value

Often there is a combination of two problems, illustrated in the Venn diagram below:

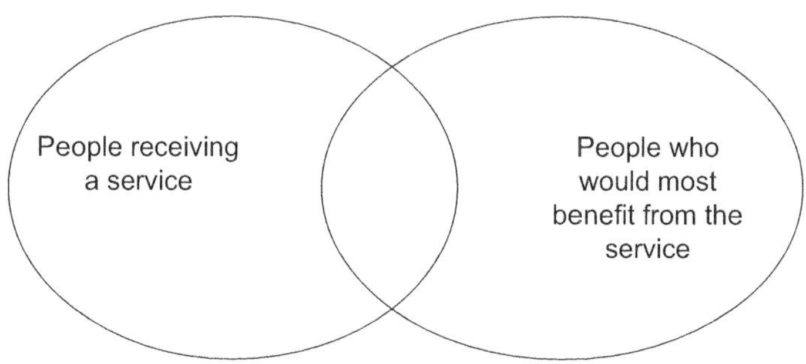

Figure Q6.3: Disparity in services

The same actions can mitigate both problems, specifically:

- Developing population-based systems of care that produce annual reports, allowing the clinicians and populations served to compare rates of intervention, identify unexplained variation and decide whether it is warranted or unwarranted
- Involving the population in a debate about over-diagnosis and over-treatment.

It is most important that this is not presented as a financial issue or a means of saving money. Priority should be given to emphasising that over-diagnosis and over-treatment are low value for individuals because of the poor balance of benefit to harm. It is appropriate to include discussion of the fact that the use of resources to diagnose and treat conditions with little prospect of benefit is of importance, not because of the finance involved but because, in the words of the report of the Academy of Medical Royal Colleges, the process of reducing waste: 'creates a higher value healthcare system where resources, cash, carbon and staff time are released from some part of the system to develop new services or support struggling services.'[71]

The next question to ask is about each individual, to ensure that personal value is optimised as well as population value.

Questions for reflection when teaching or engaged in professional and organisational development

If using these questions in network building or teaching, give one of the questions to the group and ask them to work in pairs to reflect on it for 3 minutes. Try to get people who do not know one another to work together. When taking feedback, let each pair make only one point. In the interests of equity, if you start with the pair on the left-hand side of the room for the first question, start with the pair on the right-hand side of the room for the second question.

- How can those who pay for healthcare prevent or reduce drift?
- When is a clinician justified in using a treatment for a patient who is not exactly like the type of patient in the research studies which demonstrated that the treatment does more good than harm?
- What are the principal barriers to personalised medicine?

References

65. NHS England, NHS RightCare, Public Health England. *NHS Atlas of Variation: Reducing Unwarranted Variation to Increase Value and Improve Quality.* Published September 2015. Available at: www.networks.nhs.uk/nhs-networks/staffordshire-shropshire-and-black-country-newborn/documents/documents/atlas-of-unwarranted-variation-in-maternity-care-1

66. Dartmouth Medical School, Center for the Evaluative Clinical Services. *The Dartmouth Atlas of Health Care.* 1996. American Hospital Association.

67. GIRFT: Getting It Right First Time. Available at: www.gettingitrightfirsttime.co.uk

68. Kremer JL, Genant HK, Moreland LW, *et al.* 'Effects of abatacept in patients with methotrexate-resistant active rheumatoid arthritis'. *Annals of Internal Medicine.* 2006; 144: 865–876.

69. Ridge K. Good for you, good for us, good for everybody: a plan to reduce overprescribing to make patient care better and safer, support the NHS, and reduce carbon emissions. Published 22 September 2021. Available at: www.gov.uk/government/publications/national-overprescribing-review-report

70. Tudor Hart J. 'The Inverse Care Law'. *The Lancet.* 1971; 297; 405–412.

71. Academy of Medical Royal Colleges. *Protecting Resources and Promoting Value: a Doctor's Guide to Cutting Waste in Clinical Care.* Published November 2014. Available at: www.aomrc.org.uk/wp-content/uploads/2016/05/Protecting_Resources_Promoting_Value_1114.pdf

QUESTION 7

ARE WE SURE THAT EVERY INDIVIDUAL PATIENT IS GETTING THE RIGHT INTERVENTION IN THE WAY THAT IS RIGHT FOR THEM?

This section will:

- Describe the need to identify the problem that is bothering the person most as well as their diagnosis
- Emphasise the need to personalise healthcare services.

By the end of this section you will have an understanding of:

- The need to introduce interventions to ensure that both the patient and the clinician in a consultation are clear about the problem that is bothering the patient most
- The importance of measuring outcomes that matter to the individual as well as outcomes that matter to the health service.

How's your mother, she must be mid-eighties now?
Fine, she's 86, on the waiting list for mitral valve surgery.

Mitral valve surgery? That's a big operation – what's her problem?
Well, she gets tired after 2 hours of gardening.

There is no doubt that this lady has mitral valve disease, nor about the fact that surgery is an effective intervention for mitral valve disease, though it is not an intervention that is without risk of harm, even in the very best of cardiovascular surgery units. The key issue is whether this intervention is right for this patient. The clinicians who advised this operation worked in a very good unit and had no financial interest in the decision to opt for an operation, but they had failed to identify what was really bothering her. Had they done so, they could have helped find other solutions, for example, resting for 10 minutes after one hour of gardening. In the words of Maureen Bisognono, former Chief Executive of the Institute of Healthcare Improvement, we need to move from: 'What's the matter medicine?' to 'What matters to you medicine?'[72] – and evidence-based medicine includes this principle.

Evidence- and values-based decision-making

We certainly have to have evidence-based medicine, namely, using evidence derived from research on groups of patients, which plays a centrally important part in decision-making (Figure Q7.1).

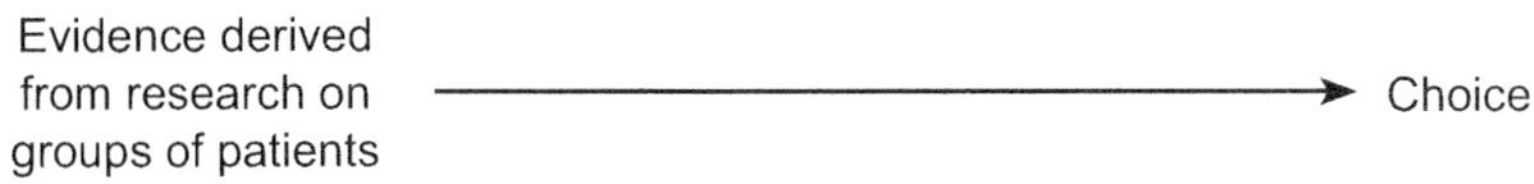

Figure Q7.1: Making choices based on evidence

Patients in RCTs and research projects are often atypical, however; for example, people who only have atrial fibrillation are included, whereas most patients with atrial fibrillation also have other diseases or risk factors (co-morbidity). The job of the clinician is to interpret the evidence taking into account the patient's unique clinical condition. Genetic information is also increasingly being added to the knowledge about an individual in an approach called precision medicine (Figure Q7.2).

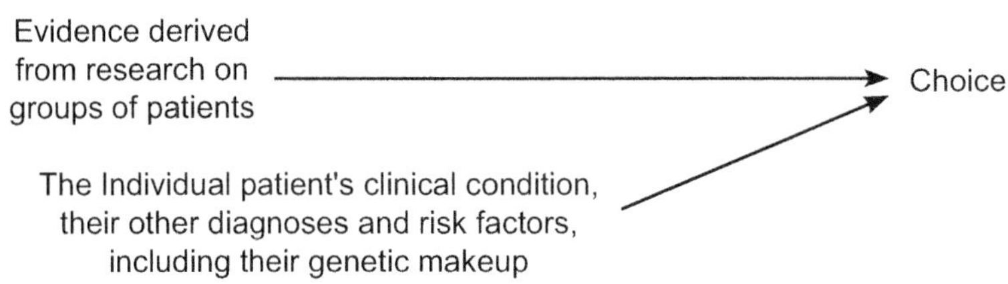

Figure Q7.2: Making choices based on evidence AND the individual patient's situation

This requires clinical skill and experience, which may be summarised into clinical decision rules:

> *Clinical prediction rules (sometimes called clinical decision rules) use clinical findings (history, physical examination, and test results) to make a diagnosis or predict an outcome. They quantify the relative importance of particular findings when evaluating an individual patient.*[73]

However, clinical decision rules are not infallible. They do not prevent error, and clinical error may result in a person receiving an intervention that is not right for them, or a person not receiving an intervention that would be right for them.

The third element in clinical decision-making relates to the patient's values (Figure Q7.3).

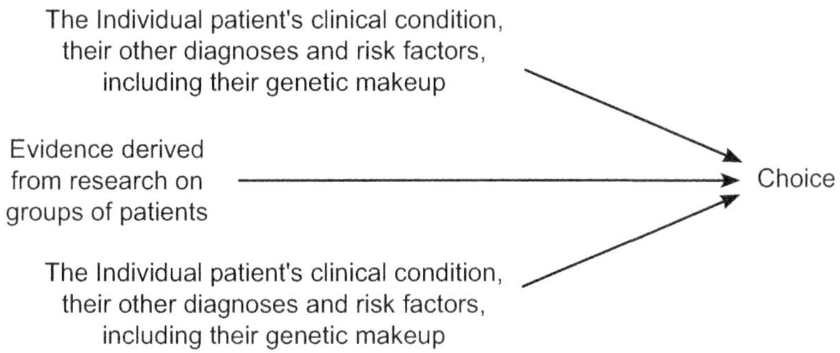

Figure Q7.3: Making choices based on evidence AND the patient's situation AND their values

Each patient has a unique value that they place on both a good outcome and a bad outcome. The value will be influenced by the nature of both good and bad outcomes and the probability of each. Individuals also have different attitudes toward risk taking: some people are reluctant to decide on an option that carries a risk because they know that if it goes wrong they will punish themselves for having made the decision that resulted in a bad outcome; other people would simply accept a bad outcome as bad luck.

Improving decision-making

Patients can be helped to understand the nature of the outcomes and their probabilities with decision aids.

> *Decision aids are evidence-based tools designed to prepare patients to participate in making specific and deliberative choices among healthcare options in ways they prefer. These tools assist decision making by providing evidence-based information about a health condition, the options for treatment, associated benefits, harms, probabilities and scientific uncertainties. Decision aids help patients recognise the value sensitive nature of the decision and clarify the value they place on the benefits, harms and scientific uncertainties. This can be done by describing the options in enough detail that patients can imagine what it is like to experience the physical, emotional and social effects; and by guiding patients to consider which benefits and harms are most important to them.*[74]

Increasingly decisions aids also include resources to help individuals reflect on what the options mean to them, for example, videos of other patients who have had good or bad outcomes reflecting on their choice and its consequences: the Healthtalk.org website is an excellent source of such videos.[75]

It is important to emphasise that the development of personalised decision-making requires not only that a health service ensures that clinicians have the skills and resources they need but also that the person called the patient has responsibilities too, and that they need to be given time, resources and support, which in turn requires the clinician and the service as a whole to be committed to personalised care. This is particularly important when providing what is known as preference-sensitive care.

> *Elective, or 'preference-sensitive' care, which Jack Wennberg in his autobiography defined as "interventions for which there is more than one option and where the outcomes will differ according to the option used". Because patients delegate decision-making to doctors, physician opinion rather than patient preference often determines which treatment patients receive. I argue that this can result in a serious but commonly overlooked medical error: operating on the wrong patients – on those who, were they fully informed, would not have wanted the operation they received.*[76]

Al Mulley, who did much of the work to analyse the issue of preference-sensitive care, and who produced resources to improve shared decision-making, has pointed out that, although we are very concerned about misdiagnosis of the presence or absence of disease, there is another type of misdiagnosis that he terms the 'silent misdiagnosis', namely failure to ascertain what patients want.[77]

Redefining the roles of clinician and patient

In legal terms the person called the patient is the Principal and the clinician is the Agent. However, to enable this in practice, the person called the patient has to be given the resources they need. Although it is common to talk about 'the Expert Patient', it is actually inappropriate to think of patients as being either expert or inexpert. In practice patients are either given the resources they need or, more usually, not given the resources they need. We need 'Resourceful Patients'.[78]

How to get better value

The delivery of high-quality, safe care consisting of evidence-based interventions does not necessarily create value for individuals, but a number of steps can increase the probability that personal value will be increased.

- Encourage patients to be clear about what is bothering them most, which may not be the presenting symptom, for example by using a simple questionnaire that not only clarifies what is bothering the patient but also their expectations:
    - What is bothering you most?
    - What do you hope we can do about what is bothering you the most?

- Be realistic about what can be achieved in the emotionally charged, time-limited, face-to-face consultation. Give as much as you can to patients before and after the consultation. Patient decision aids are now available online for many common significant decisions, for example on the NHS website.
- Ensure that clinicians are trained in the skills of patient-preference decision-making and shared decision-making. The former ensures that the patient's values are elicited and discussed; the latter clarifies the degree of patient involvement and responsibility that is right for each individual.
- Collect patient feedback, not only about their experience of housekeeping and respect but also about the degree to which their engagement with the service had impacted upon the problem that was bothering them most. Had it improved it, made no difference or made it worse?
- Give patients the resources they need to play their part.[7]

It is essential to take into account the diversity of the population being served, in particular the impact of deprivation, age and the ethnic mix of the community. All these factors – and there is considerable overlap between them – influence people's beliefs and decisions. It is therefore necessary to set up groups of patients with a particular disease/condition, not only to contribute to decision-making and service development but also to ensure that patients from all sectors of the population are represented. There is a need to redefine the relationship between healthcare services and the community they serve, and to be clear that services needs to be accountable not only to the higher level of the bureaucracy in which they operate but directly to the community they serve also.

Questions 5, 6 and 7 all address the need to deliver the right, evidence-based interventions to the right people. This is the new agenda, but it is also essential to ensure that the paradigm shifts (See Figure Q7.4 on the next page) that have taken place in the past two decades concerning the need to optimise quality, safety and efficiency are kept on the agenda because they too contribute to better value.

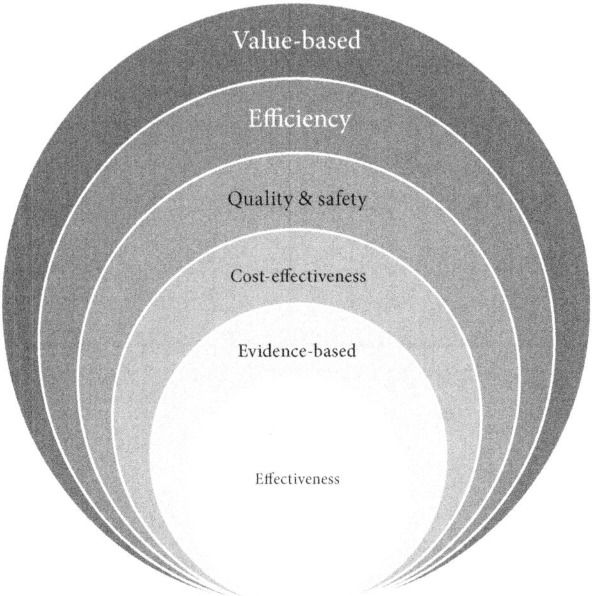

Figure Q7.4: Paradigm shifts

The final three questions address these issues.

Questions for reflection when teaching or developing networks

If using these in network building or teaching, give one of the questions to the group and ask them to work in pairs to reflect on the question for 3 minutes; try to get people who do not know one another to work together. When taking feedback, let each pair make only one point. In the interests of equity, if you start with the pair on the left-hand side of the room for the first question, start with the pair on the right-hand side of the room for the second question.

- What decisions are there in our population that we need to prioritise to ensure personal value?
- How could we reach people before they come to the health centre or hospital to enable them to think through what is bothering them most?
- Which clinical team or service is readiest to adopt this new approach?

References

72. Bisognano M. *Why "What Matters to You?" Matters Around the World.* Institute for Healthcare Improvement. Published 24 February 2017. Available at: www.ihi.org/communities/blogs/why-what-matters-to-you-matters-around-the-world

73. Reilly BM, Evans AT. 'Translating clinical research into clinical practice: impact of using prediction rules to make decisions'. *Annals of Internal Medicine.* 2006; 144: 201–209.

74. Graham ID, Logan J, Bennett CL, *et al.* 'Physicians' intentions and use of three patient decision aids'. *BMC Medical Informatics and Decision Making.* 2007; 7: 20.

75. HealthTalk.org. Available at: https://healthtalk.org

76. Wennberg JE. *Tracking Medicine: A Researcher's Quest to Understand Health Care.* 2010. Oxford University Press, p. 9.

77. Mulley A, Trimble C, Elwyn G. *Patients' Preferences Matter: Stop the Silent Misdiagnosis.* 2012. King's Fund.

78. Gray JAM. *The Resourceful Patient.* 2002. eRosetta Press.

QUESTION 8

IS THE QUALITY OF CARE AS HIGH AS IT CAN BE WITH THE RESOURCES AVAILABLE?

This section will:

- Examine the difference in benefits and harms likely to be seen in a research setting and in a service setting
- Examine the need to introduce new services carefully to maximise benefits and minimise harms
- Emphasise the need to measure outcomes as well as quality
- Introduce the need for systems of care to be established
- Review the relevance of quality assurance to value improvement.

By the end of this section you will have an understanding of:

- The importance of planning the introduction of new services or interventions to minimise the difference between the research setting and the service setting
- The key elements of a healthcare system
- How to set and re-set standards of care.

People who manage healthcare resources, most of whom are clinicians, are not usually involved in answering the first three of the value questions:

Question 1: How much money should be spent on healthcare?

Question 2: How much money should be top-sliced for nationally organised services?

Question 3: Has the money for healthcare been distributed to different parts of the country by a method that recognises variation in need?

The same people are, however, involved in decisions to allocate resources to different groups of patients, often because the force of an argument from clinicians in a speciality is an important factor influencing resource allocation. They are also closely involved with payers in deciding what resources and interventions should be provided for particular groups of patients, and which types of patients are most likely to benefit from those interventions, namely the issues covered in Questions 4–7.

Questions 8–10 are primarily the responsibility of those people who manage healthcare. If these people are to live up to the 20th century proverb that management consists of two tasks – 'Doing the right things and doing them right' – they need to address a specific set of questions about quality. The modern manager must be able to provide answers to Questions 8–10 not only to those who pay for healthcare but also to the patients who reach their service.

Question 8: Is the quality of care as high as it can be with the resources available?

Question 9: Are clinical risks being minimised?

Question 10: Why not just get a grip, improve quality and safety, and reduce costs while you are at it?

The 21st century has added a twist to the old proverb because managers are not only expected to do the right things right, they are expected to answer two supplementary questions:

- Are we doing better than last year?
- How do we plan to do even better next year?

Ensure the right things can be done well in an ordinary service setting

The first step in maximising effectiveness is, as previously described, to introduce only those interventions for which there is strong evidence that they do more good than harm. In the context of a health service, effectiveness is defined as 'the degree to which attainable improvements in health are, in fact, attained'.[79]

Effectiveness is achieved not only by deciding to provide interventions for which there is strong research evidence of benefit, that is, answering Question 5 correctly, but also by ensuring that the benefit demonstrated in the research study that produced the evidence leading to the decision to introduce the service is achieved in practice.

The magnitude of the benefit demonstrated in the research setting is sometimes referred to as the efficacy of an intervention. Research is usually conducted by people who have the following characteristics:

- A high level of commitment
- A special interest and expertise
- Experience of working to highly defined protocols
- Familiarity with having their performance continually measured
- Resources earmarked for the work.

In a busy service setting, these advantages do not exist, protocols will not be as strict and the quality of care may be lower, which means that the magnitude of benefit may well not be as great as in the research setting (Figure Q8.1, on the next page).

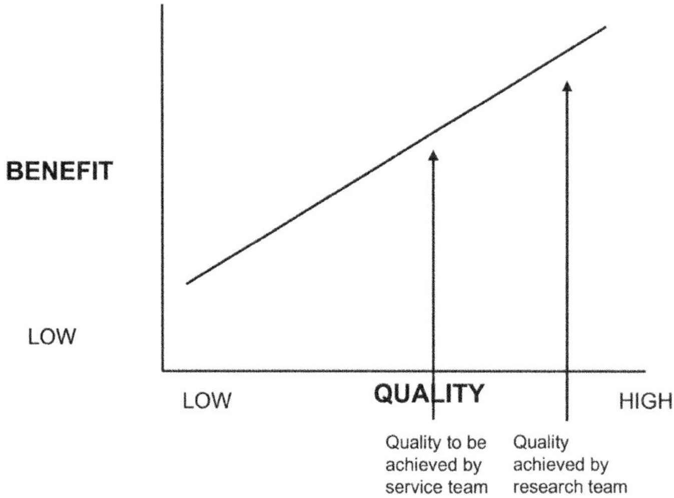

Figure Q8.1: The difference between the quality of service and research settings[80]

Thus it is not sufficient just to be able to answer Question 5, 'Are the resources that have been allocated being used on the right interventions?' in the affirmative, particularly when being pressed by an enthusiastic clinician, keen to introduce a new operation or service which they have either read about or heard discussed at a conference. It is also essential to ask:

- Does your service have, or could it develop, the skills and resources necessary to achieve a level of quality high enough to produce sufficient benefit to justify the investment of resources?

If it is not possible to achieve the level of quality necessary to produce sufficient benefit, it does not make sense to introduce a new service. Some interventions are easier to introduce with confidence that the amount of benefit shown in a research setting can be reproduced. For example, the introduction of a new statin that would lower cholesterol more effectively is relatively easy. By contrast, it would be much more challenging to introduce a new surgical operation that required a high level of skill and of experience in the operator, or a new screening programme that required high-quality system management.[81] Managing the introduction of new services in this way requires:

- A system for deciding whether to introduce a new technology
- A system for managing the introduction of new services if a decision is made to introduce them
- The publication of standards that service providers would be expected to achieve.

To ensure that the outcomes demonstrated in a research setting can be achieved in practice, it is essential to set explicit standards, and in England (and Wales) NICE is responsible for 'developing authoritative standards setting out each part of the patient pathway'.

After services are put in place, it is then necessary to ensure that there is continual improvement year on year (see Box Q8.1).

Box Q8.1: The process of continuous quality improvement

- Create a system of care, making the pathways and key decision points explicit
- Compare the performance of each service against explicit standards
- Help each service improve performance
- Re-set the standards regularly.

As we discussed in Chapter 5, a system is a set of activities with a common set of objectives. For each objective, one or more criteria must be chosen in order to allow performance to be measured, because this enables learning and improvement.

Comparing the service with other services

If managers are required to undertake continuous quality improvement, it is necessary to be clear about the yardstick against which performance will be measured. Although it is meritorious for a service to do better than it did during the previous year, such an assessment is not sufficiently rigorous. It is possible for a service to improve from a low baseline, for example, from being 'very dangerous' to being 'dangerous'. Thus it is essential for the performance of a service to be compared with that of other services. The term 'average' has come to have a meaning that implies value, in addition to its original statistical meaning, but for a service to boast that it was 'above average' would impress few patients or payers, and a comparison of performance with other services, though essential, is also insufficient. The average level of performance could be unacceptably poor, as could an 'above average' level of performance. For this reason, performance must be compared with standards.

Comparing the system with standards

> *The quality of a health service is the degree to which it conforms to pre-set standards of goodness. – Avedis Donabedian*[82]

Standards are subjective. They are value statements. What a manager regards as a good-quality service may be perceived as one of very poor quality by a patient. Conversely, a patient may think a service is of high quality, whereas the payer may assess it as unacceptably low quality. One reason for such differences in perspective is that each person may be considering different aspects of the service, and each aspect of the service has its own level of quality.

When setting standards, it is best to base decisions about the levels for specific standards on the levels of performance described in research reports and, if available, on data collected about other services. There are two standards that are essential for performance management, as outlined in Figure Q8.2:

- A minimum acceptable standard, below which no service should be allowed to operate
- An achievable standard to which all services can aspire, and which some will surpass

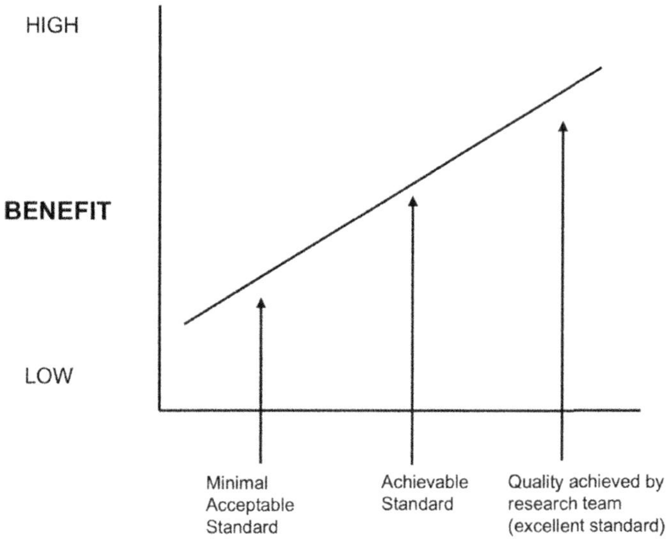

Figure Q8.2: Different levels of quality[2]

NICE standards clarify the quality of care necessary to achieve desired outcomes for both patients and clinicians.

Regular resetting of standards for continuous improvement

> *If standards are not being changed annually, it is proof they are not being used. – Kauro Ishikawa*[83]

An important component of quality assurance is the regular resetting of standards to prevent complacency and over-familiarity, even though providers may complain about the constant shifting of the goalposts.

Using methods of continuous quality improvement leads to a steady improvement in performance. All services have to be involved in a process of continuous quality improvement until the payer decides that the added value of further service improvement is less valuable than the investment of resources in another service.

How to get better value by improving quality

Quality improvement improves outcomes and therefore contributes to better value, provided the resources invested to achieve the improvement are not too great. Thus the costs of increased investment have to be taken into account. There are some simple steps that do not require investment:

- Working with other agencies to develop population-based systems of care that facilitate quality and value improvement
- Developing a quality improvement plan that covers all six of the quality dimensions:
    - effectiveness
    - efficacy
    - equity
    - access
    - safety
    - patient experience

However, it is always important to bear in mind that improving the quality of an intervention or service that is of low or zero value is not a wise move. Further, the value resulting from resource investment in quality improvement must also be considered, because quality improvement itself consumes resources that could be used for some other task or population segment.

The paradigm shift from quality to outcome

The quality and safety paradigm was launched at the turn of the 21st century with the publication of reports from the US Institute of Medicine and England's Chief Medical Officer (CMO).[84-86]

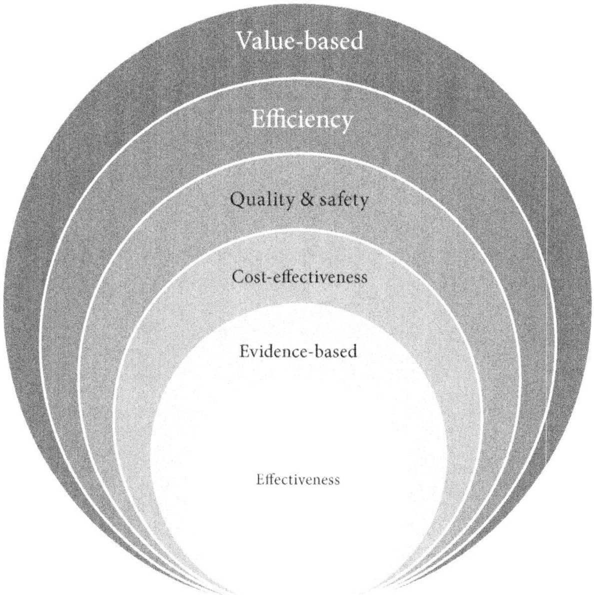

Figure Q83: Paradigm shifts

One important change resulting from the paradigm shift was a focus on the outcome of care as well as the quality of the process. Indeed, with the recognition of the fact that outcome from a patient's perspective could be radically different from that of a clinician came the realisation that a good 'clinical outcome' was not necessarily one that mattered to a patient. What was needed was not only accurate disease diagnosis but also identification of the problem that was bothering the person most and ensuring that the outcome from the patient's perspective was measured, i.e. whether the problem that had been bothering them most was better, the same or worse. For example, a person finding bending down to kneel for their beloved gardening because of arthritis of the knee might well find themselves being admitted for knee replacement surgery because significant damage has been seen on X-rays, even though some people actually find it more difficult or impossible to kneel after knee replacement surgery, even if the operation is of the highest quality. If this patient was one of these people, the problem that was bothering them most – difficulty with kneeling – would actually be made worse by the operation. If their problem, i.e. pain on kneeling to weed flower beds, had been ascertained, an alternative with no risk could have been suggested, such as raised flower beds or long-handled gardening tools.

In the penultimate question we will go on to look at one of the major issues for any health service or healthcare provider – minimising the risks to patients.

Questions for reflection when teaching or developing networks

If using these in network building or teaching, give one of the questions to the group and ask them to work in pairs to reflect on the question for 3 minutes; try to get people who do not know one another to work together. When taking feedback, let each pair make only one point. In the interests of equity, if you start with the pair on the left-hand side of the room for the first question, start with the pair on the right-hand side of the room for the second question.

- What aspects of an innovation would lead you to decide that careful preparation and planning was needed before its introduction?
- Of the services currently provided to patients, which are delivered as systems?
- In the text for this section, minimal acceptable, achievable and excellent standards are described; what other levels of standard could be chosen?

References

79. Cochrane AL. *Effectiveness and Efficiency: Random Reflections on Health Services.* 1972. Nuffield Provincial Hospitals Trust.

80. Gray JAM. *How to Build Healthcare Systems.* 2011. Offox Press.

81. Meakins J, Gray M. *Evidence-Based Surgery, An Issue of Surgical Clinics – The Clinics: Surgery.* 2006. Saunders.

82. Donabedian A. *An Introduction to Quality Assurance in Healthcare.* 2002. Oxford University Press.

83. Ishikawa K. *What is Total Quality Control? The Japanese Way.* 1985. Prentice-Hall.

84. Institute of Medicine (US) Committee on Quality of Health Care in America. *Crossing the Quality Chasm: A New Health System for the 21st Century.* 2001. National Academies Press.

85. Institute of Medicine (US); Committee on Quality of Health Care in America; Linda T. Kohn, Janet M. Corrigan, Molla S. Donaldson (Eds). *To Err is Human: Building a Safer Health System.* 2000. National Academies Press.

86. Department of Health (UK). *An Organisation With a Memory: Report of an expert group on learning from adverse events in the NHS chaired by the Chief Medical Officer.* 2000. The Stationery Office. Available at: https://qi.elft.nhs.uk/wp-content/uploads/2014/08/r_02-an-organisation-with-a-memory-l-donaldson.pdf

9

ARE CLINICAL RISKS BEING MINIMISED?

This section will:

- Review the different causes of harm in healthcare
- Explore the relationship between quality, safety and value.

By the end of this section you will have an understanding of:

- The causes of harm in healthcare
- The distinction between harm caused by poor-quality care and the harm caused by medical error
- How harm reduces value.

> *Punters, we just call them punters, because – let's face it – they are taking a chance every time they use the health service!*

In a debate at a meeting in Belfast about what term should be used to refer to people who use health services – patients or consumers – the term 'punter' was suggested by one of the doctors. The definition of a punter is someone one who takes a gamble, and in the context of healthcare reflects the fact that all healthcare can cause harm and everyone who uses health services runs the risk of harm. This harm affects not only the patient but also clinicians, managers and those responsible for paying for healthcare, because harm reduces value.

Avoidable and unavoidable harm

There are two types of harm: avoidable and unavoidable. Avoidable harm has been the main focus of measures designed to improve the safety of healthcare, and again there are two different types:

- Harm caused by doing the wrong thing, usually referred to as medical error
- Harm caused by doing the right thing badly, that is, problems with the quality of care.

Amputating the wrong leg is a medical error; amputating the correct leg but doing it so badly that the patient needs a second operation is harm from poor-quality care. The harms that result from poor-quality healthcare and those that result from medical errors are inter-related because errors are less likely to occur in high-quality services.[87]

Minimising avoidable harm caused by doing the right thing badly

The benefit and harm caused by doing the right things well or badly are functions of the quality of care provided. Therefore, the balance between benefit and harm is better if the quality of care if high. The service should be stopped, however, if it falls below a level of quality at which the harms are greater than the benefits, known as the minimal acceptable level of quality.

Minimising avoidable harm caused by doing the wrong things (errors)

Although some medical errors will always occur, the incidence can be minimised and there are a number of ways in which a health service can achieve this, notably the development of systems and creation of a strong safety culture.

To maximise the likelihood of benefit and minimise that of harm and errors, professionals need standard operating procedures (SOPs), defined in Wikipedia in 2022 as: 'a set of step by step instructions compiled by an organization to help workers carry out routine operations.'[88]

In his annual report for 2005,[89] the CMO for England, Professor Sir Liam Donaldson, emphasised the need for SOPs because they have a major contribution to make to patient safety. Donaldson had put the need to reduce errors on the map in England with the production of a report titled 'An Organisation With A Memory' in 2000,[90] authored by an 'expert group learning from adverse events'. The 2005 Annual Report recognised that SOPs – 'doing everything exactly the same way all the time' – was 'counter-cultural in healthcare', meaning counter to the culture of clinical autonomy. The challenge is illustrated by the story of an encounter between Sir Liam and a surgeon who told him: 'If you introduce that approach, it will be like working in a factory, not being a doctor,' to which the CMO replied robustly that there was new evidence from many specialities that SOPs are '. . .compatible with high-quality clinical practice by highly trained, highly skilled professionals who continue to exercise judgement in vast areas of their practice.'

To improve quality and safety, it is necessary to have a style of general management that will increase effectiveness and reduce harm, for example the:

- Promotion of a safety culture
- Use of systems, including SOPs
- Establishment of clear lines of accountability for risk management and safety
- Collection of data about risk factors, medical errors and near-misses.

It is also necessary to introduce risk management procedures, targeting those activities or environments where medical errors are most common and serious, such as:

- High-risk activities:
  - prescribing
  - handover of care from one clinician to another
  - patient identification
- High-risk areas:
  - intensive care
  - operating theatres
  - emergency departments.

When new hazards about adverse events and near-misses are identified through research or the collection and analysis of data, an organisation needs to respond quickly and sensitively, meeting the concerns of any patient who has been harmed and reducing the risk that other patients could be harmed in the same way, a response desired by many patients when harm occurs. The '100,000 Lives Campaign' of the Institute of Healthcare Improvement (IHI) offers an excellent example of the potential beneficial impact of applying what is known but not always done by getting research results into practice.[91] It encouraged US hospitals to take a number of practical steps to minimise harm to patients, such as deploying 'rapid response teams' if patients showed signs of decline, preventing adverse drug reactions by implementing medication reconciliation, and preventing surgical site infections and ventilator-associated pneumonia.

Minimising unavoidable harm caused by over-diagnosis and over-treatment

Side effects are an inevitable consequence of almost all healthcare interventions, thus even the highest quality care can do harm, as Avedis Donabedian's classic diagram reminds us (Figure Q9.1). When care is necessary or appropriate, the risk of harm is acceptable, provided the patient understands the nature of the risk. However, there is increasing concern about unavoidable harm, namely, the harm that will inevitably affect a proportion of people who receive interventions, which is increased if there is over-diagnosis or over-treatment.

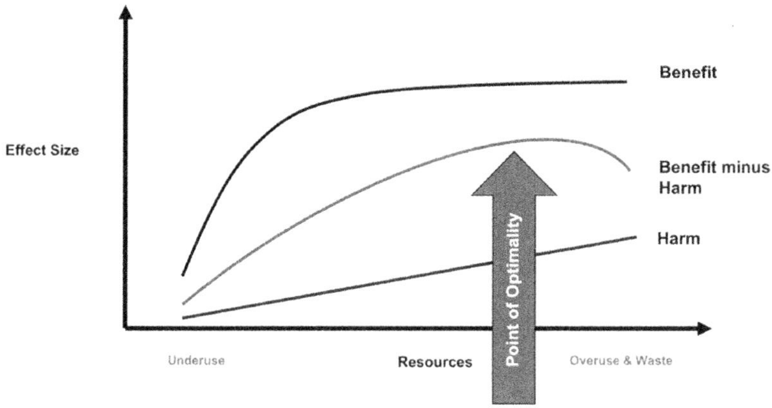

Figure Q9.1: Donabedian's depiction of the relationship between investment benefit, harm and value

Over-diagnosis and over-treatment are modern epidemics that were central to the 'Too Much Medicine' campaign run by the *British Medical Journal*.[92] If harm from healthcare is to be reduced, over-diagnosis and over-treatment need to be tackled. Furthermore, utilising resources to undertake interventions that will do no good and may cause harm can be classified as producing zero or negative value in healthcare.

How to get better value by reducing risk

Safer care contributes to better value in two ways. It reduces the probability of a bad outcome and minimises the cost of dealing with complications. Some simple steps are listed below, though this topic really requires a separate book – try *Patient Safety* by Charles Vincent.[93]

- Look at the IHI and NHS England websites for safety projects and techniques that could be adapted and adopted
- Create a plan for safer care based on the principles in Vincent's book Patient Safety, covering both systems and culture
- Implement the safety plan, focusing particularly on the key role of clinical microsystems, which are defined in the following way:

> *Organizational units built around the definition of repeatable core service competencies. Elements of a micro-system include (1) a core team of health care professionals, (2) a defined population of patients, (3) carefully designed work processes, and (4) an environment capable of linking information on all aspects of work and patient or population outcomes to support ongoing evaluation of performance.*[87]

It is essential to improve safety and reduce errors but it is also essential to remember and communicate the message that all healthcare does harm.

In our final question, we tackle the challenges to implementing many of the ideas discussed in this book and one of the biggest enemies of achieving value in healthcare – waste.

Questions for reflection when teaching or developing networks

If using these in network building or teaching, give one of the questions to the group and ask them to work in pairs to reflect on the question for 3 minutes; try to get people who do not know one another to work together. When taking feedback, let each pair make only one point. In the interests of equity, if you start with the pair on the left-hand side of the room for the first question, start with the pair on the right-hand side of the room for the second question.

- If you were reducing harm, would you give priority to the prevention of error or to improving quality? Give your reasons why.
- In an interview on local radio, how would you explain the phenomenon that all healthcare causes harm?
- What is the best way to explain to patients the balance of benefit and harm? Give the reasons for your choice.

References

87. Institute of Medicine (US); Committee on Quality of Health Care in America; Linda T. Kohn, Janet M. Corrigan, Molla S. Donaldson (Eds). *To Err is Human: Building a Safer Health System*. 2000. National Academies Press.

88. Wikipedia. Standard operating procedure. Available at: https://en.wikipedia.org/wiki/Standard_operating_procedure

89. Department of Health (UK). *The Chief Medical Officer on the state of public health: Annual Report 2005*. Published July 2006. Available at: www.researchgate.net/publication/319998930_On_the_state_of_public_health_Annual_report_of_the_Chief_Medical_Officer_2005

90. Department of Health (UK). *An Organisation With a Memory: Report of an expert group on learning from adverse events in the NHS chaired by the Chief Medical Officer*. 2000. The Stationery Office. Available at: https://qi.elft.nhs.uk/wp-content/uploads/2014/08/r_02-an-organisation-with-a-memory-l-donaldson.pdf

91. Berwick DM, Calkins DR, McCannon CJ. 'The 100,000 Lives Campaign: Setting a goal and a deadline for improving health care quality'. *Journal of the American Medical Association*. 2006; 295; 324–327.

92. *British Medical Journal*. Too much medicine. Available at: www.bmj.com/too-much-medicine

93. Vincent C. *Patient Safety*. 2010. BMJ Books/Wiley-Blackwell.

QUESTION 10

WHY NOT JUST GET A GRIP, IMPROVE QUALITY AND SAFETY, AND REDUCE COSTS WHILE YOU ARE AT IT?

This section will:

- Review the terms used in describing the use of resources
- Introduce the concept of sustainability
- Examine the different techniques that can be used to reduce waste.

By the end of this section you will have an understanding of:

- The difference between efficiency and productivity
- The principal causes of wasted resources
- How to define sustainable healthcare
- How increased productivity need not decrease the ability of a care provider to personalise care.

The Japanese term *kaizen*, meaning continual improvement, is now part of the management vocabulary. The term *muda*, meaning waste, is less well known, and even less well known is the Japanese word *mottainai*, which means a feeling of remorse for having wasted resources, a word for which there is no English equivalent. Waste can be defined as 'any human activity which consumes resources but produces no value.' Taiichi Ohno, who hated waste, described seven categories of waste in industrial systems (see Box Q10.1).[94]

Box Q10.1: Taiichi Ohno's seven categories of waste in industrial systems
• Over-production • Waiting time • Transportation • Wasteful processing • Too much stock • Too much movement on the factory floor • Defective products

Ohno's work on reducing waste, and his concept of 'lean thinking', which flowed from it, is of central importance to those who pay for or manage health services.[95,96] The five 'whys?' of Ohno – outlined in the checklists section – are worth asking frequently in healthcare, particularly in what is called 'Accident & Emergency' (A&E). However, there are some important differences between healthcare and manufacturing that need to be taken into account, in particular the need to distinguish between productivity and efficiency.

Increase both productivity and efficiency

Productivity relates the processes of care such as operations and MRI examinations, the outputs in the economists' term, to inputs, i.e. the number of surgeons and MRI machines respectively.

Efficiency relates what economists call inputs, such as money, staff, beds or other resources, to outcomes.

For example, the productivity of a cataract service is measured by the number of cataract operations per bed. The efficiency of the same service is measured by the proportion of people reporting that the problem that had been bothering them most was solved or significantly improved after the operation, related to resources used.

The seven steps to improving productivity

Those who pay for and manage healthcare services that are doing the right things to the right patients can address the seven causes of low productivity in health services by adapting Ohno's principles (see Box Q10.2).

Box Q10.2: Seven causes of low productivity in health services
1. Under-use of buildings and equipment
2. Too much stock
3. Too much cost for non-essential non-clinical staff
4. Too much wasted time, for clinicians *and* patients
5. Care in hospital instead of at home
6. Staff too skilled and scarce for the task in hand
7. Equipment and tools of unnecessary expense

1. Can we make more use of buildings and equipment?

'Sweat the assets' is an industrial proverb, meaning that it is important to use buildings and plant facilities to the maximum. This of course has been greatly complicated by the constraints resulting from the COVID-19 pandemic, which have reduced the usability of many buildings, but it is still an important issue.

2. Can we carry less stock?

Just-in-time delivery of equipment as needed was one of the great achievements of the Toyota productions systems. In contrast, most health services buy not only too much but also too many types of equipment and store it for too long. Such waste can be prevented and cured by better procurement strategies.

3. How can we reduce the cost of non-clinical staff?

Clinical staff consult with individual patients or groups of patients. However, the fulfilment of clinical duties requires the support of non-clinical staff, including technical, procurement, and administrative and management staff. The important issue is to identify ways to reduce costs while retaining the capacity to undertake essential support tasks for clinical practice. Different approaches have been taken to reduce costs, for example:

- Outsourcing non-clinical services – many private contractors pay lower wages or provide fewer benefits than public service employers, which can be viewed as a moral, as well as a productivity, issue
- Reducing the number of tasks that administrative staff have to do, for example, by reducing demands for data
- Reorganisation.

Of these methods, the last appears to be the least effective, and may increase costs in both the short and the long term.

4. Can the waste of clinician and patient time be reduced?

The scarcest resource that clinicians possess is time. For most clinicians, the work from which the greatest value can be derived for their time is clinical practice, followed by research, then education.

Spending a clinician's time on activities other than clinical practice, research and education can sometimes represent good value, for example, if a physician is reimbursed for half a day managing resources or relating a service to a population in need. Many other activities, however, are a great waste of time, such as meetings without purpose or conclusion, or tracking down lost notes, data, new identity card or parking space.

Clinical practice is of high value, but within the course of clinical work the time of clinicians and patients is often wasted if, for example, a patient's notes are missing, key data, such as laboratory results, are not available, or there is unnecessary waiting time, for example between operations in a theatre.

All clinicians have their own lists of what they consider to be a waste of time, but their perspective may not be shared. Attendance at management meetings may be classified as a waste of time by a clinician, but regarded as high value by a manager. It would require independent evaluation to determine whether the clinician's perspective was correct and the meeting was unfocused and unproductive, or whether the manager's perspective was correct and the clinician came to a good meeting with the wrong attitude.

Education and research can also be unproductive and of low value. Education is of low value if:

- It is not determined by the formally ascertained learning needs of clinicians, as opposed to their wants; thus there is evidence that if clinicians are interested in a topic and want to learn about it, they will seek out the learning they want, while resources for training should be reserved for areas in which clinicians are not delivering good quality care
- It is not delivered using methods that have evidence of effectiveness; for example, lectures to large numbers of attendees are usually of low value.

As we described in the answer to Question 2, research is of low value if:

- The answer to the research question is already known but the researchers have not conducted a systematic review
- The study design is inappropriate or inadequate
- The conduct of the research is sloppy

- The reporting is biased.

5. Is care being delivered in the most appropriate place?

Many patients are treated in facilities with levels of staffing and equipment they do not need. 'Bed blockers' are usually elderly patients who have recovered from the acute phase of a disease but cannot be discharged because they are too disabled to return home and are unable to be placed in a nursing home; this is a matter of concern both for those who manage or pay for care and for the patients themselves – who are at high risk of hospital-acquired infection, institutionalisation and malnutrition. Another example is patients who attend a clinic with a problem that might have been resolved if their primary care clinician could have phoned, e-mailed or had other means of accessing the expertise of a specialist.

The 19th century term 'out-patient' should be discontinued because it simply means 'not an in-patient'; systems of care need to be designed with pathways that indicate clearly why and when a person needs to attend hospital for a face-to-face encounter.

The term 'A&E' arguably could be replaced by 'SFS' – System Failure Service – because the term accident implies nothing could be done to stop it and emergency that it came out of the blue, but many of the problems could have been prevented if appropriate systems were in place.

6. Could this care be provided by less highly trained staff?

Highly trained staff are scarce, and it is a waste of their time to carry out tasks that could be undertaken equally well by staff who have not been trained to perform all the tasks of a highly skilled person but who *have* been trained specifically to carry out a finite range of tasks. Sometimes staff trained in a finite range of tasks perform these with greater attention to detail and better results than the most highly trained staff – to whom such tasks are, at best, boring.

7. Can we procure good equipment and drugs at cheaper cost?

> *When asked what passed through his mind the minute before take-off, the astronaut replied: 'I could not stop thinking that I am sitting on top of the cheapest tender!'*

Some people prefer the term 'low cost' to 'cheap', and 'lower cost' to 'cheaper', but who cares about the niceties of language? The key question is, 'Why pay more than is necessary?' Costs can be reduced by:

- Skilful procurement
- Bulk purchase
- The use of generic rather than branded drugs
- Sometimes 'making' rather than 'buying'.

These activities are ethically important because they reduce waste, increase productivity and release resources for clinical care.

In the words of Don Berwick, waste is an ethical issue for everyone, particularly for people in healthcare, because the cost needs to be counted in carbon as well as in pounds, dollars or euros.[97] We need not only efficient but also sustainable healthcare. This is especially important in light of the health impacts of climate change.

Act with Urgency – Get a Grip, Go for GIRFT

After a business dinner with good food, plentiful drink and bonhomie, it is usually time for a welcome night's sleep. It was a different ending to the story, however, when Taiichi Ohno, the recently retired creator of the world-famous and highly efficient Toyota production system, finally agreed to advise an American company on how to reduce waste.

After this business dinner, any thought of rest was postponed. To the host's farewell, 'See you in the morning,' Ohno replied that, if they were serious, they should make an immediate start on reducing waste: call in staff, reorganise the production line and ignore the possible protests of unions. This they did. Ohno moved from the dinner table to the shop floor – jackets off, sleeves up, machinery moved, waste slashed and productivity increased.

In 2014, the NHS in England decided that they needed a workstream to improve quality and safety and reduce the variation between specialist clinical services. The acronym GIRFT was adopted – Getting It Right First Time – itself an old industrial principle, but even more important was finding the right leader, and an orthopaedic surgeon was recruited who had just the right personality for the job. Like Ohno rising from the dinner table, Tim Briggs rose from the operating table and launched the GIRFT programme in 2016 with the same passion and credibility.[98] The GIRFT programme started with three actions:

- A broad data-gathering and analysis exercise, performed by health data analysts, which generated a detailed picture of current national practice, outcomes and related factors
- Direct clinical engagement via visits or virtual meetings between clinical specialists and individual hospital trusts, based on the data – providing an unprecedented opportunity to examine individual trust behaviours and performance in the relevant area of practice, in the context of the national picture. This would enable trusts to understand where they were performing well and what they could do better – drawing on the input of senior clinicians
- A national report, which drew on both the data analysis and the discussions with hospital trusts to identify opportunities for improvement across relevant services.

There followed:

- An implementation phase, in which the GIRFT team supported trusts, commissioners and integrated care systems to deliver the improvements recommended
- The introduction of best practice guidance and support for standardised, integrated patient pathways and elective recovery work in 'high volume/low complexity' specialities.

The key to the success of GIRFT has been its leadership – not just of Briggs but also of the people who were motivated to follow his lead in creating and promoting the right culture. The importance of culture is that it influences behaviour and how clinicians think, feel and act to make decisions. It is culture that motivates or demotivates clinicians.

How to motivate clinicians

Promoting cost reduction is a poor way of motivating clinicians. Cost reduction needs to be promoted as a means of treating more patients better. The following steps may be helpful:

- Promoting a culture of resource stewardship by introducing the language of stewardship, value and waste, using the Toyota definition of waste or *muda* as anything that does not add value to an outcome
- Promoting a culture of stewardship through the development of programme budgets, for example for people with cancer, and systems budgets within each programme budget, for example budgets for lung cancer, breast cancer and colorectal cancer, to encourage stewardship at the level of individual conditions. The same can be done with sub-groups of the population identified by a common characteristic such as age, for example programmes for children with mental health problems or elderly people with frailty.

- Focusing on carbon costs as well as financial costs, because an appeal to change based on sustainability will attract people who are unmoved by appeals based on funding crises.

Minimise the burden of treatment

Finally, though perhaps this should come first, remember that for patients and carers there are also costs in terms of time and inconvenience, brilliantly named 'the burden of treatment'. Multiple appointments for tests that could be delivered at one appointment with a little bit of thought, difficult journeys to reach distant clinics at inconvenient times, and a general lack of consideration for the fact that, although patients and carers are grateful for the technical interventions delivered, they also have lives to lead and jobs to do. Patient-centred care, therefore, can reduce and not increase the amount of resources used.

As we have emphasised, personal value and population value are two sides of the one coin. We need to create a culture in which the sharp and often hostile distinction between clinicians and managers becomes a thing of the past as everyone involved in healthcare works together to increase value and reduce waste – motivated not by their professional background but by a common culture of stewardship.

Questions for reflection when teaching or developing networks

If using these in network building or teaching, give one of the questions to the group and ask them to work in pairs to reflect on the question for 3 minutes; try to get people who do not know one another to work together. When taking feedback, let each pair make only one point. In the interests of equity, if you start with the pair on the left-hand side of the room for the first question, start with the pair on the right-hand side of the room for the second question.

- What are the principal sources of waste in a hospital?
- What are the principal sources of waste in the relationship between primary and secondary care?
- How could staff best be motivated to reduce the carbon footprint of the care they provide?

References

94. Ohno T. *Toyota Production System: Beyond Large-Scale Production*. 1988. Productivity Press.

95. Liker JK. *The Toyota Way*. 2004. McGraw-Hill.

96. Womack JP, Jones DT. *Lean Thinking: Banish Waste and Create Wealth in Your Corporation*. 1996. Simon & Schuster.

97. Berwick DM. *Promising Care: How We Can Rescue Health Care by Improving It*. 2014. Jossey-Bass.

98.GIRFT: Getting It Right First Time. Available at: www.gettingitrightfirsttime.co.uk

VALUE IMPROVEMENT CHECKLISTS

Every soldier in the SAS carries a small booklet, about the size of Filofax (though long before Filofaxes were invented), everywhere and always. This little book, the Tactical Aide Memoire, contains all the key facts about issues such as how to build a bridge or set a mortar. It is carried by everyone from the newest recruit to most senior officer and has huge symbolic as well as practical value.

After the pages of flowing prose we include a set of checklists as a Value-Based Healthcare Aide Memoire.

WHAT?	How to reduce both the number of errors and low-value healthcare
WHY?	Because errors cause harm to patients and cost healthcare, and low-value healthcare always causes harm and may not cause any benefit
WHEN?	This needs to be a continuous process, but should have both an annual cycle and specific actions as serious errors are identified
WHO?	This needs to be a responsibility of every person who manages resources
HOW?	☑ Promote continuous quality improvement, because improvement in quality will reduce the incidence of errors ☑ Ask the Chief Knowledge Officer to review knowledge about the types of errors likely to occur and evidence about interventions that reduce risk ☑ Identify lower-value interventions and reduce their number ☑ Set up a Risk Reduction Group, with a clearly accountable leader ☑ Ask the group to develop and implement a risk reduction plan ☑ Ensure there are clear protocols for investigating errors and involve patients in the resolution of problems caused by errors.

WHAT?	How to engage patients and improve their experience
WHY?	Because the engagement of patients will improve the value of healthcare
WHEN?	This is a continuous process, part of general management, but an annual patient engagement conference can highlight and focus the process
WHO?	Every person who manages resources needs to be given this as a clear responsibility
HOW?	☑ A person who can speak as a patient should be enrolled on the board or management team ☑ Review and improve complaint management ☑ Use the immediate feedback offered by www.iwantgreatcare.org ☑ Reduce resources used in measuring patient satisfaction and increase resources used to measure patient experience ☑ Review the written information given to patients, and assure and improve its quality by adopting the Information Standard: www.informationstandard.org ☑ Ensure managers conduct experience surveys at least once a year and act on their results; high-quality surveys done for a short period are better value than continuous poor-quality surveys.

WHAT?	How to improve productivity
WHY?	Because increased productivity frees resources for high-value healthcare without adverse effects
WHEN?	Continuously, obsessively, but highlighted by an annual productivity workshop and celebrations
WHO?	Every person who manages resources. A Productivity Interest Group (PIG) to generate and support ideas can pull together leads from all the divisions (PIGs are very productive creatures!).
HOW?	☑ Ensure everyone is clear about the distinction between efficiency and productivity, and that productivity does not mean a reduction in quality but an improvement in value ☑ Develop and implement a communication plan ☑ Set up projects to: ◦ make more use of buildings and equipment ◦ improve procurement ◦ reduce stock ◦ launch a hospital-at-home project ◦ reduce the use of paper ◦ prevent the waste of resources on poor-value research ◦ make better use of the time of the most experienced staff ☑ Require an Annual Value Improvement Report.

WHAT?	How to create a culture of stewardship
WHY?	Because a culture of stewardship is essential for increasing value
WHEN?	The process needs to be started from the first time the need to increase value as well as improve quality is agreed
WHO?	The development of culture is one of the core functions of leadership, but leadership does not necessarily mean only the top of an organisation – there are leaders scattered throughout it.
HOW?	☑ Agree and promote the glossary and the culture of stewardship ☑ Make it clear which behaviours are desired and which are unacceptable ☑ Ensure all public documents have a clear statement of intent ☑ Think of practical ways in which good stewardship could be made visible, for example having information about the carbon footprint of the service in the entrance hall.

WHAT?	How to design a population-based system
WHY?	Because this is the third dimension of healthcare, complementing the levels of care and the necessary bureaucracies, and is essential for measuring and increasing value
WHEN?	As soon as a decision is made to focus on value
WHO?	Always work with a keen team of clinicians and patient representatives to design the first system
HOW?	☑ Define the scope of the system, i.e. is it all ages with type 2 diabetes or just people aged 18 and over? ☑ Define the population to be served, i.e. is it geographically defined or people registered with a group of health service providers? ☑ Reach agreement on the aim of the service ☑ Reach agreement on the more detailed objectives of the service ☑ For each objective, find one or more criteria ☑ For each of the objectives identify levels of performance that can be used as quality standards ☑ Identify all the resources used in the system, thus creating a system budget ☑ Define all the partners that need to be engaged in the network

WHAT?	How to increase effectiveness
WHY?	Because increased effectiveness increases value
WHEN?	Continuous process, built into annual planning and reporting and of the same status as finance
WHO?	Clinical leaders, including those in imaging, pharmacy and laboratory services, and all people who manage resources
HOW?	☑ Set up an Innovation Group to ensure that no ineffective technology slips into use ☑ Use the IDEAL (Identify the problem; Define and represent the problem; Explore possible strategies or solutions; Act on a selected strategy or solution; Look back and evaluate) methodology for innovations without randomised controlled trial evidence, e.g. novel surgical operations ☑ Require the Chief Knowledge Officer to produce monthly knowledge briefings about new evidence that should be put into practice ☑ Develop systems of care, with care pathways for all common procedures and conditions ☑ For each new condition, ask the relevant clinical lead to identify evidence-based measures of processes and outcome measures of relevance to patients ☑ Require each service to produce an Annual Effectiveness Plan, based on the annual review of their service and care ☑ Require all annual reports to describe effectiveness compared with the performance of other services and explicit national standards ☑ Introduce the methods of continuous quality improvement.

WHAT?	How to get to the root of problems
WHY?	Because short-term solutions to immediate causes are of lower value than solutions that tackle root causes
WHEN?	Whenever there is a problem or an opportunity for value improvement that 'can't be done'
WHO?	Whoever has a problem
HOW?	Use the 'Five Whys' method of Taiichi Ohno, who always asked 'Why?' five times, for example: ☑ Why is this patient at the clinic? (Because we have the reports of his investigations) ☑ Why could the results not be sent to him? (Because a clinical decision needs to be made) ☑ Why could he not make that decision with his primary care physician? (Because the physician does not know how we manage this problem) ☑ Why do they not know how this problem is managed? Is it too difficult? (No, it is not too difficult, but they are new to the area and not familiar with how we do things) ☑ Why do we not identify and brief GPs about our new procedures? (Good question. . .)

WHAT?	How to carry out a systematic review
WHY?	A systematic review of all the evidence is necessary to minimise bias and errors in reports of research
WHEN?	Before significant resources are invested
WHO?	The scale of a systematic review and the skills required should not be underestimated. Those who pay for or manage healthcare should commission someone who has experience to do the review.
HOW?	☑ Make the question as precise and possible, e.g. instead of asking for a systematic review of positron emission tomography (PET) scanners, ask 'What is the added value of PET scanning for patients with advanced cancer?' ☑ Search the scientific literature with the assistance of a librarian and keep a copy of the search strategy ☑ Use explicit quality criteria to decide which research reports should be included in the review and which should be excluded ☑ Ask a statistician how the data in the individual high-quality research reports should be combined ☑ Publish the results of the review, including references to reports that were excluded for reasons of quality as well as references of reports included in the review.

WHAT?	**How to transform healthcare using information technology**
WHY?	For two reasons. First, because technology creates tools that by themselves change culture and practice – reflect on the lessons of history as described by Lynn White Jr in *Medieval Technology and Social Change.*[i] Second, because investing in IT simply to do the same things digitally is of very low value – reflect on the lessons of 'How New Technologies Cause Great Companies to Fail' in *The Innovator's Dilemma* by Clayton Christensen.[ii]
WHEN?	Before every investment in IT
WHO?	Everyone must be involved, but someone needs to take the lead in 'The Transformation of Care', not a project called 'The Introduction of IT'
HOW?	☑ Send information to patients digitally, linked to email if they have it, before and after every consultation ☑ Encourage patients to record the consultation on their mobile phones ☑ Offer email consultations ☑ Train clinicians how to relate with empathy to their patient whilst simultaneously typing information into/referring to notes on a computer in the consulting room ☑ Describe all care pathways and standard operating procedures digitally

WHAT?	**How to transform healthcare using information technology**
HOW?	☑ Use IT to help multidisciplinary teams work smarter ☑ Make all knowledge available online ☑ Create clinical networks that are sustained on the web, not by a bureaucracy ☑ Put laboratory IT in charge of chronic disease monitoring ☑ Get the Chief Executive to produce a blog

References

i. White Jr, L. *Medieval Technology and Social Change*. 1996. Oxford University Press.

ii. Christensen CM. *The Innovator's Dilemma: When New Technologies Cause Great Firms to Fail*. 1997. Harvard Business Review Press.

WHAT?	How to respond to a bid for a new treatment or service
WHY?	Because management for better value requires tight control of innovation combined with rapid adoption of high-value interventions
WHEN?	As part of the annual planning process or as new technologies emerge
WHO?	The person who holds the funds, the clinician making the bid and the person who manages their resources
HOW?	☑ The team that wants the service should be asked to provide information about both the evidence base and the relative value of the proposed information ◦ Is the proposal based on a systematic review of the evidence? ☑ The bidder should be required to prepare a systematic review if one is not available. If the evidence base is inadequate, the bidder can be encouraged to bid for research funds. ☑ The bidder should provide data about: ◦ The number of patients in the group or population they serve who would be helped (or harmed) by the new service ◦ How added benefits from the innovation compare with added benefits that would result if the existing service were delivered at higher levels of quality

WHAT?	How to respond to a bid for a new treatment or service
HOW?	☑ The relative value should be appraised by asking the bidder to compare the value of the proposed addition to their service with: ◦ Other innovations that the service might introduce in the next year ◦ Lower-value interventions for the same group of patients that could be stopped to fund the innovation ☑ The response to high-value innovation should be enthusiastic – provided the proposer is willing to take responsibility for releasing the necessary resources. This approach is called 'hitting them with the carrot'.

WHAT?	How to conduct an annual population value review
WHY?	To ensure that resources are allocated between different budgets to maximise value and identify the need for movement of resources from one budget to another
WHEN?	In the middle of the financial year, when expenditure for the previous year is clear and expenditure for the next financial year is being planned
WHO?	People responsible for allocation of resources
HOW?	☑ Separate out research and education costs ☑ Use a simple system of classification such as the ICD (this is the basis of programme budgeting in NHS England) ☑ Allocate all other costs to the programme budgets proportionally, including primary care, laboratory and imaging ☑ Distribute the budget analysis ☑ Respond to criticisms by asking for suggestions about how allocation can be improved, but also by reminding people that it is their data and any quality problems start with them!

WHAT?	How to conduct an annual population value review
HOW?	☑ For each budget, payers and managers should ask what would be the effect on the value derived from resources if we: ◦ Increased the allocation to this programme by 5%? ◦ Decreased the allocation to this budget by 5%? ☑ Produce a report of these discussions and a proposal for reallocation of resources for the next financial year

WHAT?	How to conduct a review of expenditure on a disease
WHY?	Because the main focus of healthcare management, competition and value improvement should be on diseases, not on hospitals or insurance schemes
WHEN?	Because this activity requires energy and focus, and, since there are about 50 'big' problems such as epilepsy or diabetes, plan one a week throughout the year
WHO?	All those involved in managing resources for a particular condition, patients' representatives and payers
HOW?	☑ Produce a Value Review Pack containing data on: ◦ Hospital admissions compared with other services ◦ Prescribing rates compared with other services ◦ Outcome data, if available ◦ Any other data on variations in the care provided, from audit studies, for example ◦ Financial data, if available ◦ New high-quality evidence produced in the preceding year ☑ Look at the website for the STAR Tool and consider using this method of analysis and redistributing along the core pathway ☑ Present the pack to a workshop ☑ Accept criticisms of the data, reminding participants that 'These are the data you submitted'

WHAT?	How to conduct a review of expenditure on a disease
HOW?	☑ Ask the workshop to focus on their existing resources and ask: ◦ What should we do more of, or better? ◦ What should we do less of? ☑ Ask the workshop to advise: ◦ What would be their top priority if new money became available? ◦ What would be their lowest priority if cuts had to be made?

WHAT?	How to manage knowledge
WHY?	Because the implementation of what we know from research, data and experience will have a bigger impact on health and healthcare than any new drug or technology likely to be developed in the next decade
WHEN?	The management of knowledge needs to be reported to executive boards and management teams as frequently as financial reports
WHO?	The Chief Executive, boards and management teams
HOW?	☑ The Chief Executive should identify one board member as being responsible for knowledge and give that person the title of Chief Knowledge Officer (CKO) ☑ Each significant management team in the organisation should also have one person on their team responsible for getting knowledge into practice ☑ A librarian should be free from library management duties to support the CKO ☑ Require the CKO to prepare a plan, describing how: ◦ The knowledge coming into the organisation can be improved ◦ More knowledge from experience can be created within the organisation ◦ Important new knowledge can be more effectively implemented ◦ The knowledge disseminated by the organisation, e.g. patient information leaflets, can be improved ☑ Implement the plan

WHAT?	**How to improve sustainable value and reduce the carbon footprint of patient pathways**
WHY?	Because climate change is the greatest threat to human health of the 21st century, and we have a responsibility to future generations of patients and healthcare professionals to develop sustainable healthcare systems
WHEN?	Now! Think about one thing you can do tomorrow. . .
WHO?	Everyone involved in the design and delivery of healthcare services has a role to play
HOW?	☑ First consider disease prevention and health promotion. Are there opportunities to look upstream and prevent individuals becoming patients or optimise health conditions? Collaborate with colleagues in primary care and public health. ◦ Especially consider areas where there are co-benefits to patient and planetary health, e.g. active transport, reduction of red and processed meat consumption, and improved home insulation ☑ Empower individuals to make decisions about their own healthcare. Work closely with patients to understand their personal goals and determine the best path forward for them, in line with GIRFT principles

WHAT?	**How to improve sustainable value and reduce the carbon footprint of patient pathways**
HOW?	☑ Consider all steps in the patient pathway (you can use a value process map to help here, co-developed with all relevant stakeholders, including patient representatives). Seek to streamline this, removing steps that do not add value for patients, for example: ◦ Consolidate appointments into one-stop clinics ◦ Use virtual clinics where appropriate ◦ Avoid unnecessary investigations that are unlikely to change management ☑ Where treatment is necessary consider the use of low-carbon alternatives: ◦ Use low-carbon alternative medications, e.g. dry powder inhalers rather than metered dose inhalers, inhalational anaesthetics with the lowest global warming potential, where clinically appropriate ◦ Reduce unnecessary single-use items wherever possible. Don't open items 'just in case'! ◦ Switch single-use items to reusable alternatives where available ◦ Encourage active maintenance and repair of equipment ◦ Where single-use items are unavoidable seek reprocessed alternatives ◦ Use low-carbon waste streams where appropriate (e.g. recycling, domestic waste and non-infectious offensive waste streams).

GLOSSARY

Language creates social reality. Here is the new language for the new reality, namely that everyone has to feel a sense of stewardship for optimising value and minimising waste from the resources available for health and social care. This is a distillation of the Oxford Value and Stewardship Programme (OVSP) Glossary.

Appropriate, necessary and futile

A treatment is:

» Necessary if everyone agrees it is essential even though there is a risk
» Appropriate if almost everyone agrees the benefits outweigh the risks and that the intervention is justified
» Inappropriate if almost everyone agrees that the risks outweigh the benefits and that its use is not justified
» Futile if everyone agrees the intervention would do more harm than good.

Cost-effectiveness, productivity and efficiency

» Productivity relates the outputs of a service to the inputs
» Efficiency relates the outcomes of care to the inputs
» Cost-effectiveness relates the outcomes of a technology or intervention to the costs.

Culture

> *'Culture is the shared tacit assumptions of a group that it has learned in coping with external tasks and dealing with internal relationships.'* [1]

Efficacy and effectiveness

- Efficacy is the magnitude of the benefit demonstrated in the research setting
- Effectiveness is the degree to which an intervention, the efficacy of which has been proven in the research setting, delivers benefit in the ordinary service setting.

Empathy

Empathy is different from sympathy or compassion. It is the ability to understand what another is thinking from their perspective and communicate to the other person that you have managed to do this.

Equity, equality and health inequalities

- Inequality is an objective difference in mortality, morbidity or service provision
- Inequity is a difference in service access or use that is deemed unfair.

Integrated care – system, network and pathway

- A network is a set of organisations and individuals that deliver the system's objectives
- A system is a set of activities with a common aim, a common set of objectives and a set of criteria against which progress towards the outcomes that matter can be measured

- A pathway is the course an individual follows as they go through the system.

Leadership, management and accountability

- Leadership creates and changes culture
- Management achieves the objectives of an organisation working within that culture
- Accountability is a relationship based on the provision of information about performance from those who have it to those who have a right to it.

Outcomes that matter to health and social care

These outcomes are the results of health and social care interventions which indicate that high value is being realised for individuals and populations.

Outcomes that matter to individuals

These outcomes are the results people care about most, and they often differ from the outcomes regarded as important by clinicians and people who manage health services.

Overuse, underuse and optimality

> *'Overuse is the provision of medical services for no benefit or for which harms outweigh benefits.'* [2]

Population health terms

- Population health means the health status of a defined group of people

- Population healthcare focuses primarily on segments of the whole population defined by a common need, which may be a symptom such as breathlessness, a condition such as arthritis or a common characteristic such as frailty in old age – and not by institutions, specialities or technologies
- Population health management is a method that stratifies the population by levels of risk, allowing resources to be focused on those sub-groups at highest risk.

Precision, personalised and stratified medicine

- Personalised medicine considers the patient's unique beliefs, preferences and environment as well as clinical findings
- Precision medicine uses information about the patient's genome in addition to other clinical measures
- Stratified medicine focuses on the person's level of risk, considering their genetic profile as well as their clinical condition.

Programme budgeting and marginal analysis

- Programme budgeting, sometimes called service line accounting in industry, is budgeting based not on institutions but on segments of the population defined by need, for example budgets for people with respiratory problems or people in the last year of life. Within a budget for such a segment there may be budgets for sub-segments; for example, within the respiratory disease, budgets for people with both asthma and COPD.
- Marginal analysis is a technique for estimating the effects of shifting resources from the budget for one segment or sub-segment to another.

Quality and safety

> *'The quality of a service is the degree to which it conforms to pre-set standards of goodness.'* [3]

Shared decision-making

> *'In a shared decision, a health care provider communicates to the patient personalized information about the options, outcomes, probabilities, and scientific uncertainties of available treatment options, and the patient communicates his or her values and the relative importance he or she places on benefits and harms.'*

Stewardship

Stewardship is a culture in which people who do not own something are committed to ensuring its survival for future generations.

Structure, process and outcome

» The structure is the organisation, which may be a bureaucracy, market or network

» The process is the activities, for example the number of operations done

» The outcome is the result of the process.

Value

Value is assessed by weighing up the benefits received by an individual or a group of people with a common need or by a population, considering the resources that have been used. The European Union Expert Panel on Effective Ways of Investing in Health has defined four types of value:

» Personal value: appropriate care to achieve a patient's personal goals
» Allocative value: equitable resource distribution across all patient groups
» Technical value: achievement of best possible outcomes with available resources
» Social value: contribution of healthcare to social participation and connectedness.

Variation

> *'Unwarranted variation is variation in the utilization of health care services that cannot be explained by variation in patient illness or patient preferences.'* [4]

Waste

Waste is the use of resources that would produce more value if used for another purpose or another subgroup of the population.

References

1. Schein EH. *The Corporate Culture Survival Guide.* 1999. John Wiley & Sons, p. 186.

2. Korenstein D, Falk R, Howell EA, Bishop T, Keyhani S. 'Overuse of healthcare services in the United States: an understudied problem'. *Archives of Internal Medicine.* 2012; 172: 171–178.

3. Donabedian A. 'The definition of quality: a conceptual exploration'. In: *Explorations in Quality Assessment and Monitoring. Volume 1: The Definition of Quality and Approaches to its Assessment.* 1980. Health Administration Press.

4. Wennberg JE. *Tracking Medicine: A Researcher's Quest to Understand Health Care.* 2010. Oxford University Press.

CO-AUTHOR BIO'S

Gwyn Bevan

Emeritus Professor of Policy Analysis, London School of Economics & Political Science.

Gwyn Bevan is Emeritus Professor of Policy Analysis in, and former Head of, the Department of Management at the London School of Economics and Political Science; and an Affiliate Professor in the Istituto di Management of the Scuola Superiore Sant'Anna, Pisa. He is, or has been, an adviser to the Inspectorate of police and fire services in England and Wales; the Education Commission of the Rockefeller Foundation on research in developing countries; allocating resources for health care and public health in England; the reform of publicly-financed legal services in England ands Wales; and funding research into overseas aid. He was a Director at the Commission for Health Improvement which was responsible for inspections of quality of care in the NHS in England and Wales.

Chantelle Rizan

Clinical Lecturer in Sustainable Healthcare

Chantelle Rizan is a Clinical Lecturer in Sustainable Healthcare at Brighton and Sussex Medical School, and was appointed in 2022 following her PhD evaluating ways to mitigate the carbon footprint of products used in the operating theatre. Her interest in sustainability developed as a junior doctor concerned about volumes of single-use plastics used, alongside through her Masters of Research in which she used lean management techniques to streamline patient pathways and maximise resource use. Chantelle seeks to translate her research into practice and policy, as founding member of the Royal College of Surgeons of England Sustainability in Surgery working group, and is an academic advisor for a national report on Greener Surgery in collaboration with UK Health and Climate Change Alliance. Key achievements include receiving the Hillary International Health and Care Leadership Award (2022), and the Adam Weiler Doctoral Impact

Walter Ricciardi

Professor of Public Health, Università Cattolica del Sacro Cuore Rome

Walter Ricciardi is Past President of the World Federation of Public Health Associations.

President of Mission Board for Cancer of European Commission.

Member of the Scientific Advisory Board of the Pan-European Commission on Health and Sustainable Development World Health Organization–Regional Office for Europe.

Member of the Scientific Board, Santé Publique France.

Ordinary Member of Pontificia Academia pro Vita, Vatican.

Founder and Director of Osservatorio Nazionale per la salute delle Regioni Italiane (Italian Observatory on Healthcare).

Editor of European Journal of Public Health and of Oxford Handbook of Public Health Practice.

Caroline Clarke

Group CEO of the Royal Free London NHS Foundation Trust, and past president of the HFMA

Caroline Clarke studied economics at University and then joined the NHS to work in finance. She worked for a number of NHS organisations, and for KPMG, before becoming the Director of Finance at the Royal Free Hospital NHS Foundation Trust. She became Deputy Chief Executive and then in 2019 Chief Executive of the hospital.

Caroline was President of the Healthcare Finance Managers Association and developed a major initiative designed to bring clinicians and finance staff closer together by understanding each other's role and culture.

In 2023 Caroline was appointed Regional Director of the NHS for London.

Rachel Stancliffe

Founder and Director of The Centre for Sustainable Healthcare, which is supporting health systems to transform for a sustainable future.

Rachel Stancliffe has over 20 years experience of leading strategic development in complex settings. She has worked across silos and disciplines at national and international level with practitioners and academics. After an undergraduate degree in Human Sciences at Oxford and an MSc in Demography at LSE, she first worked in public health in the UK, and then in the former Soviet Union delivering change and strategy development programmes for public health in a politically sensitive and complex environment with UNICEF, Save the Children and others. She then helped to develop The Cochrane Library for 10 years, working with researchers and publishers worldwide to ensure that best evidence informs clinical decisions.

Rachel contributes to international roundtables and expert groups on sustainable healthcare, SDGs and net zero, has partnered extensively with academics and has authored and co-authored articles in this area.

Anant Jani

Scientific Director of the Oxford Value and Stewardship Programme

Anant Jani has a PhD in immunology from Yale University and his experience in healthcare started when working in on the QIPP Right Care programme at the Department of Health. This involved helping localities across England to design and implement high-value population-based healthcare systems, including building the first national system for stroke prevention for patients with atrial fibrillation. He currently works on understanding how we can improve population health through social prescriptions and by addressing social determinants of health dand is a Research Fellow at Heidelberg University as well as working with the Oxford Martin School Future of Cooling Programme and CAMS Oxford Institute.

Alison Tonge

Director of Integrated Services Development, Arden Gem Care System Support

Alison Tonge has over 30 years Executive leadership in Finance, PHM Strategy, Performance. Leading roles in Healthcare within NHS England, Commissioning, Consulting and Integrated Care Canada. She specialises in integrated planning and releasing value.

INDEX

A

B

C

D

N

O

P

T

W

Printed in Great Britain
by Amazon

45539538R00178